Python Robotics Projects

Build smart and collaborative robots using Python

Prof. Diwakar Vaish

BIRMINGHAM - MUMBAI

Python Robotics Projects

Commissioning Editor: Gebin George
Acquisition Editor: Shrilekha Inani
Content Development Editor: Nithin Varghese
Technical Editor: Komal Karne
Copy Editors: Safis Editing, Dipti Mankame, Laxmi Subramanian
Project Coordinator: Virginia Dias
Proofreader: Safis Editing
Indexer: Pratik Shirodkar
Graphics: Tom Scaria
Production Coordinator: Nilesh Mohite

First published: May 2018

Production reference: 1240518

Published by Packt Publishing Ltd.
Livery Place
35 Livery Street
Birmingham
B3 2PB, UK.

ISBN 978-1-78883-292-2

www.packtpub.com

`mapt.io`

Mapt is an online digital library that gives you full access to over 5,000 books and videos, as well as industry leading tools to help you plan your personal development and advance your career. For more information, please visit our website.

Why subscribe?

- Spend less time learning and more time coding with practical eBooks and Videos from over 4,000 industry professionals

- Improve your learning with Skill Plans built especially for you

- Get a free eBook or video every month

- Mapt is fully searchable

- Copy and paste, print, and bookmark content

PacktPub.com

Did you know that Packt offers eBook versions of every book published, with PDF and ePub files available? You can upgrade to the eBook version at `www.PacktPub.com` and as a print book customer, you are entitled to a discount on the eBook copy. Get in touch with us at `service@packtpub.com` for more details.

At `www.PacktPub.com`, you can also read a collection of free technical articles, sign up for a range of free newsletters, and receive exclusive discounts and offers on Packt books and eBooks.

Contributors

About the author

Prof. Diwakar Vaish is a robotics scientist and the inventor of Manav (India's first indigenous humanoid robot), the world's first mind-controlled wheelchair, brain cloning, and the world's cheapest ventilator. He has also been a guest lecturer at over 13 IITs and various other institutions. He is the founder of A-SET Robotics, a leading robotics research company based in New Delhi.

A huge thank you to the open source community for their contribution.

I would like to thank my family who has supported and given me the freedom to follow an unexplored path. Also, thanks to Packt, who has helped me through all the stages of writing, my team and especially Ms. Udita Dua, who has worked hard to implement the projects.

Finally, thank you God for giving me the power to do everything I am doing right now.

About the reviewer

Ruixiang Du is a PhD candidate in mechanical engineering at Worcester Polytechnic Institute (WPI). He currently works in the Autonomy, Control, and Estimation Laboratory, with a research focus on the motion planning and control of autonomous mobile robots in cluttered and dynamic environments.

Ruixiang has general interests in robotics and in real-time and embedded systems. He has worked on various robotic projects with robot platforms, ranging from medical robots and unmanned aerial/ground vehicles to humanoid robots. He was a member of Team WPI-CMU for the DARPA Robotics Challenge.

Packt is searching for authors like you

If you're interested in becoming an author for Packt, please visit authors.packtpub.com and apply today. We have worked with thousands of developers and tech professionals, just like you, to help them share their insight with the global tech community. You can make a general application, apply for a specific hot topic that we are recruiting an author for, or submit your own idea.

Table of Contents

Preface

In this book, you will learn the basics of robotics using Raspberry Pi as our hardware and Python as our programming language. The projects we undertake will help readers to understand the basics of the language and the hardware we are using. The technologies we are exploring in this book are the ones that act as a baseline for most of the robots we use. By going through this book, readers will not only understand how to make the projects mentioned in this book but also move a step ahead and give shape to their imagination. In this book, we will be using very cheap hardware and software that are open source, making it easy to afford. In this, we will start with Python, so even a 12-year-old will be able to understand and implement it. Besides this, we will be exploring different hardware and their working principle so that you just don't interface the hardware but get to know it to the most minute detail. For those who have a will to explore robotics using the latest technology and language, this could be the perfect place to start.

Who this book is for

This book is for those who have a will to learn robotics and get familiar with the latest technology using the latest programming language. Age is no limit whether you are 12 years young or 60 years old; you can read this book and convert your ideas into reality.

What this book covers

Chapter 1, *Robotics 101*, will make you understand the basics of our hardware and Python. Using simple LEDs, we will start to make simple programs in Python.

Chapter 2, *Using GPIOs as Input*, will discuss how to connect various sensors, starting with interfacing a switch through an ultrasonic range finder and finally to a light sensor (LDR) using an analog-to-digital converter.

Chapter 3, *Making a Gardener Robot*, will use various sensors, such as a soil humidity sensor, and a temperature sensor to sense the climate, and using a solenoid valve controlled by a relay, we will be making a robot that waters the garden whenever required.

Chapter 4, *Basics of Motors*, will discuss the working of motor and how it can be driven by a motor driver, how a full H bridge motor driver works, and also how the speed control mechanism works in the motor driver. While doing all this, we will control a motor and make it move in a different direction at different speeds.

Chapter 5, *Making a Pet Feeding Robot*, will teach you how to make a robot that will feed your pet whenever you have programmed it using motors and other sensors. It would also sense if the pet is there or not, and until such time as the pet eats its food, the buzzer will always be left on to make sure that the pet understands that the food is dispensed. Also, using force sensors, we will be able to make out how much food has been eaten. After a sufficient quantity of food has been consumed, the buzzer will be deactivated.

Chapter 6, *Bluetooth-Controlled Robotic Car*, will teach more about steering and controlling a robotic vehicle, and the concepts of a skid-steer mechanism will be implemented. You will also learn how to use the Bluetooth onboard our Raspberry Pi and connect it to your mobile phone. Finally, using an app, we will control our robotic vehicle using our mobile phone.

Chapter 7, *Sensor Interface for Obstacle Avoidance*, will provide an insight into how we can use IR proximity sensors to determine distances. Also, we will make smart algorithms to sense distance on all sides and then move in the direction where the distance is greatest.

Chapter 8, *Making Your Own Area Scanner*, will teach you the basics of servo motors and how they can be controlled. Using servo motor, we will make an area scanner, in other words, a homemade LIDAR. Using this home-built sensor, we would make a self-navigating car.

Chapter 9, *Vision Processing*, will teach you how to prepare the Raspberry Pi to capture images using the camera and how processing takes place.

Chapter 10, *Making a Guard Robot*, will teach you how to make a vision processing powered system that will be able to recognize faces using insights from the previous chapter. It would then be trained to recognize a specific face and react differently when it recognizes the face familiar to it. Finally, we will make a guard robot that will guard your house; when it recognizes your face, it will let you in. If it recognizes an unknown face, then it will raise an alarm.

Chapter 11, *Basic Switching*, will control the equipment at your home with simple logic. Finally, we will make an alarm that will wake you up in the natural way by lights. This will have a smart automatic snooze.

Chapter 12, *Recognizing Humans with Jarvis*, will teach you how to control devices at your home with a room occupancy sensor that we will build at home using an IR proximity sensor. We will then make this occupancy sensor smart and ready to count the number of people in the room and only switch off the lights or other equipment once no one is left in the room.

Chapter 13, *Making Jarvis IoT Enabled*, will provide you with insights into the concepts of IoT and MQTT server through which we will be able to monitor our home based on events. Also, you will learn how to control the devices in our home while sitting anywhere in the world.

Chapter 14, *Giving Voice to Jarvis*, will teach you how the system can be made capable of synthesizing speech. Also, you will learn how you can make the system recognize our speech, and based on it, everything in the home can be controlled.

Chapter 15, *Gesture Recognition*, will make you identify the gestures made on the board using electric waves, and based on those gestures, the smart home will be controlled.

Chapter 16, *Machine Learning*, will make you understand the concepts of machine learning and especially the k-nearest algorithm. Using this algorithm, you will understand how data can be given to the system and predictions can be made based on it . Finally, you will execute a program to generate its own data by the inputs of the users over the course of time, and based on that data, it will start automatically controlling the home without any human intervention.

Chapter 17, *Gesture-Controlled Robotic Vehicle*, will teach you how to build a robot that will be controlled based on the tilt of your hand. The concepts of accelerometer and gyroscope will be understood and implemented.

Chapter 18, *Making a Robotic Arm*, will help you make a robotic hand. You will understand how to set the physical limits of the servos for protection purposes, and we will then make a program in which you will control the robot will be controlled based on different frames. Finally, you will go ahead and understand how to control speed of motion of the robot.

To get the most out of this book

There is no need of prior Python knowledge though having a prior experience will accelerate your learning curve. Readers will have to download and install RASPBIAN STRETCH WITH DESKTOP; this will give us the GUI interface for Raspberry Pi.

Download the example code files

You can download the example code files for this book from your account at www.packtpub.com. If you purchased this book elsewhere, you can visit www.packtpub.com/support and register to have the files emailed directly to you.

You can download the code files by following these steps:

1. Log in or register at `www.packtpub.com`.
2. Select the **SUPPORT** tab.
3. Click on **Code Downloads & Errata**.
4. Enter the name of the book in the **Search** box and follow the on-screen instructions.

Once the file is downloaded, please make sure that you unzip or extract the folder using the latest version of:

- WinRAR/7-Zip for Windows
- Zipeg/iZip/UnRarX for Mac
- 7-Zip/PeaZip for Linux

The code bundle for the book is also hosted on GitHub at `https://github.com/PacktPublishing/Python-Robotics-Projects`. In case, there's an update to the code, it will be updated on the existing GitHub repository.

We also have other code bundles from our rich catalog of books and videos available at `https://github.com/PacktPublishing/`. Check them out!

Download the color images

We also provide a PDF file that has color images of the screenshots/diagrams used in this book. You can download it from `https://www.packtpub.com/sites/default/files/downloads/PythonRoboticsProjects_ColorImages.pdf`.

Conventions used

There are a number of text conventions used throughout this book.

`CodeInText`: Indicates code words in text, database table names, folder names, filenames, file extensions, pathnames, dummy URLs, user input, and Twitter handles. Here is an example: "We have to multiply 2 and 3 we simply write `Multiply(2,3)`."

A block of code is set as follows:

```
import RPi.GPIO as GPIO
from time import sleep
GPIO.setmode(GPIO.BOARD)
GPIO.setup(23,GPIO.OUT)
```

When we wish to draw your attention to a particular part of a code block, the relevant lines or items are set in bold:

```
import RPi.GPIO as GPIO
from time import sleep
GPIO.setmode(GPIO.BOARD)
GPIO.setup(23,GPIO.OUT)
```

Any command-line input or output is written as follows:

```
sudo apt-get update
sudo apt-get upgrade
```

Bold: Indicates a new term, an important word, or words that you see onscreen. For example, words in menus or dialog boxes appear in the text like this. Here is an example: "Then select **I2C** to enable it. Then select **Yes**."

Warnings or important notes appear like this.

Tips and tricks appear like this.

Get in touch

Feedback from our readers is always welcome.

General feedback: Email feedback@packtpub.com and mention the book title in the subject of your message. If you have questions about any aspect of this book, please email us at questions@packtpub.com.

Errata: Although we have taken every care to ensure the accuracy of our content, mistakes do happen. If you have found a mistake in this book, we would be grateful if you would report this to us. Please visit www.packtpub.com/submit-errata, selecting your book, clicking on the Errata Submission Form link, and entering the details.

Piracy: If you come across any illegal copies of our works in any form on the Internet, we would be grateful if you would provide us with the location address or website name. Please contact us at copyright@packtpub.com with a link to the material.

If you are interested in becoming an author: If there is a topic that you have expertise in and you are interested in either writing or contributing to a book, please visit authors.packtpub.com.

Reviews

Please leave a review. Once you have read and used this book, why not leave a review on the site that you purchased it from? Potential readers can then see and use your unbiased opinion to make purchase decisions, we at Packt can understand what you think about our products, and our authors can see your feedback on their book. Thank you!

For more information about Packt, please visit packtpub.com.

Robotics 101

1

Hello world! As soon as we say the word robot, thoughts of science fiction start to surround us. We may recall the cartoon serial *The Jetsons* or think of the movie *Terminator*. But, as a matter of fact, robots as a species do not belong to science fiction anymore. They are as real as they can get. Look around you and point out any object; it probably wouldn't have been made without a robot. The modern era has been shaped by robots.

But then, you can also take a step back and think, wait a minute, aren't the things he is talking about called machines and not robots? Well, yes, you are very correct, yet very mistaken at the same time. It is cartoons and science fiction that have imparted an image of a human-like robot that is called a **robot**. But robots are much more than that.

Unfortunately, we do not have a concrete, universally agreed definition of robots, but, as I like to say, *Any machine capable of performing physical as well as intellectual tasks can be called a robot.*

Now, you may say that, according to my definition, even an automatic washing machine can be called a robot. Well, technically, yes, and why should we not call it a robot? Think of the things it is doing for you and what kind of automation has been adapted over the years. After you feed in the type of cloth it automatically washes, rinses, and dries as you would have done yourself in the 19th century. The point I am trying to make is that there is a huge variation of robots that we can think of, which can radically change the way we live. We need to think with a wider perspective—not just limit robot to look as a human adaption in form of humanoid robots.

We live in the golden era of robotics and automation in which the development of new products is as simple as it can get. What a decade back might have taken a team of engineers, can now be done by a person sitting in bedroom in just a few minutes, thanks to the open source world. At the very same time, there is hardware horsepower available to you by which you can literally build a super computer in your own home with just a few hundred dollars. We are surrounded by problems, some simple and others complex, which are waiting to be solved. The only missing chain in the whole process is you: an innovative mind that has the capability to exploit these technologies to solve the world's problems.

To make your mind capable of doing so, we will be starting of by understanding the roots and the basics of robotics. The goal of this book is not only to make the projects that are mentioned in the book but to make you understand how to exploit the resources to build your dream projects.

Finally, I would like to congratulate you on entering this amazing and futuristic field at the correct time. I always tell my students a rule, which I would like to share with you as well:

- First is a scientist
- Second is a researcher
- Third is an engineer
- Fourth is a technician
- Last is a mechanic

What it means is that the earlier in the life cycle you enter any field, the higher in the hierarchy you can get. The later you come, the harder it is to climb to the top.

Enough talking—now let's get straight to business! We will cover the following topics in this chapter:

- The hardware arsenal
- Setting up Raspberry Pi
- Programming
- Playing with voltage

The hardware arsenal

Talking of robots, there are a few basic tangible components that they are made up of, which are as follows:

- Computing Unit
- Sensors
- Actuators
- Chassis
- Power source

Firstly, we will be discussing the microcontroller and, during the course of book, we will be discussing the rest of the tangible components in detail as and when required.

Whenever you have been to buy a laptop or a computer, you must have heard the word microprocessor. This is the primary unit that has to make all the decisions. I call it the *king*, but what is a king without an empire? For the king to work, he needs some subordinates that can do the things for him, the same way in which the microprocessor needs a few subordinates such as RAM, storage, I/O devices, and so on. Now, the problem is that when we put in all these things the overall unit gets expensive and bulky. But, as we know, subsequently weight and size are very important factors when it comes to robots, so we cannot afford to have a big bulky piece of system running a robot.

Hence, we made something called a SoC. Now, this is a one man show as this small chip, has all the necessary systems for it to work inside that small little chipset itself. So, now you don't need to add RAM or storage or any other thing for it to work. These small microcontrollers can get really powerful but a downside is, once a manufacturer has made an SoC, thereafter no changes can be done to it. The size of storage, RAM, or the I/O cannot be changed. But we generally can live with these limitations as when programming the robots, you might not be using the entire juice of the microcontroller until the time you are running some serious artificial intelligence or machine-learning code.

One such great piece of hardware is Raspberry Pi. Yes, it sounds very tasty, but there is so much more to it. This is a super small yet extremely powerful microcontroller. It is often referred to as a prototyping board because of the fact that it is used by roboticists everywhere to bring out their ideas and to make them a reality in a quick time span. It is available all across the globe and is extremely cheap. You can literally stream HD movies, surf the internet, and do much more on just a $10 device. I can't think of something as ludicrous as this. It is fairly easy to use and you can use Python to program it.

So, basically, it ticks all our boxes. This will be the primary weapon we will be using throughout the book.

So let me introduce you to Raspberry Pi! This is what it looks like:

There are various models of Raspberry Pi available on the market. But we will be using Raspberry Pi Zero W; this will cost you around $10 and it is easier to purchase than a Big Mac burger. Do make sure you buy the Raspberry Pi Zero with a W, which supposedly stands for wireless capabilities such as Wi-Fi and Bluetooth. There are a few more things that you will have to order or arrange for it to work. Here is a list of items:

- Micro USB to standard USB adapter
- Keyboard
- Mouse
- Micro SD memory card, 16 or 32 GB
- Micro SD card reader
- Micro USB power adapter (2 amp or more)
- Micro HDMI to HDMI port
- Breadboard
- Bunch of jumper wires (male to male, male to female, and female to female)
- 3V LEDs

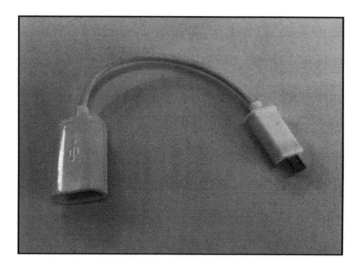

As you will instantly make out from the image, there is a micro HDMI port onboard, over which you can hook up your HD monitor or a TV screen. Second there is a micro SD card slot. This will be the primary storage device for this computer. Other than that, you will also find two USB sockets and a camera bus. You may think this is it, but the best is yet to come. Raspberry Pi has something called **GPIO**, which stands for **general purpose input/output**. These are disguised as small 40 through-hole ports on one corner of the Raspberry Pi; this is what makes it super special.

Now, conventionally you would attach things to your computer that are compatible with it. So, hooking up a mouse, keyboard or a joystick is as easy as inserting a USB port, but what if you need to connect your computer to your light bulbs or your air-conditioner? Exactly, you can't. That's where GPIO comes in to save the day. These are pins which are very useful when it comes to robotics, as these can be used to connect various components such as sensors/motors. The beauty of these pins is that they can be used as either input or output based on what we program them for. So, as we will later see, each of these pins can be defined in the program to be either input or output based on our needs.

Now, out of these 40 pins, 26 are GPIO. The rest of the pins are generic power or ground ports. There are two more ports called **ID EEPROM** which at this point of time we do not require:

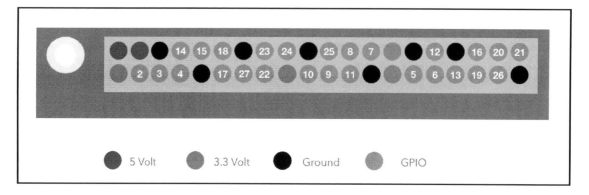

As you can see, Raspberry Pi is capable of giving us two types of power supply: 3.3V and 5V. These basically cater for most of our purposes.

Setting up Raspberry Pi

We will talk about the GPIO and other things to do with Raspberry Pi in a while. Firstly, we will understand how to set up this board for the first time.

The first thing you need to do is to make sure that the operating system of Raspberry Pi is ready. I am assuming that you are using a Windows PC, but if you are doing it on another OS as well, then there will not be much of a difference.

To install the OS, start your PC and follow these steps:

1. Go to www.raspberrypi.org and click on **DOWNLOADS**
2. Now click on **RASPBIAN**, you will see the following two options:
   - **RASPBIAN STRETCH WITH DESKTOP**
   - **RASPBIAN STRETCH LITE**
3. We will be downloading **RASPBIAN STRETCH WITH DESKTOP**; this will give us the GUI interface for Raspberry Pi
4. After downloading, unzip the package into a folder

Now we need to copy it to the memory card of Raspberry Pi. The memory card over which you need to copy must be formatted by low level formatting. There are basically two types of formatting. one which simply erases the index the other one which we know as low level formatting is the one in which we remove all the data from both the index and their physical memory location. There would be a button to toggle a low level format. Make sure it is clicked before you format your memory card for this function. I would recommend using the SD card formatter by `www.sdcard.org`. Now open the formatter and you simply have to format it using the 32 KB option.

 Find more details and more up-to-date information here: `https://www.raspberrypi.org/documentation/installation/installing-images/README.md`.

Once done, you have to copy the image onto the SD card. The easiest way to do that is by using WinDisk Imager. You can download it online without any problems. Then simply select the image and the location on your SD card and start copying the image.

This could take a few minutes. After it is done, your SD will be ready. Plug it into Raspberry Pi and we will be ready to power it up. But before you power it up, plug in your monitor using the Micro HDMI to HDMI wire, connect the keyboard and mouse to Raspberry Pi using the Micro USB, and power it up by using the Micro USB adapter to standard USB adapter. Now, use the other USB port on Raspberry Pi to power it up using the micro USB power adapter.

Once you start it up, you will see a boot-up screen and within a few seconds you will be able to see the desktop. So, finally, our Raspberry Pi is up and running.

Go ahead and explore a few options, surf the internet, look at some cat videos on YouTube, and get yourself familiar with this mighty device.

By now, you must already be appreciating the power of Raspberry Pi. It may be slightly slower than your average computer. But, come on, this thing costs just $10!

Let's program

In this chapter, we will get you familiar with Python and how you can use the GPIOs on this device. To do this, go ahead and click on the Raspberry icon in the top left-hand corner. You will see the Python console 3.0. There could be an older version of Python as well. We will be using the newer version in this book.

Once the window opens, you will see the playground where you would be doing the coding. So now we are ready to write the first code for Python Robotics. Now let's see how it's done.

The first thing we will write is:

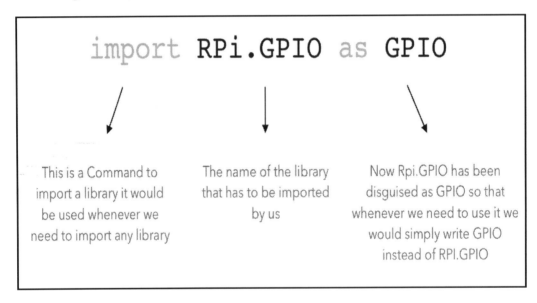

Almost all of the time when we start writing a program, we will start by writing the preceding line. Now, before we understand what it does, we need to understand libraries. Often while we are writing code, we will have to write the code again and again in multiple places. This takes a lot of time and certainly is not cool!

So, to solve this problem, we created functions. A function is a miniature program that we might think would be used over and over again. In this miniature program itself, we also mention what it would be called.

Let's say that there is a code in which we need to multiply two numbers again and again. So, what we do is we write the code once and make it a function. We also name this function `Multiply`.

So now, whenever we need to multiply two numbers, we don't have to write its code again; rather, we simply have to call the function to do it for us instead of writing the code to multiply. The problem is, how do we tell which number has to be multiplied?

There is a solution to that as well. As you might see later, whenever a function is called we put opening and closing brackets after it, such as `multiply()`.

If the brackets are empty that means no user input has been given. If, for example, we have to multiply 2 and 3 we simply write `Multiply(2,3)`.

We are giving the input as 2 and 3. The position of the input in the brackets is also important as the position in the brackets will define where in the program it will go.

Now, let's say you make functions such as:

- Add
- Subtract
- Multiply
- Divide

Say you stack them together. Then the pile of functions grouped together will be called a library. These libraries can have hundreds of functions. There are some functions which are already in the Python language so that the job is made simpler for the programmers. Others can be defined as open source or developed by you at your convenience.

Now, getting back to the point. We are calling the library `RPi.GPIO`; this is a library defined by Raspberry Pi. This will have functions that will make your life easier when it comes to programming Raspberry Pi. So, in the program, once we call the library, all the functions are at your disposal and ready to be used.

In the next line, we write `Import.time`. As you must have guessed, this is used to import a library time. What it does we will learn shortly.

The next line of code would be as follows:

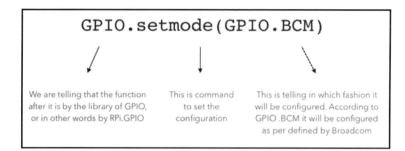

Before we understand what it does, let's learn a bit more about GPIOs. These pins are hard numbered according to their physical positions in Raspberry Pi. However, we can change the numbering of the pins in the software for our understanding and convenience. But in this code, we will not be playing around with this and will set it do the default set by Broadcom, which is the manufacturer of the microcontroller of Raspberry Pi.

This line uses a function of the RPi.GPIO library called setmode. What this function does is that it sets the pin configuration of the setmode to (GPIO.BCM)—BCM is further a function of GPIO.

Now we can use the base pin configuration. Further to this, a specialty of the GPIO pins is that it can be used both as input and output. But the only condition is that we have to specify whether it has to be used as input or output in the program itself. It cannot do both functions at the same time. Here is how it is done:

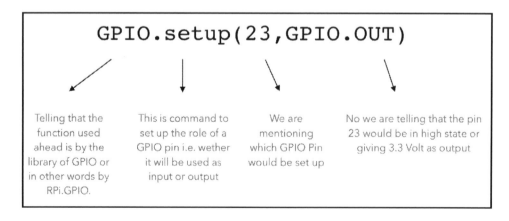

The next line of code will be as follows:

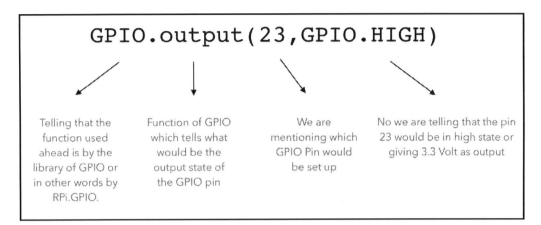

Again, we are using a function of the library GPIO called output. What this does is that it sets up a specific pin of the board in a state which we want. So, here we have mentioned that the pin number 23 has to be set high. Just for the sake of clarity, high means on and low means off.

The next line of code will be as follows:

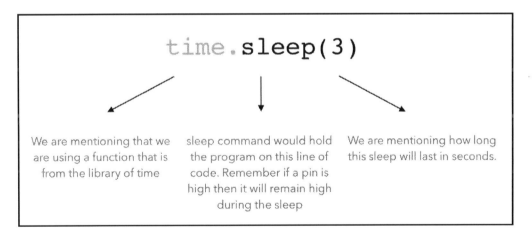

In this line, we are using a function from the library time. The function sleep basically freezes the state of all the GPIO pins. So, for example, if the pin 23 is high then it will remain high until the time the function sleep is executed. In the function sleep, we have defined the value as 3 seconds.

Hence, for 3 seconds, the pin state of Raspberry Pi will remain as it was before this line of code.

Finally, the last line of the code will be:

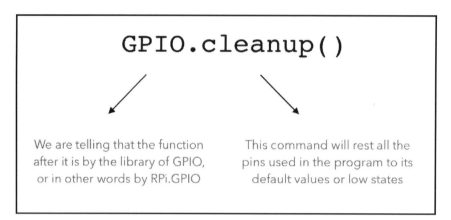

This will be a common sight after every program. This function of the GPIO library will reset the state of every pin that has been used in the program—the state of all the pins will be low. Remember, it will only affect the pins that are used in the program and not any other pins. So, for example, we have used the pin 23 in the program, so it will only affect pin 23 and not any other pin in Raspberry Pi.

Finally, your program will look something like this:

```
import RPI.GPIO as GPIO
import time

GPIO.setmode(GPIO.BCM)

GPIO.setup(23,GPIO,OUT)

GPIO.out(23,GPIO.High)

time.sleep(3)

GPIO.cleanup()
```

Now, one thing that you must remember is that whatever code we are writing will be executed one line after the other. So, let's say we keep `import RPI.GPIO as GPIO` at the bottom, then the whole program will not work. Why? Because as soon as it goes to `GPIO.setmode(GPIO.BCM)` it will not understand what `GPIO` is, neither will it understand what `setmode` is. Hence, we always import the libraries as soon as we start writing the code.

Now, working on the same concept, it will execute the program in the following way:

- `GPIO.out(23,GPIO.High)`: It will turn pin 23 high/on
- `time.sleep(3)`: It will wait for 3 seconds while pin is still high
- `GPIO.cleanup()`: Finally, it will set the state of the pin 23 to low

Now, to see whether the program is working, let's attach some hardware to check whether what we have written is actually happening.

 I am assuming that readers are already aware of how breadboard is used. If you are not familiar with it, just go ahead and google it. It will take 5 minutes to understand. It is super easy and will come in handy.

Now go ahead and connect the LED on breadboard, then connect the ground of the LED to the ground pin in Raspberry Pi, and set the positive/VCC to pin number 23 (refer the pin diagram).

You can also refer to the following diagram:

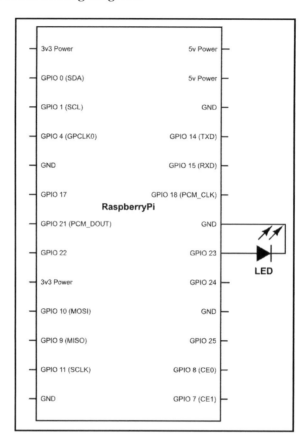

Once you are done, go ahead run the code and see what happens!

The LED will glow for 3 seconds and then turn back off again, exactly as we expected it to do. Now let's just play around with the code and do a slight modification. This time, we will add a few more lines marked in bold:

```
import RPi.GPIO as GPIO
from time
import sleep
GPIO.setmode(GPIO.BOARD)
GPIO.setup(23, GPIO.OUT)
while True:
  for i in range(3):
  GPIO.output(23, GPIO.HIGH)
sleep(.5)
```

```
GPIO.output(23, GPIO.LOW)
sleep(.5)
sleep(1)
GPIO.cleanup()
```

Before understanding what's inside the code, you will notice that not every line is aligned, they have been intended. What does this mean ?

A line indented together with other lines of code is called a block. So for example if you have a statement such as

```
while True:
    for i in range(3):
    GPIO.output(23, GPIO.HIGH)
sleep(.5)
GPIO.output(23, GPIO.LOW)
sleep(.5)
sleep(1)
GPIO.cleanup()
```

Now in this line lets see how the code will run.

- A while true loop would run, this will run the code that is inside it i.e.

```
for i in range(3):
    GPIO.output(23, GPIO.HIGH)
sleep(.5)
GPIO.output(23, GPIO.LOW)
sleep(.5)
sleep(1)
```

- Thereafter the code `for I in range (3):` would run. It will run the code inside the for loop until the value of `I` is in range, Hence the code below would run.

```
GPIO.output(23, GPIO.HIGH)
sleep(.5)
GPIO.output(23, GPIO.LOW)
sleep(.5)
```

The above code can be referred to a block of code, which is inside the `for` loop. The block of code can be made by indenting the code.

Now, let's see what it does. `While True` is a loop, it will run the `for` loop inside it again and again until the time the condition is not false. The condition we are using here is:

```
for i in range(3):
```

The maximum range is 3 and every time the statement runs it increments the value of the i by +1. So it basically acts as a counter. Let's see what the program will actually do.

It will check for the value of i and increment it by 1 thereafter. As the code progresses, it will glow the LED high for 0.5 seconds and then shut it off for 0.5 seconds. And then it will wait for 1 second. This will repeat until the while loop is false, as in the value of i becomes greater than 3 where it would get out of the program and terminate. Run the program and see if it actually happens.

By now, you understand how easy the programming is in Raspberry Pi. To go a step further, we will make another program and make some changes to the hardware.

We will be connecting five more LEDs from pin numbers 7 through to 12. We will make them switch on and off in a pattern.

Once connected, we will write the code as follows:

```
import RPi.GPIO as GPIO
from time
import sleep
GPIO.setmode(GPIO.BOARD)
GPIO.setup(7, GPIO.OUT)
GPIO.setup(8, GPIO.OUTPUT)
GPIO.setup(9, GPIO.OUTPUT)
GPIO.setup(10, GPIO.OUTPUT)
GPIO.setup(11, GPIO.OUTPUT)
while True:
  for i in range(7, 12):
  GPIO.output(i, GPIO.HIGH)
sleep(1)
GPIO.cleanup()
```

Now the code is fairly simple. Let's see what it means:

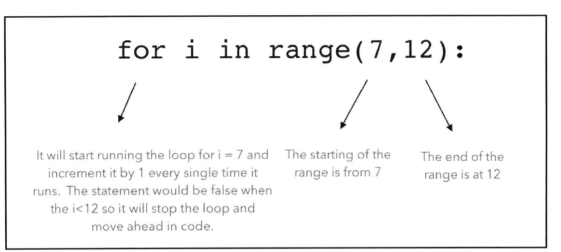

Before I tell you something more about the code, let's go ahead and run it.

When you run it, you will understand that as per the statement it is addressing the pins one by one and switching them to high after every 1 second.

Playing with voltage

So far so good! But did you notice one thing? We have been using Raspberry Pi as a switch—simply switching the various components on and off. But what if we need to vary the intensity of the LEDs that we have just programmed? Is it possible? The answer is no. But we can still get it done somehow!

Let's see how. Computers work in binary which means that they can represent either 0 or 1. This is because of the fact that the primary computing unit in any system is based on a transistor which can either be on or off representing 0 or 1. So, if we see this technically, computers are only capable of switching due to the binary architecture. However, there is a trick. This trick is called **pulse width modulation (PWM)**.

Now, before I explain any of it in detail, let's go ahead plug in an LED on pin number 18, then copy this code into Raspberry Pi and run it:

```
import RPi.GPIO as GPIO
import time
GPIO.setmode(GPIO.BCM)
```

```
GPIO.setup(18,GPIO.OUT)

pwm= GPIO.PWM(18,1)
duty_cycle = 50
pwm.start(duty_cycle)

time.sleep(10)

GPIO.cleanup()
```

What did you notice? The LED will be blinking at once a second. Now let's tweak it a bit and change the PWM(18,1) to PWM(18,5). Let's run and see what happens.

You will have noticed that it is now blinking five times in a second. So the number 5 is basically representing the frequency as the LED is now flickering five times in a second. Now, again, rewrite the code and increase 5 to 50. Once you increase it to 50, it switches the LED on and off 50 times in a second or at 50 Hertz. So, it appears to you as if it is always on.

Now comes the interesting part. Go over to your code and change duty_cycle = 50 to duty_cycle = 10.

What did you notice? You must have seen that the LED is now glowing way lower in intensity. In fact, it will be half of what it originally was.

Let's see what is actually happening:

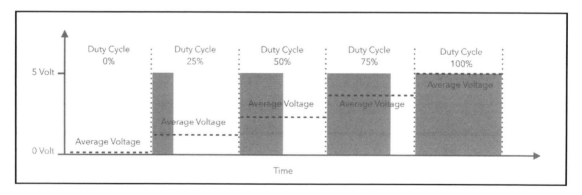

As you can make out from the diagram, the function is basically creating a pulse, the characteristics of which we are changing. The first characteristic is the frequency, the pulses generated in a second. In the code line `pwm= GPIO.PWM(18,1)`, we are basically telling the microcontroller to generate one pulse every second on pin number `1`. In the second line, duty cycle is a percent value. It determines for how much percent of the time the pulse will be high. For the rest of the time of the pulse the output of the pin will be off. So, for the following code, the below bulleted points would be the characteristics:

```
pwm= GPIO.PWM(18,1)
duty_cycle = 50
```

- Time/width of every pulse is 1 second
- Percent of time it would on is 50%
- Percent of time it would be off is 50%
- Time it would be on is 0.5 seconds
- Time it would be off is 0.5 seconds

When we increase the frequency more than 50 hertz then it is very hard for the human eye to make out if it is actually switching on or off. Theoretically, for 50% of the time the pin will remain high, and for the rest of the time it will be low. So, if we take an average then we can easily say that the overall voltage would be half of the original. Using this method, we can modulate the voltage output of any pin as per our requirements.

Summary

Now you must have understood how the GPIOs can be used as output and how, by applying conditions, we can change their behaviors.

In the next chapter, we will understand how these pins can be used as input as well. So come back, and see you there!

2
Using GPIOs as Input

In the previous chapter, we understood how GPIOs are used for output. But, as the name suggests, the GPIO can be used for both input and output purposes. In this chapter, we will see how you can go ahead and use these pins to input the data over to Raspberry Pi.

The topics which we will cover in this chapter are:

- A deeper dive into GPIOs
- Interfacing the PIR sensor
- Interfacing the ultrasonic proximity sensor
- Interfacing through I2C

A deeper dive into GPIOs

I am sure you remember this line of code from the previous chapter:

```
GPIO.setup(18,GPIO.OUT)
```

As explained earlier, this basically tells us how GPIO the pin will behave in a certain program. By now, you must have guessed that by changing this single line of code we can change the behavior of the pin and convert it from output to input. This is how you would do it:

```
GPIO.setup(18,GPIO.IN)
```

Once you write this line of code in your program, the microcontroller will know that during the time that the program is being run, the pin number 18 will only be used for input purposes.

To understand how this would actually work, let's head back to our hardware and see how it can be done. Firstly, you need to connect an LED to any of the pins; we will be using pin number 23 in this program. Secondly, you need to connect a switch on pin number 24. You can refer the diagram that follows for making the connections:

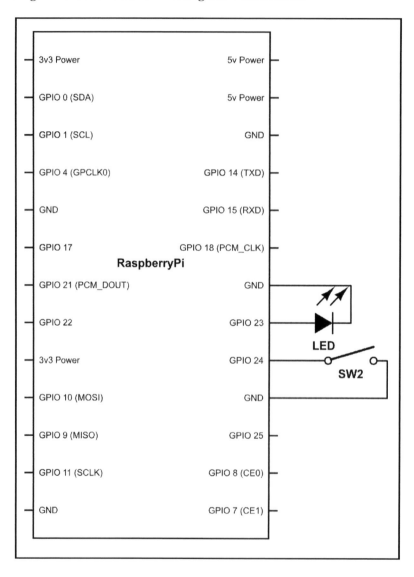

Once you connect it, you can go ahead and write this program:

```
import time import RPi.GPIO as GPIO
GPIO.setmode(GPIO.BCM)
GPIO.setup(24,GPIO.IN)
GPIO.setup(23,GPIO.OUT)
while True:
   button_state = GPIO.input(24)
      if button_state == True:
        GPIO.output(23,GPIO.HIGH)
      else:
        GPIO.output(23,GPIO.LOW)
   time.sleep(0.5)
GPIO.cleanup()
```

Once the program is uploaded, then, as soon as you press the push button, the LED will turn itself on.

Let's understand what exactly is happening. `while True:` is basically an infinite loop; once you apply this loop, the code running inside it is repeated over and over again until something breaks it, and by break I mean some interruption that causes the program to stop and exit. Now, ideally we exit the program by pressing *Ctrl* + *C* whenever there is an infinite loop.

```
button_state = GPIO.input(24)
```

In the above line, the program understands where it has to look; in this program. In this line we are telling the program that we are looking for GPIO 24, which is an input:

```
if button_state == True:
    GPIO.output(23,GPIO.HIGH)
```

If the button is high, in other words when the button is pressed and the current is reaching the pin number 24, then the GPIO pin number 23 will be set to high:

```
else:
    GPIO.output(23,GPIO.LOW)
```

If the pin number 24 is not true, it will follow this line of code and will keep the pin number 23 low, in other words switched off.

So, there it is, your first program for using the GPIOs for input purposes.

Interfacing the PIR sensor

So far, so good! In this unit, we will go ahead and interface out first sensor, which is a passive infrared, commonly known as a PIR sensor. This sensor is a very special sensor and is used very commonly in automation projects. Its low energy consumption makes it a superb contender for IoT projects as well. So let's see how it works.

You must have noticed that when we heat a metal to a high temperature, it slowly gets dark red in color, and when we heat it further, it gets brighter and slowly goes from red to yellow as depicted in the below diagram which shows a red hot steel tab. Now, as the temperature increases, the wavelength of the emitted radiation decreases; that is why with the increase in temperature the color changes from red to yellow, as yellow has a shorter wavelength compared to red.

But the interesting part is that even when the objects are not heated enough, they emit radiation; in fact, any object that is above the temperate of absolute zero emits some form of radiation. Some we can see with the naked eye, others we can't. So, at room temperature, objects emit infrared radiation which has a higher wavelength compared to visible light. Hence, we don't see it with our eyes. Nonetheless, it is still there.

What this PIR sensor does is that it senses the infrared light from the objects around it and whenever an object moves, it can sense the overall change in its pattern and, based on that, can detect if there is any movement that has happened in its proximity.

We assume that whenever there is someone in a room there will be some inherent movement that will happen, and hence this sensor is very commonly used as an occupancy sensor. Now, let's connect this sensor and see how we can use it:

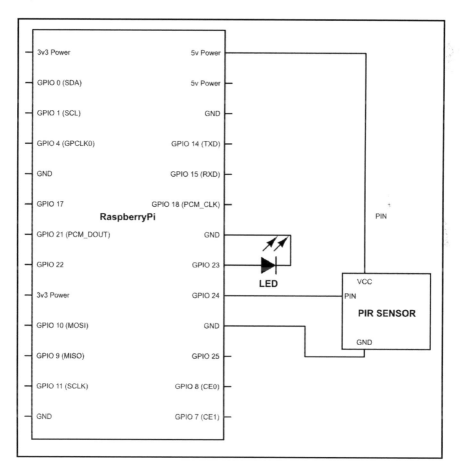

Once you have connected it as per the preceding diagram, go ahead and upload the code: :

```
import time import RPi.GPIO as GPIO
GPIO.setmode(GPIO.BCM)
GPIO.setup(23,GPIO.IN)
GPIO.setup(24,GPIO.OUT)
while True:
 if GPIO.input(23) == 1:
  GPIO.output(24,GPIO.HIGH)
 else:
  GPIO.output(24,GPIO.LOW)

 time.sleep(1)
GPIO.cleanup()
```

Now, let's see what is happening. The logic is very simple. As soon as the PIR sensor detects movement, it turns its output pin to high. All we have to do is to monitor that pin and that's basically it.

The logic is entirely similar to that of a push-button switch, and it will also work in a similar manner. So not much explaining is needed.

Interfacing the ultrasonic proximity sensor

First, the basics. A proximity sensor is a type of sensor that senses the proximity of an object from it. There is a universe full of sensors that are available to accomplish this task and numerous technologies that allow us to do so. As the name says, the ultrasonic proximity sensor works on the principal of ultrasonic sound waves. The working principle is quite easy to understand. The ultrasonic sensor sends a beam of ultrasonic sound waves; these waves are inaudible to human ears, but nonetheless it is still a sound wave and it also behaves like a sound wave.

Now, as we know, sound bounces off different surfaces and forms an echo. You must have experienced this echo when speaking in an empty room. You can hear your own sound but with a slight delay. This delay is caused by the property of sound. A sound is a wave, hence it has a speed. Sound waves have a set speed of travel. So, to cover a specific distance, they take some time. By calculating this time, we can derive how far the sound waves are going before getting bounced off from a surface.

Similarly, in this sensor, we shoot ultrasonic sound waves in a specific direction and then sense the echo which bounces back. Naturally, there would be a delay in receiving the echo; the delay would be directly proportional to the distance of the object from the sensor and, based on this delay, we could easily compute the distance.

Now, to work with the proximity sensor, we need to understand the physical architecture of the sensor to wire it correctly. There are four pins in the sensor, which are:

- VCC (positive)
- Trigger
- Echo
- GND (ground)

I obviously don't have any need to explain what VCC and ground does. So, let's move on straight to trigger. Whenever the pin is high for 10 microseconds, the ultrasonic sensor will send eight cycles of 40 kHz sound waves to the target. Once the trigger cycle is completed, the **ECHO** is set to high. Once it receives the echo signal back, the **ECHO** pin is set back to low. Here is a diagram to show how it actually happens:

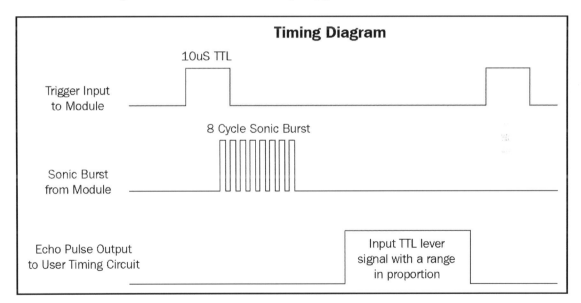

That is all we need to know for now. Subsequently, we will learn more as we move along. Now, to go ahead and make it live, connect it as per the diagram:

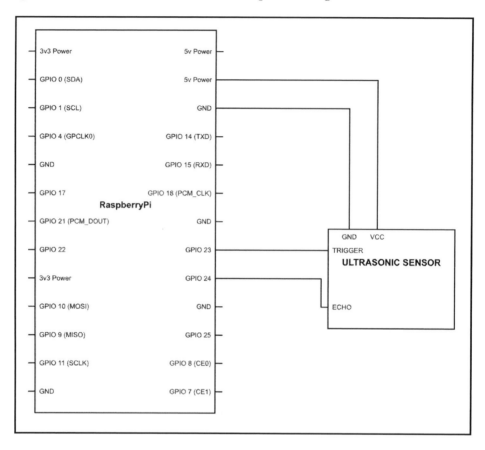

Once the connection is made, the following is the code that you need to run:

```
import RPi.GPIO as GPIO
import time

GPIO.setmode(GPIO.BCM)
GPIO.setup(23,GPIO.OUT)
GPIO.setup(24,GPIO.IN)

while True:
    pulse_start = 0
    pulse_stop = 0
    duration = 0
    distance = 0
```

```
GPIO.output(23,GPIO.LOW)
time.sleep(0.1)
GPIO.output(23,GPIO.HIGH)
time.sleep(0.000010)
GPIO.output(23,GPIO.LOW)

while GPIO.input(24)==0:
    pulse_start = time.time()

while GPIO.input(24)==1:
    pulse_stop = time.time()

duration = pulse_stop - pulse_start

distance = duration*17150.0
distance = round(distance,2)
print ("distance" + str(distance))

time.sleep(0.2)
}
```

Now, once you run this program, the output on your screen will be showing you the distance of the object once in every 0.2 seconds. Now, you must be wondering how this is communicating all these readings:

```
GPIO.setup(23,GPIO.OUT)
```

We are assigning pin 23 to give pulse to **TRIGGER** pin of the sensor when required:

```
GPIO.setup(24,GPIO.IN)
```

We are assigning pin 24 to receive the logic to confirm the receipt of the echo signal:

```
pulse_start = 0
pulse_stop = 0
duration = 0
distance = 0
```

We will be using the preceding as variables, and every time the loop starts we are assigning them a value which is 0; this is to wipe off the previous reading that we would have stored during the course of program:

```
GPIO.output(23,GPIO.HIGH)
   time.sleep(0.000010)
   GPIO.output(23,GPIO.LOW)
```

We keep the trigger pin number 23 high for 0.000010 seconds so that the ultrasonic sensor can send a brief pulse of ultrasonic waves:

```
while GPIO.input(24)==0:
pulse_start = time.time()
```

This while statement will keep noting down the time of the `pulse_start` variable until the time pin number 24 is low. The final reading of the time will be stored in the `pulse_start` variable, as in noting down the time when the pulse was sent:

```
while GPIO.input(24)==1:
pulse_stop = time.time()
```

The `while` statement in this loop will start noting the time when the input on pin number 24 is high and it will keep noting the time until the pin number 24 remains high. The final reading of the time will be stored in the `pulse_stop` variable, as in noting down the time when the pulse is received:

```
duration = pulse_stop - pulse_start
```

In this statement we are calculating the overall time it took for the pulse to travel from the sensor to the object and bounce back to the receiver on the sensor:

```
distance = duration*17150.0
```

This is an arithmetic formula given by the manufacturer to convert the time duration it took for the ultrasonic waves to travel into the actual distance in centimeters. You may ask how did we get to this equation?

Let me give you a brief about it. With elementary physics we would remember this simple equation: *Speed = Distance / Time*.

Now you may also recall that the speed of sound is 343 meters per second. Now 1 meter has 100 centimeters hence to convert this speed into centimeters per second, we would have to multiply the speed by 100, hence the speed would be 34,300 centimeters per second.

Now we know one element of the equation which is the speed. So lets put the value of speed into the equation. Now the equation would look something like this: *34,300 = Distance / Time.*

Now we know one thing that the distance which the sound is travelling is twice the actual distance. How ? Because the sound first goes from the sensor to the object. Then it bounces off that surface and reaches back to the sensor. So essentially it is covering twice the distance. Hence we to adapt this equation we have to make a small change: *34,300 / 2 = Distance / Time*

Now what we want out of this equation is distance So lets take all other part to the other side. Now the formula would look something like this: *17,150 * Time = Distance*

So here we have it the formula for the distance.

```
distance = round(distance,2)
```

As the distance the ultrasonic waves have traveled is twice the actual distance (once for going towards the object and second for bouncing back to the sensor), we divide it by half to get the actual distance:

```
print 'Distance = ',distance
```

Finally, we will print the measured distance via the following statement. Anything that is in the quotation marks ' . . . ' will be written the way it has been written. However, `distance` is written without quotation marks, and distance is a variable. Hence, the variable stored in the distance will be written in the final output on the screen:

```
time.sleep(0.25)
```

The code will pause on this line for a time of 0.2 seconds. If we did not have this pause, then the values would come out at an incredible speed which would be hard for us to read or understand. If you are tinkering around, I would recommend removing this statement and running the code to see what happens.

Interfacing through I2C

So far, so good. Electronic circuits can be very interesting and, while they seem very complex, often we find that the working can be very simple. In the previous section, we interfaced one sensor at a time. We can go ahead and interface multiple sensors, but we are limited by the number of GPIOs that are present. We have also seen that some sensors such as ultrasonic sensors may use more than one GPIO pin for their working. This further reduces the number of sensors that we can interface with the microcontroller. Once we move on to more complex circuits, we will also realize that the wiring can be really messy and if a problem occurs then finding what's wrong becomes one tedious task.

Now, there is an even bigger problem that we face while designing robotic systems and that's the problem of timing—all the work done in a system has to be synchronized. Most of the systems are currently sequential in nature, as in the output of one unit becomes the input of another:

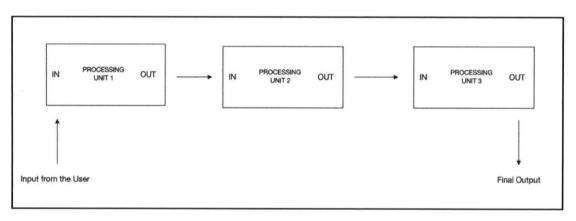

Now, for the task to be completed, the **PROCESSING UNIT 1** has to deliver the input to **PROCESSING UNIT 2** when needed, and the same goes for **PROCESSING UNIT 3**. If the data is not timed perfectly, then either the **PROCESSING UNIT 2** will keep waiting for the input from **PROCESSING UNIT 1** or, even worse, the **PROCESSING UNIT 1** will send the data to **PROCESSING UNIT 2** at a time when it does not need it. In which case, the data will get lost and the process will have some errors.

Hence, to solve this problem, the computer scientists back in the day invented a system of pulsing. The clock pulse is a very simple square wave which has a 50% duty cycle (recollect **pulse width modulation (PWM)**). The circuits are designed to do one operation at either the rising or the falling edge of the clock pulse. Due to this synchronization, every part of the circuit knows when to work. Here is what the clock pulse looks like:

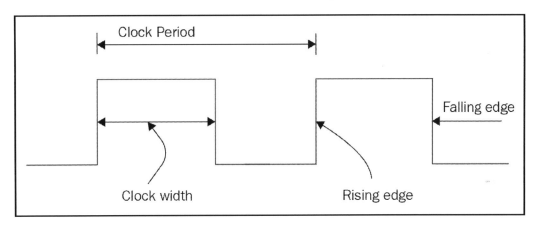

Now, coming back to the point, we have two problems:

- There is a physical limit to how many devices/sensors can be connected to the robot
- How to time the sensors and interconnected circuits to work in harmony

To solve these problems, we use a very commonly used protocol called **I2C**, which stands for **Inter-integrated Circuits**. This protocol is extremely useful when we need to connect multiple devices on the same set of GPIOs, such as when we have only one set of GPIO pins over which multiple sensors can be linked. This is made possible due to unique addresses allocated to each hardware. This address is used to identify a sensor and then to communicate with it accordingly. Now, to implement the I2C protocol we need two lines; these lines are as follows:

- Data
- Clock

As you may have guessed, the clock line is used to send a clock pulse to the devices attached to it and the data is the bus over which the data flows to and fro.

Now, the entire I2C architecture works on a master-slave configuration, wherein the master generates the clock signal all the time for the slave devices and the slave devices have to constantly look for the clock pulse and the data packets sent by the master devices. Let's see how it's done.

As mentioned earlier, there are two lines: the data line, which is referred to as **Serial Data (SDA)**, and the clock line, which is referred to as **Serial Clock (SCL)**. From now on, we will be using the terms SCL and SDA:

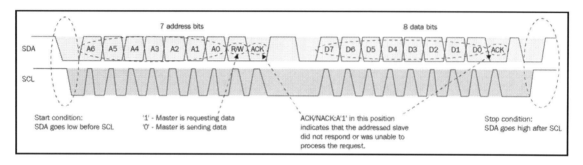

Lets look at the main pointers shown in the diagram:

- **Start condition**: To start a communication, a start condition is created indicating that the communication is about to happen. This condition is depicted by the master by keeping the SDA line low before the SCL. This indicates all the slave devices are ready for communication.

- **Address frame**: Once the communication is started the master sends the address of the device that needs to be communicated with. This is a 7-bit address. In every clock pulse, a bit is sent, hence it takes seven clock pulses to send the 7-bit address. After that 7-bit address is a read/write bit. This indicates to the device whether the master would like to write in this operation or if it wants to read some data. Hence, the total address frame is of 8 bits, which takes eight clock pulses to be sent. After these eight pulses, during the ninth clock pulse, the master waits for the acknowledgement from the device. This acknowledgement is sent by the slave device when the SDA line is pulled low by the slave device which is being addressed. With this strategy, the master knows that the address sent by it has been received and the slave device is now ready for the communication. If the acknowledgement is not sent back, then it is up to the master what has to be done.

- **Data frame**: Once the acknowledgement is sent, depending on if it is a read or write operation, the data is either written by the master onto the slave or, in read operation, the data is sent by the slave over to the master. The length of this data frame can be arbitrary.
- **Stop frame**: Once the data transfer is completed, the stop condition is made by the master to indicate that the communication has to stop. This condition is done when the SDA line goes from low to high after the SCL line goes from low to high.

So this is basically how I2C communication works. For every device we have a 7-bit address, hence we can connect up to 128 devices on a single bus. That's a lot of devices. The chances of running out of physical limits is almost negligible. Now let's go ahead and see how we can connect the sensors via this protocol. Generally, it is not required to do the core programming for the I2C, as it is lengthy and cumbersome. That's where the magic of open source comes in. There are a lot of developers across the globe who are working on these sensors and most of them are generous enough to make a library and share it for ease of programming. These libraries are available online and most of them take care of the complex process of communication.

Now is the time that we interface our first I2C device, which is an analogue to digital converter. You must be wondering why we use this converter in the first place. Recall the time when we started understanding GPIO pins. These magic pins can be used both as input and output; you may also remember that these pins can either be on or off—these are all digital pins, not only when it comes to output but also for input. But there are a huge amount of sensors that work over analogue communication. Due to the digital architecture of Raspberry Pi, it is difficult to interface these sensors directly. Hence, we use an **analogue to digital converter** (**ADC**), this converter converts the analogue value of the sensors to the digital bits that are understandable by Raspberry Pi.

We will be connecting an LDR, the resistor will change the value of resistance based on how much light is falling onto it. Hence, the voltage will be dependent upon how much light is falling over the LDR.

Now let's see how it is practically done. Take up your Pi and let's get going. To start, firstly we need to enable I2C on our Raspberry Pi; follow the steps listed here:

1. Open the terminal (*Ctrl + Shift + T*)
2. Type `sudo raspi-config`
3. Select the interfacing options:

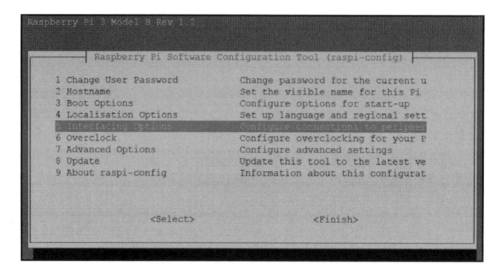

4. Then go to **Advanced Options**:

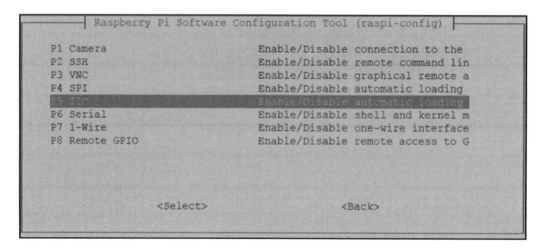

5. Then select **I2C** to enable it. Then select **Yes**:

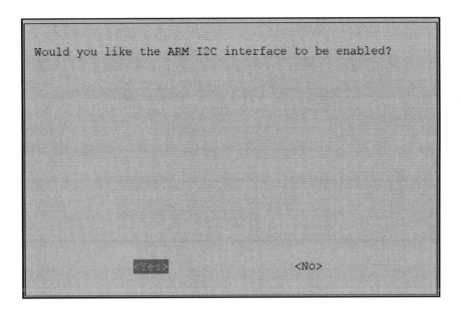

Now install the `adafruit` library to interface the ADC1115:

1. Open the terminal and copy the following command:

   ```
   sudo apt-get install build-essential python-dev python-smbus
   python-pip
   ```

   This command downloads the libraries and the dependencies over to Raspberry Pi

2. Now type the following:

   ```
   sudo pip install adafruit-ads1x15
   ```

This command installs the libraries and the dependencies over to Raspberry Pi.

Now that the software is set up, let's get the hardware ready. Connect Raspberry Pi to the ADS1115 as shown in the following diagram:

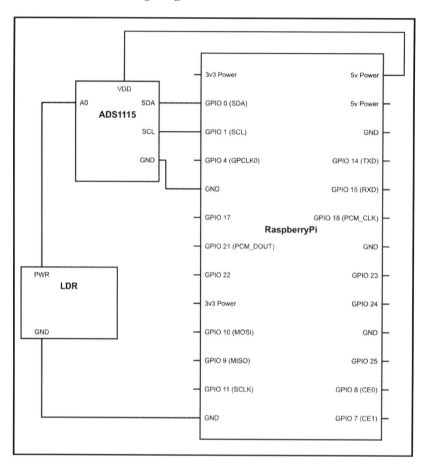

Once you are ready, go ahead and upload this code in Pi:

```
import time
import Adafruit_ADS1x15
import RPi.GPIO as GPIO
LED =14

GPIO.setmode(GPIO.BCM)
GPIO.setup(LED,GPIO.OUT)

adc = Adafruit_ADS1x15.ADS1115()
GAIN = 1
```

```
channel=0
adc.start_adc(channel, gain=GAIN)

while True:
    value = adc.get_last_result()
    print(str(value))
    time.sleep(0.1)
    if value >= 100:
        GPIO.output(LED,1)
    else :
        GPIO.output(LED,0)

adc.stop_adc()
```

Note that there can be times when this code may not work, in which case try tweaking the value of threshold:

```
if value >= 100:
```

What you might have noticed is that whenever the LDR is faced towards a light source, the LED also switches on, and whenever it is away from light, the LED switches off.

So now you have interfaced an I2C device. Let's understand how this code is actually working:

```
import Adafruit_ADS1x15
```

The preceding line of code imports the `Adafruit_ADS1x15` library in the code so that we can use all its functions during the program.

```
adc = Adafruit_ADS1x15.ADS1115()
```

The preceding line of code creates the instance of the library `Adafruit_ADS1x115`. The line `.ADS1115()` is the function for creating the instance as `adc`. Understood anything? Let me put it in English.

Now, instead of writing `Adafruit_ADS1x15` all the time, we can simply write `adc` to call the library functions. Further, you can use any word instead of `adc`; it can be your cat's name or your neighbor's name, and it would still work:

```
GAIN = 1
```

This is the value to which the sensing would be done. 1 depicts that the sensing would happen in full range. Which for our ADC is from a voltage range of 0V to +/-4.096V. Now changing the gain would result in change of the sensing range. I.e. if we change the value of gain to 2 Then the Range in which the sensing would happen would be Half of the original range i.w. 0 to +/- 2.048 Volts.

Now you must be asking what is the voltage range and why are we changing the gain ?

The reason is simple. There are different types of analog sensors. Which give output in a wide variety of voltage range. Some sensors can give you output in the range of 0.5 volt to 4 volt others can give you from 0.1 volt to 0.98 volts. Now if we set the gain to 1 then the all of these sensors could be easily interfaced. As all of them fall in between the sensing range of 0 to 4.098 Volts. However as it is a 16 bit ADC hence the total number of discrete values that the ADC can provide would be in between 2^{16} or 65,536 readings. Hence at the gain of 1 the minimum voltage change that the ADC could detect would be: *4.096 / 65536 = 0.000062.*

But if increase the gain to 4 then the sensing range would reduce to a mere 0 to +/- 1.0245. So this would be able to work with the output range between 0.1 volt to 0.98 volt. But now lets see the minimum voltage change that it could detect: *1.0245 / 65536 = 0.00001563.*

Now as you can see the minimum voltage that can be detected is very low. Which is a good thing for the compatibility with sensor.

Now, it is up to you as to what gain value you want. The LDR is working on 5V, hence it is better for us to use the entire gain reading of 1:

```
channel=0
```

When you look closely at the ADC hardware, you will notice that there are various pins including **A0**, **A1**, **A2**, and **A4** This is a four-channel ADC—it can convert four analogue inputs and convert them into digital data. As we are only using one single data stream, we will be letting Pi know which pin it is connected on. With the following line, we are telling Pi to start the process of converting the data:

```
adc.start_adc(channel, gain=GAIN)
```

In the following line, we are instructing the ADC to stop the conversion, and that's where the code ends.

```
adc.stop_adc()
```

Summary

This chapter was all about interfacing sensors with GPIOs so that the data can be retrieved by sensors. Moving forward, in the next chapter, with the help of these learned topics, we will learn how to make a pet-feeding robot.

3
Making a Gardener Robot

All right my friends, you have understood some of the basics of input and output; now it's the time to make something to which we can hand over some of our daily responsibilities. This robot might not really look like a robot, but trust me, it will make your life easier. Most of all the plants in your garden will be blessing you for making it.

We will be covering the following topics:

- Working with solenoids
- Making the robot
- Making it more intelligent
- Making it truly intelligent

Working with solenoids

What we are going to make is an automation system that will water your plants whenever they need it. So technically, once it is set up, you don't really have to worry ever about watering your green creatures. Whether you are at your home, at the office, or on a vacation, this will keep doing its job no matter what.

Now, you must be wondering how it will water the plants, so let me tell you, for every problem in this world, there exists a solution. In our case, that solution is called a solenoid valve. What it essentially does is switch the flow of liquids. There are various solenoid valves available in the market; some of the identifying features are as follows:

- **Size**: They come in various sizes such as half an inch, three quarters of an inch, 1 inch, and so on. This basically will determine the flow rate of the solenoid valve.

- **Medium**: Whether it is meant for fluid, gas, vapor, and so on.
- **Normal condition**:
    - **Normally opened**: This valve will allow the flow of liquids in the off state—when no power is supplied to the valve
    - **Normally closed**: This valve will stop the flow of liquids in the off state—when no power is supplied to the valve
- **Number of ways**: A simple valve will have an inlet and an outlet. So, when it is open, it will allow the liquid to flow from the inlet to the outlet. However, there can be other types of valve such as a three-way valve which might have two outlets and one inlet. It would regulate where the flow of the liquid would happen.

There can be some more specifics in terms of the valves as well, but for now that's all we need to know. One thing to notice about the solenoid valve is that these valves can either be opened or closed. Achieving any state in between or controlling flow via these valves is not possible. For this we can use a servo valve or motor valve. But as of now, we don't need it.

What we will be using in this chapter is a half inch valve for water/fluid, which is normally closed. When you look closely at this valve you will see that it operates at 12 volts and the current consumption is close to 1 amp. This is a lot of current for Raspberry Pi. The upper limit of current that Raspberry Pi can provide per pin is about 50 milliamp. So if we connect this valve to Raspberry Pi then it's surely not going to work.

What do we do now? The answer to this question is a relay. The basic job of a relay is to re-lay the circuits. Basically, it's an electronically controlled switch. The basic job of a relay is to switch devices that have a higher current/voltage consumption than what can be given by a controlling unit on and off. This is a fairly simple device, as you can see in the diagram. There are two circuits. One is depicted in blue, which is a low voltage and low current circuit. This circuit is powering up a coil. The other circuit is depicted in red and black. This circuit is a high voltage, high current circuit.

In the initial stages, as you can see, the high voltage high current circuit is not complete and the oven will not work:

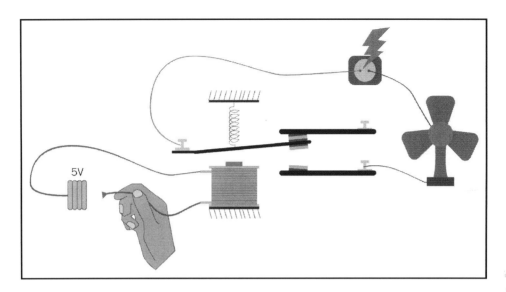

Now, in this second diagram, you can see that the blue circuit is connected to the 5V power source and that the coil is energized. Whenever a coil gets energized, it forms an electromagnet and attracts the metal leaf of the high power circuit to make the circuit complete, hence powering up the oven:

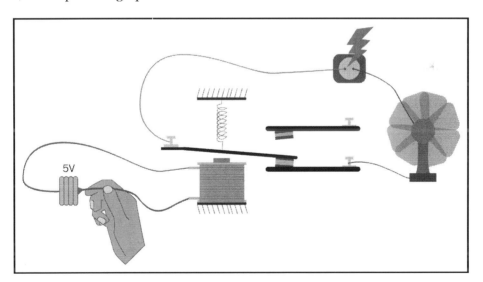

This is how a solenoid works. The consumption of the coil is hardly a few milliamps, hence it is very easy to actuate a coil via a micro-controller. This in turn makes a contact between the final circuit.

There are various kinds of relays available on the market; some of the identifying features are as follows:

- **Max output voltage**: The maximum voltage that it can handle
- **Maximum output current**: The maximum current that it can bear for any output device connected to it
- **Signal voltage**: The voltage that it requires switch the components on or off
- **Normal condition**:
    - **Normal off**: This will not allow any current to flow until the time the signal is not received
    - **Normal on**: It will allow the current to flow until the time the signal is not received

Now, coming back to our gardening robot, the solenoid attached to it will be working on 1 amp and 12V, so any relay which can supply equal to or more than 1 amp and 12V would work.

Commonly, the relays available on the market are 120V and 12 amp DC. One important thing to remember is that there will be two separate ratings for AC and DC voltage and current. As our solenoid will be working at 12V, we will only be considering the DC upper limit.

Making the robot

Now, let's get down to making the robot. Firstly, you need to make the water connection from the tap to the solenoid and from the solenoid to the sprinkler. You also have to make the connection, as follows:

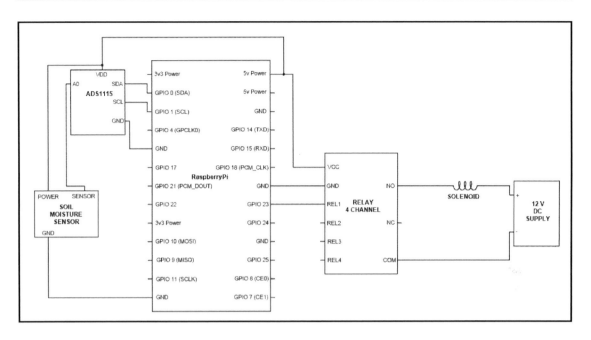

Now let's start programming. We will be interfacing a soil moisture sensor in this robot. The job of this sensor is to determine the amount of water in the soil. By determining this, we can understand if the garden needs water or not. This soil moisture sensor is an analogue sensor, hence we will be using an ADC to convert the analogue reading to Pi-understandable digital values. So let's get going:

```
import time
import RPi.GPIO as GPIO
import Adafruit_ADS1x15
water_valve_pin = 23
moisture_percentage = 20
GPIO.setmode(GPIO.BCM)
GPIO.setwarnings(False)
GPIO.setup(water_valve_pin, GPIO.OUT)
adc = Adafruit_ADS1x15.ADS1115()
channel = 0
GAIN = 1
while True:
 adc.start_adc(channel, gain=GAIN)
 moisture_value = adc.get_last_result()
 moisture_value= int(moisture_value/327)
 print moisture_value
 if moisture_value < moisture_percentage:
 GPIO.output(water_valve_pin, GPIO.HIGH)
 time.sleep(5)
```

```
    else:
        GPIO.output(water_valve_pin, GPIO.LOW)
```

Before you run this code, let's understand what it is actually doing:

```
    moisture_percentage = 20
```

`moisture_percentage` = `20` is the percentage that will act as a threshold; if the moisture level in the soil becomes less than 20% then your garden needs water. It is this condition that your robot will keep looking for; once this condition is met then appropriate action can be taken. This percentage can also be changed to `30`, `40`, or any other value as per your garden's needs:

```
    moisture_value = int(moisture_value/327)
```

The ADC is a 16-bit device—there are 16 binary digits that can represent a value. Hence, the value can be between 0 and 2^{15} or, in other words, between 0 and `32768`. Now, it is simple math that for every percentage of moisture the ADC will give the following reading: `32768/100`, or `327.68`. Hence, to find out the percentage of moisture in the soil, we would have to divide the actual value given by the ADC by `327.68`.

The rest of the code is fairly simple and, once you go through it, it won't be very hard for you to understand.

Making it more intelligent

Congratulations on making your first robot! But did you notice one problem? The robot we made was continuously looking for a moisture value and, as soon as it noticed that the moisture value was low, it suddenly pumped water and made sure that the humidity of the soil was always more than 20%. However, this is not required. In general, we water the garden once or twice a day. If we water it more then it might not be good for the plants.

So, let's go ahead and make it slightly more intelligent and make it water the plants only when the moisture level is low at a certain time. This time, we won't need to make any changes to the hardware; we simply need to tweak the code.

Let's go ahead and upload the following code, and then see what exactly happens:

```
from time import sleep
from datetime import datetime
import RPi.GPIO as GPIO
import Adafruit_ADS1x15
water_valve_pin = 23
moisture_percentage = 20
GPIO.setmode(GPIO.BCM)
GPIO.setwarnings(False)
GPIO.setup(water_valve_pin, GPIO.OUT)
adc = Adafruit_ADS1x15.ADS1115()
GAIN = 1
def check_moisture():
 adc.start_adc(0,gain= GAIN)
 moisture_value = adc.get_last_result()
 moisture_value = int(moisture_value/327)
 if moisture_value < moisture_level:
 GPIO.output(water_valve_pin, GPIO.HIGH)
 sleep(5)
 GPIO.output(water_valve_pin, GPIO.LOW)
 else:
 GPIO.output(water_valve_pin, GPIO.LOW)
while True:
 H = datetime.now().strftime('%H')
 M = datetime.now().strftime('%M')
 if H == '07' and M <= '10':
 check_moisture()
 if H == '17' and M <= '01':
 check_moisture()
```

This code might look a little alien to you, but trust me, it is as simple as it can get. Let's see what's happening step by step:

```
from datetime import datetime
```

This line of code is importing daytime instances from the date time library. This is a library which is by default in Python. All we need to do is to call it. Now, what it does is that without any hustle and bustle, it helps us determine the time within our code:

```
def check_moisture():
```

There are several times when we have to do something over and over again. These sets of code can be a few repetitive lines or multiple pages of code. Hence, rewriting that code doesn't make sense at all. We can create a function. In this function, we can define what will happen whenever it is called. Here in this line, we have created a function by the name of `check_moisture()`; now, whenever this function is called within a program, there will be a set of activities that will be performed. The set of activities that will be performed is defined by the user. So, whenever we write `def`, then it means that we are defining a function; thereafter, we write the name of the function that needs to be defined.

Once done, then whatever we write in the indentation following it will be done once the function is called. Do remember that whenever we call or define a function, it is denoted by an open and a closed `()` bracket at the end of the name of the function:

```
moisture_value = adc.get_last_result()
```

`adc.get_last_result()` is a function of `adc`. The activity it does is to simply take the result from the pin defined earlier (pin number 0) and fetch the reading to a variable `moisture_value`. So, after the line `moisture_value` will be the reading of the pin number 0 of the ADC or, in other words, the reading of the moisture sensor:

```
H = datetime.now().strftime('%H')
```

The code `datetime` is an instance and a method of `.now()`. What this function does is that it updates the time. Now, the `date time.now()` has updated all the parameters of date and time which includes the hours, minutes, seconds, and even the date. It is up to us whether we want all of it or any specific part of the date and time. At present, we want to put the value of hours in the variable `H`, hence we are using a `.strftime('%H')` method. `strftime` stands for string format of time. So whatever value it outputs is in string format. `('%H')` means that it will give us the value of the hours only. Similarly, we can also get the time in minutes by using `('%M')` and `('%S')`. We can also get the value of the date, month, and year with the following syntax:

- For getting the date: `('%d')`
- For getting the month: `('%m')`
- For getting the year: `('%Y')`

```
if H == '07' and M <= '10':
```

In the preceding condition, we are checking if the time is 7 o'clock or not; further, we are also checking if the time is less than or equal to 10 minutes or not. So this piece of code will only run the statement in the `if` statement when the time is 7 hours and between 0 and 10 minutes.

One thing to particularly note is that we have used an `and` between both the conditions, hence it will only run the code inside it once both the statements are absolutely true. There are some other statements we can use inside it, as well, such as `or`, in which case it will run the code if either of the statements is true.

If we replace `and` with `or` in this `if` statement, then it will run the code for every 0 to 10 minutes of every hour and will run the code continuously for the entire time between 7:00 a.m. and 7:59 a.m.:

```
check_moisture()
```

As you may remember, previously we defined a function by the name of `check_moisture()`. While defining that function, we had also defined the set of activities that would happen every time this function is called.

Now is the time to call that function. As soon as the program reaches this end of the code, it will execute the set of activities that was earlier defined in the function.

So there we have it. Now, as soon as you run this code, it will wait for the time defined by you in the program. Once the specific time has been reached, then it will check for the moisture. If the moisture is less than the set value then it will start to water the plants until the time the moisture reaches above that threshold.

Making it truly intelligent

Amazing work! We have started building things that are smarter than us by ourselves. But now we want to take it a step further and make it even smarter than us—that's what robots are here for. Not only to do what we do but to do all that in a better way.

So, what can we improve? Well, we do not require a lot of water on a chilly winter day, but when it's summertime we need way more than what we drink in winter. The same thing happens with plants as well.

In winter, the amount of water they need is way less. Furthermore, even the rate of evaporation of water in the soil is slower. Hence, in both the conditions, we need to supply varying amounts of water to the garden. The question is, how do we do that?

Well, firstly, to know if it's hot or cold outside we require a sensor. We will be using a sensor named DHT11. It is a cheap yet robust sensor that gives us the readings of both the temperature and humidity. The best part is, it is super cheap at a rate of around $2.

It has four pins. But if you presume that it will work to I2C protocols, then you would be wrong. It has its own data transfer methodology. It is good to have one single protocol for all the sensors, but often you will also find that there are various sensors or devices which work on a different or an altogether new protocol. DHT11 is one such sensor. In this case, we have the choice of either understanding the entire methodology of communication or to simply get the library from the manufacturer and use it at our disposal. At present we will be opting for the latter.

Now let's see what the pins of the DHT11 look like:

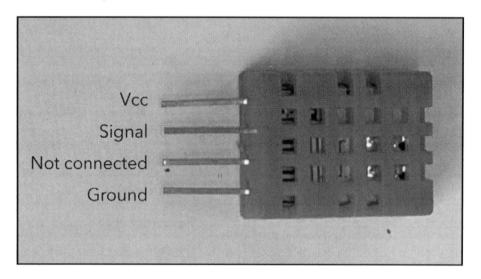

What you can see here is that there is only one signal pin which will do all the communication digitally. There are two pins for power and one of the pin is not in use. I.e. there is no significant purpose of the pin. It might be there just for soldering or for future use. This sensor works on a 5V supply and only needs a few milliamps, hence we can simply power it up by using Raspberry Pi. Now, for the data communication, we will connect the signal pin to GPIO pin number 4.

Before we start writing the code, let's first install the libraries for the communication between DHT11 and Raspberry Pi. We have done this before with the library of ADS1115, but in this one there are a few little tricks that we need to take care of. So let's get started.

Firstly, we need to make sure that the operating system of your Raspberry Pi is up to date. So connect Raspberry Pi to the internet, open the command prompt in Raspberry Pi, and type the following command:

```
sudo apt-get update
```

This command will update the raspbian OS of your Raspberry Pi automatically. Then go ahead and type in this:

```
sudo apt-get install build-essential python-dev python-openssl
```

In this command, we are installing the following packages:

- `build-essential`
- `python-dev`
- `python-openssl`

You must be wondering why we are installing all of these. Well, to cut a long story short, these are the dependencies for the library that we are about to install for the communication of DHT11. We will not be able to use the library if these packages are not installed on Raspberry Pi.

Finally, we have to install the library; this is a generic library in which the function of communicating with the DHT11 sensor is also available. This should suffice for our needs of easy communication. Here is the command to install it:

```
sudo python setup.py install
```

All right then, we are good to go. Our system is ready to talk to DHT11. Let's first just see if what we have done up until now works the way we want. To do that, connect the DHT11 as follows; you can leave the rest of the components such as the solenoid and the soil humidity sensor connected as they are. They should not interfere. Now upload the the following code in Pi:

```
from time import sleep
from datetime import datetime
import RPi.GPIO as GPIO
import Adafruit_DHT
sensor = 11
pin = 4
GPIO.setmode(GPIO.BCM)
GPIO.setwarnings(False)
while True:
  humidity, temperature = Adafruit_DHT.read_retry(sensor, pin)
  print("Temperature: " +temperature+ "C")
```

```
print("Humidity: " +humidity+ "%")
time.sleep(2)
```

Once you upload this code, you will see readings of the sensor on your screen. This code is simply providing you with the raw readings of the sensor. This code is super simple and everything written here will be well understood by you, except for a few lines of the code, which are:

```
import Adafruit_DHT
```

In this line of the code, we are importing the `Adafruit_DHT` library in our code. This is the same library that will be used to communicate with the DHT11 sensor:

```
sensor = 11
```

There are different versions of DHT available, such as DHT11, DHT22, and so on. We need to tell the program which sensor we are using. Hence, we have allotted a value to the variable sensor. Later, you will see how we will be using it:

```
pin = 4
```

In this line, we are assigning the value 4 to a variable called `pin`. This variable will be used to tell the program on which pin of the Raspberry Pi we have connected the DHT11:

```
humidity, temperature = Adafruit_DHT.read_retry(sensor, pin)
```

In this line, we are using a method of the `Adafruit` library named `Adafruit_DHT.read_retry()`. Now, what this does is that it reads the DHT sensor and gives the reading of the sensor to the variables `humidity` and `temperature`. One thing to note is that the DHT11 gives a reading which is updated every 2 seconds. Hence, the readings that you will be receiving will be refresh after every 2 seconds.

Once this code is through, then we can be sure that the sensor is working the way we want. Finally, the time has come to integrate all of the sensors together and make an entirely intelligent robot. As the solenoid, humidity sensor, and temperature sensors are already connected, all we need to do is to upload the code over to Pi and see the magic:

```
from time import sleep
from datetime import datetime
import RPi.GPIO as GPIO
import Adafruit_ADS1x15
import Adafruit_DHT
water_valve_pin = 23
sensor = 11
pin = 4
GPIO.setmode(GPIO.BCM)
```

```
GPIO.setwarnings(False)
GPIO.setup(water_valve_pin, GPIO.OUT)
Channel =0
GAIN = 1
adc = Adafruit_ADS1x15.ADS1115()
def check_moisture(m):
 adc.start_adc(channel, gain=GAIN)
 moisture_value = adc.get_last_result()
 moisture_value = int(moisture_value/327)
 print moisture_value
 if moisture_value < m:
 GPIO.output(water_valve_pin, GPIO.HIGH)
 sleep(5)
 GPIO.output(water_valve_pin, GPIO.LOW)
 else:
 GPIO.output(water_valve_pin, GPIO.LOW)
while True:
 humidity, temperature = Adafruit_DHT.read_retry(sensor, pin)
 H = datetime.now().strftime('%H')
 M = datetime.now().strftime('%M')
 if H == '07' and M <= '10':
 if temperature < 15:
 check_moisture(20)
 elif temperature >= 15 and temperature < 28:
 check_moisture(30)
 elif temperature >= 28:
 check_moisture(40)
 if H == '17' and M <= '10':
 if temperature < 15:

 check_moisture(20)
 elif temperature >= 15 and temperature < 28:
 check_moisture(30)
 elif temperature >= 28:
 check_moisture(40)
```

Pretty long code, right? It might look so, but once you write it line by line, you will certainly understand that it might be longer than all the code we have written so far, but it's anything but complex. You might have understood most of the program, however let me explain a few new things that we have used here:

```
def check_moisture(m):
   adc.start_adc(channel, gain = GAIN)

moisture_value = adc.get_last_result()
moisture_value = int(moisture_value / 327)
print moisture_value
```

```
if moisture_value < m:
  GPIO.output(water_valve_pin, GPIO.HIGH)
  sleep(5)
  GPIO.output(water_valve_pin, GPIO.LOW)
else :
  GPIO.output(water_valve_pin, GPIO.LOW)
```

In this line, we are defining a function named `check_moisture()`. Previously, if you remember, while we were making the function `check_moisture`, we were basically checking if the moisture value was either more or less than 20%. What if we have to check the moisture for 30%, 40%, and 50%? Would we make a separate function for that?

Obviously not! What we do is we pass an argument to the function, an argument is basically a variable placed within the brackets of the function. Now we can assign values to this variable for, for example, `check_moisture(30)`—now the value of the m will be 30 during the time that function is executing. Then again, if you call it as `check_moisture(40)` then the value of that m would be 40.

Now, as you can see, we are comparing values of m throughout the function:

```
if moisture_value < m:
```

The `if` statement will be checking the value of the m which is assigned while calling the function. This makes our job very easy and simple.

Let's see what the rest of the program is doing:

```
if temperature < 15:
    check_moisture(20)
```

Every time the desired time is reached it will go ahead and check for the temperature. If the temperature is less than 15 it will call the function `check_moisture` with the value of the argument as 20. Hence, if the moisture is less than 20%, then the water will be fed to the garden:

```
elif temperature >= 15 and temperature < 28:
        check_moisture(30)
```

The `elif` or the `else if` statement is used after an `if` statement. This in common words means that if the previous `if` statement is not true, then it will check for this `if` statement. So, in the preceding line it will check if the temperature is between 15 and 28 degrees Celsius. If that is true, then it will check the moisture of the soil. The argument to the function is 30 in this line. Hence, it will check if the moisture is less than 30. If so, then it will supply the water to the garden:

```
elif temperature >= 28:
            check_moisture(40)
```

Similarly, in this line of code we are checking the temperature, and if it is equal to or more than 28 degrees Celsius then it will pass the value 40 as an argument to the function `check_moisture`. Hence this time it will check for moisture if it is 28 or more than that.

As you can see, now the system will be checking the ambient temperature and, based on that, the amount of water to the plants is regulated. The best part is that it is consistent and will provide the right amount of water needed by the plants.

The values mentioned in this entire chapter are simply assumed values. I would strongly recommend to tweak it based on where you live and what kind of plants you have in your garden to get the best out of the system.

Summary

In this chapter, we covered certain topics such as solenoid integration and soil humidity sensors to build a robot that waters your backyard garden automatically. Next up, we will cover the basics of motors.

4
Basics of Motors

All right then! We have made a robot that takes care of your garden and I hope it's working fine. It's time to take things to another level.

We have always thought that robots are like WALL-E, moving around and doing things for us. Well, my friend, now that dream is not far away. In fact, in this chapter we will be going ahead and making one. Let's see how it's done.

We will be covering the following topics:

- The basics
- Getting it rolling
- Changing the speed

The basics

Whenever we talk about moving from one place to another, we think about wheels and similarly whenever we think about moving the wheels of a robot, we think about motors. There are various different types of motors that exist. So let's firstly look at the most basic type of motor, which is called a brushed DC motor. As the name suggests, it works on a direct current. You may find such motors like this:

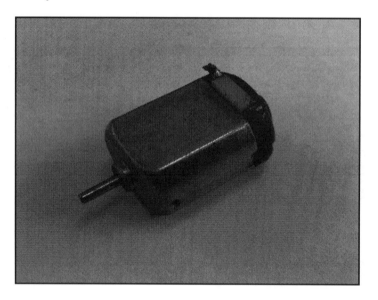

Trust me, these things are omnipresent, from the Christmas gift you bought for your neighbor to the biggest baddest machines out there—you will find these motors hiding under the hood. These motors are common for a reason and that is because they are very, very simple. So simple that powering them up only requires a battery and two wires. Simply connect the positive to one terminal and negative to the other, and the motor will start spinning. Interchange those connections and the direction of the rotation will change. Take two cells and double the voltage and the motor will spin even faster. It is that simple.

Now you might assume that we would simply connect this motor to Raspberry Pi and that we would be good to go. But unfortunately this is not going to be the case. As you may remember from the previous chapters, Raspberry Pi can only supply around 50 milliamps, but the consumption of a motor can be much higher. Hence, to run one we need an intermediate device.

The first thing that will come to your mind will be to use a relay, and why not? They can channel a huge amount of current and can handle high voltages. This should be the ideal choice. You would be right if you thought so, but only to some extent, and that is because a relay is simply a switch we can use to turn the motor on or off. We would not be able to control the speed or the direction of rotation of the motor. Now, you would think that this problem is not new and that we can very easily solve it by using **pulse width modulation (PWM)**, right? Well, the answer is no! Because these relays are mechanical devices, and due to their mechanical nature, there are some maximum limits in terms of it being switched on or off in a second. Hence, it would not be able to cope with the frequency of PWM. Finally, we would still be left with the problem of changing the direction and the speed of the motor. So what do we do now?

As I always say, the beauty of a problem is that it always has a solution, and the solution here is called a motor driver. A motor driver is primarily a set of electronic relays—a switch that can allow high currents yet is not mechanical. Hence, we can switch it hundreds of times every second. These electronic relays are either made of simple transistors or, in high power applications, they can even use MOSFETs for switching. We can simply give PWM to these electronic switches and get the voltage to modulate while making sure that enough current is being delivered to the circuit. Further, as I mentioned earlier, the motor driver is made of a set of these electronic relays. The most common and workable fashion in which they are arranged is called a full bridge or an H Bridge. Before I explain any further, let's see what this is, exactly:

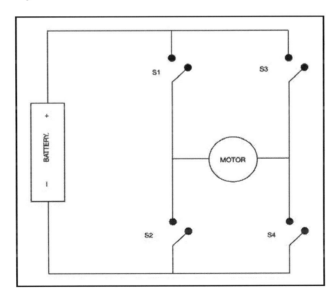

In a full bridge we have four switching circuits across the connected motor; these can be independently switched on or off based on the requirements. In the off state, all of these switching circuits are in an open state, hence keeping the motor switched off. Now, whenever we want to start the motor, we will have to switch on two switches in such a way that the circuit is complete and the motor starts working. So let's see what it would look like:

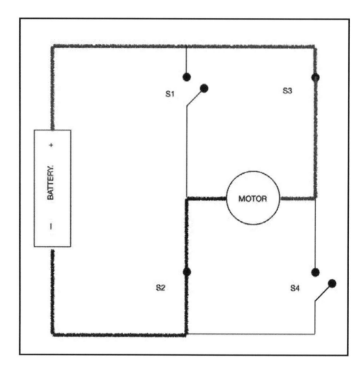

Here, we have switched on the switching circuit **S2** and **S3**; this in turn completes the circuit and lets the current flow in the motor. Now, to control the speed, these same switching circuits can be switched on and off at a very high frequency at varying duty cycles to achieve a specific mean voltage. Now that we can achieve a specific speed for the motor by changing the voltage via these two switching circuits, let's see how we are going to change the direction of rotation of the motor:

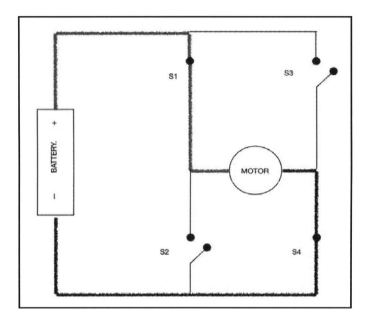

In this circuit we have switched off the previously connected **S2** and **S3** and instead switched on **S1** and **S4**, hence the polarity to the motor is reversed. As we discussed earlier, whenever the polarity of a DC-brushed motor is changed, the direction also changes subsequently. There are various types of motor drivers you can find on the market. What we have understood here is called a brushed DC H-bridge motor driver; there are other types of motor drivers as well for controlling other types of motors, but currently we will stick to the brushed motor only. While selecting a motor driver, you should examine the specification sheet of the motor driver very carefully. Some of the key specifications that will be mentioned are as follows:

- **Voltage rating**: There will be a minimum and maximum limit to the voltage that the motor driver can handle and modulate between. Make sure your motor lies in between this specific voltage range.
- **Current rating**: There will be an absolute maximum current that the motor driver can handle; going anywhere beyond it will burn or damage the motor driver. This can be a little deceptive. Let's see why. Except for the absolute maximum, there will be many other current ratings that might be specified. These might be:

- **Repetitive maximum current**: This is the current rating that can be the maximum current the motor driver can handle, but not continuously. This rating is given because at times the load on the motor might increase and there might be a higher current requirement for a brief moment. The motor driver will provide the adequate current on a repetitive basis without getting damaged. But this current requirement should not be continuous.

- **Burst maximum current**: This is the absolute maximum current that the motor driver can handle; anything beyond it will damage the motor driver. The DC motors might have a very high current requirement when it starts from a standstill. Hence, the motor drivers are designed to handle these currents. But this surge of current should not be repetitive, otherwise heating and subsequent damage can happen. Often, burst maximum current is referred to as the maximum current by the manufacturers.

- **Continuous maximum current**: This is the real deal; the continuous maximum current is the maximum continuous current that the motor driver can mange on a continuous basis.

- **Supply voltage**: This is the operating voltage of the motor driver—this voltage must be given to the motor driver for its own internal workings.

- **Logic supply voltage**: This is the control signal given to the motor driver, and can be given at various voltages such as 5V, 3.3V, and 12V. Hence, the motor driver will specify the maximum logical voltage that it can accept in the signal line.

Now, let's see what we have got. During the course of this book, we will be using the L298N motor driver module, which currently is one of the most common motor driver modules available on the market. It has two channels—you have two H-bridges and hence you can connect two motors onto it. Further, the specifications for this motor driver are also decent for the price. Here are the specifications:

- **Voltage rating**: 2.5V to 46V
- **Repetitive maximum current**: 2.5 amp
- **Burst maximum current**: 3 amp
- **Continuous maximum current**: 2 amp
- **Supply voltage**: 4.5V to 7V
- **Logic supply voltage**: 4.5V to 7V

Once you have the physical motor driver with you, you will notice the following pins:

- **Motor A**: This is channel 1 of the motor driver. You can connect the first motor to this port.
- **Motor B**: This is channel 2 of the motor driver. You can connect a second motor to this port. If you only have one motor, you can simply leave this port unconnected.
- **GND**: This is the ground of the power supply that you will attach for the motor. It is very important that you not only connect the ground of the power supply but also connect the ground of Raspberry Pi to this port so that the circuit is complete between Raspberry Pi and the motor driver.
- **VCC**: This is the positive port of the motor driver. This is where the positive terminal of your battery or power adapter will go.
- **IN 1 and IN 2**: These are the two logical inputs that we need to provide from the microcontroller for motor A. Whenever IN 1 receives the signal, one part of the H-bridge is activated—the motor starts spinning in one direction. Whenever IN 2 receives the signal, the other part of the H-bridge is activated, making the motor spin in the opposite direction.
- **IN 3 and IN 4**: This is the logical input of the motor B, which will work in exactly the same way as IN 1 and IN 2.
- **EN A and EN B**: These are the enable pins for both the channels. If these pins are not high, the respective channels will not work despite any signal that you give over the input ports. You might notice that there is a small cap on the EN ports. This is called a shunt. What it does is that it makes contact between the two pins that it has been connected on. This cap, when present over the EN pin, means that it would permanently be high as long as this shunt is connected.

Getting it rolling

OK, that's a lot of theory, so now let's fire up one of our motors via Raspberry Pi. To do that, go ahead and connect the motor and the motor driver as shown:

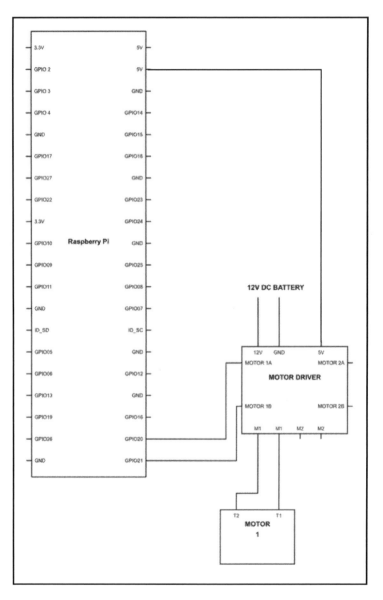

Now, once you are done with it, let's upload the code and see what happens:

```
import RPi.GPIO as GPIO
from time import sleep
GPIO.setmode(GPIO.BCM)

Motor1R = 20
Motor1L = 21

GPIO.setup(Motor1R,GPIO.OUT)
GPIO.setup(Motor1L,GPIO.OUT)


GPIO.output(Motor1R,GPIO.HIGH)
GPIO.output(Motor1L,GPIO.LOW)

sleep(5)

GPIO.output(Motor1R,GPIO.LOW)
GPIO.output(Motor1L,GPIO.HIGH)

sleep(5)

GPIO.cleanup()
```

Now, let's understand the code a bit:

```
Motor1R = 20
Motor1L = 21
```

Pin number 20 is connected to IN 1 of the motor driver. For convenience, we have changed motor 1 right to Motor1R; in reality, the motor can spin in any direction but we have just written this for convenience and understanding. Similarly, we have done this for Motor1L as well. This is connected to IN 2, hence this will lead to the motor spinning in the other direction:

```
GPIO.output(Motor1R,GPIO.HIGH)
GPIO.output(Motor1L,GPIO.LOW)
```

Here, we are making the Motor1R or the pin number 20 high, which means that the input motor driver is getting is:

Motor	Pin	Input	State
Motor 1R	Pin number 20 of Raspberry Pi	IN 1	HIGH
Motor 1L	Pin number 21 of Raspberry Pi	IN 2	LOW

Now, after a delay of 5 seconds, the following code will run, which will change the state of the pins as depicted in the below table:

```
GPIO.output(Motor1R,GPIO.LOW)
GPIO.output(Motor1L,GPIO.HIGH)
```

Motor	Pin	Input	State
Motor 1R	Pin number 20 of Raspberry Pi	IN 1	LOW
Motor 1L	Pin number 21 of Raspberry Pi	IN 2	HIGH

Now, let's see what happens once we run it. The motor will spin firstly in one direction and then it will go in the other direction. The code is very straightforward and I don't think there is any need for explanation. All we are doing here is simply turning either of the two GPIOs connected to the motor driver on and off. Once the input IN 1 of the motor driver is activated, a part of the H-bridge is switched on, causing the motor to spin in one direction. Whenever the IN 2 of the motor driver is high, then the opposite part of H-bridge is turned on, causing the polarity at the output end of the motor driver to change, and hence the motor turns in the other direction.

Changing the speed

Now that we have understood how to change the direction of the motor using the motor driver, it's time to take it a step further and control the speed of the motor using the motor driver. To do this, we don't really have to do much. The motor drivers are built to understand the PWM signals. Once the PWM signal to the motor driver is provided, then the motor driver in turn adjusts the output voltage for the motor and hence changes the speed of the motor driver. The PWM has to be provided on the same input ports IN 1 and IN 2 for motor A, and IN 3 and IN 4 for motor B. It is obvious that the pin on which the PWM is provided will decide the direction in which the motor will move, and the duty cycle of the PWM will decide the speed at which the motor will be spinning.

Now we have understood how speed control in motor driver works. It's time to do it by ourselves. To do so, we do not need to make any changes to the connections; all we need to do is to upload the following code:

```
import RPi.GPIO as GPIO
from time
import sleep
GPIO.setmode(GPIO.BCM)

Motor1R = 20
Motor1L = 21
```

```
GPIO.setup(Motor1R, GPIO.OUT)
GPIO.setup(Motor1L, GPIO.OUT)

pwm = GPIO.PWM(Motor1R, 100)
pwm.start(0)

try:
while True:
  GPIO.output(Motor1L, GPIO.LOW)
for i in range(0, 101):
  pwm.ChangeDutyCycle(i)
sleep(0.1)

except KeyboardInterrupt:

  pwm.stop()
GPIO.cleanup()
```

What happened after you ran this code? I'm sure the motor started slowly and then started increasing its speed and, upon reaching its top speed, it eventually stopped—exactly what we wanted it to do. If you remember, this code looks very familiar. Remember changing the brightness of the LED in the first chapter? It is almost the same; there are a few differences, though, so let's see what they are:

```
pwm = GPIO.PWM(Motor1R, 100)
```

In this line, we are simply defining the pin we have to give the PWM on—as in, on Motor1R, which corresponds to pin number 20. Also, we are are defining the frequency of the PWM as 100 hertz or 100 times in a second:

```
pwm.start(0)
```

If you remember, the preceding command from the previous chapters, pwm.start(), is primarily used for defining the duty cycle of the signal. Here, we are giving it the duty cycle as 0 that is the pin would be off:

```
GPIO.output(Motor1L, GPIO.LOW)
```

As we are running motor in one specific direction and which is `1R` hence the other half of the H bridge should be turned off. this would be done by the above line by putting the line `1L` LOW. If we don't do this then the pin `21` can be in an arbitrary state, hence it can be either on or off. This might conflict with the direction in which the motor is moving and the hardware would not work properly:

```
for i in range(0,101):
```

Here comes the real deal; this line, `for i in range(0,101):`, will keep on running the program contained in it until the time the value of `i` is between `0` to `101`. It will also increment the value of `i` every time this loop runs. Here, every time, the value will increase by one:

```
pwm.ChangeDutyCycle(i)
```

Now, this is a slightly new command. Previously, we have used the line `pwm.start(0)` to assign a duty cycle to the PWM. As we have already assigned a duty cycle value to the PWM, to change it we would use the previously mentioned command. The duty cycle would be the same as the value of `i`.

Hence, every time the code passes through the `for` loop, the value or the duty cycle will increase by one. Super easy, isn't it?

Everything in robotics is very easy if you do it right. The idea is to break your problem into small pieces and solve them one by one; trust me, once you do that, nothing will look difficult to you.

Summary

In this chapter, we worked on the various aspects of a motor. Moving on, by using all the basics, we will study the interaction of Bluetooth with mobile devices and build a Bluetooth-controlled robotic car.

5
Making a Pet Feeding Robot

In this chapter, we will take a step further in terms of integrating the sensors to make a robot that feeds your pet whenever you have programmed it to. It is fairly simple to build; you might need some DIY skills and a few old cardboards to prepare this project. Keep scissors and adhesives handy, as they might be needed here.

There are times when you are not at home throughout the day and your pet keeps waiting for you to feed him. For such a situation, this robot would be of great help; it will feed your pet at specific times and also make sure that your pet gets the right quantity of food every single time. This can even be helpful on a daily basis. As it will never forget to feed your pet, no matter what.

Force measurement

Force is one of the fundamental units that is applied to objects, either due to gravity or some external factors. Force measurements can give us a lot of insight about the environment or the object. If you have an electronic weight scale, then every time you step on to the weight scale, the weight being told to you happens because of a force sensor. This happens because your body has a mass. Due to the mass, the gravity pulls the object toward the center of the earth. The force being applied by the gravity to any physical object is referred to as the weight of the object. Hence, with the force sensor, we are basically sensing how much force gravity is applying to a body.

Now when we talk about force measurements, it can be done using multiple ways. There are various types of complex load cells that can precisely tell us how many milligrams of weight have changed. There are also much simpler sensors that can simply give us a rough estimate of how much force is being applied. From this data, we can calculate the relative weight of the object. You must be asking why are we not using the load cell. The reason is that it can be slightly complicated for the present scenario, and it's always good to start with basics.

So, let's see what we have. The load sensor we are talking about is a resistive force sensor. The way it works is very simple. It consists of polymer whose resistance changes with the change of force applied to it. In general, the more force you apply, the lower would be the resistance. Hence, due to change in this resistance, we can simply calculate the resultant voltage. This resultant voltage would be directly proportional to the weight being put on the force sensor.

Constructing the robot

Now, to make this robot, we would need a few cardboard cartons. We need to make two parts of it:

- A food dispenser
- A collecting bowl with a force sensor

First, let's see how the dispenser has to be made. You need to follow these steps:

1. Take a medium-sized carton that can carry up to about four and a half pounds of pet food.
2. Then, go ahead and make a small cutout.
3. This cutout should be big enough to dispense food but not so big that a lot of food comes out of it at once.
4. Now, once that is done, you need to make a lid that covers that through-hole.
5. This lid should be slightly bigger than the through-hole itself.
6. Install the lid over the shaft of the motor.

7. Fix the motor on to the cardboard, as shown in the following diagram. Make sure that the position of the motor should be such that the lid covers the entire through-hole on the cardboard.

8. Finally, install ends-stops. These are simple pieces of cardboard that will restrict the movement of the lid in either direction.

9. The first end-stop should be at a position that it should stop the lid exactly where it covers the entire through-hole.

10. The second should be at a position where the lid is entirely opened, and there is no obstruction when the food comes down from the container.

To help you with the construction, refer to the following diagram; you can devise other ways to control the opening or closing as well if you want:

Now, the second part is the bowl. This part is pretty straightforward. You simply need to paste the force sensor using a mild adhesive onto the bottom of the bowl, where it makes contact with the ground. Once this is done, add another layer of adhesive and attach it exactly below the dispenser.

Once this constitution is done, go ahead and wire it up, as shown here:

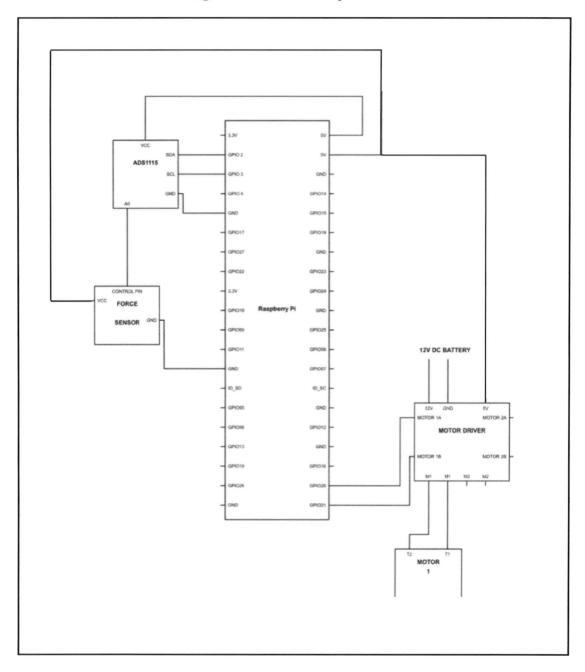

Perfect! Now we are ready to upload our code and make this thing work. So, go ahead and upload the following code; then I will tell you what exactly is happening:

```
import Adafruit_ADS1x15
import RPi.GPIO as GPIO

adc = Adafruit_ADS1x15.ADS1015()

GAIN = 1
channel = 0

adc.start_adc(channel, gain=GAIN)

while True:
    print(adc.get_last_result())
```

Now, once you upload this code, you will start to get the raw reading of the force sensors. How? Let's see:

```
import Adafruit_ADS1x15
```

Here, we are sporting the library for ADS1x15 using the command `import Adafruit_ADS1x115`; this will help us read the value from the ADC:

```
adc = Adafruit_ADS1x15.ADS1015()

GAIN = 1
channel = 0

adc.start_adc(channel, gain=GAIN)
```

You should know what this line does; however if you are not sure, refer to `Chapter 2, Using GPIOs as Input`:

```
    print(adc.get_last_result())
```

In this line, the raw reading that has been received by the ADC will be shown to you.

You must be wondering why we are doing this. Till now, you must have been feeding your pet based on visual quantity, instead of a specific weight. Hence, what we are doing here is printing the value of the force sensor. Once this value is printed, then you can correct quantity of the food in the container and measure the reading. This reading will act as a threshold. That is, this is the quantity that would be dispensed.

Now, once you have noted this reading, we will change the code slightly. Let's see what it is:

```
import time
import Adafruit_ADS1x15
import RPi.GPIO as GPIO
Motor1a = 21
Motor1b = 20
Buzzer = 14
FSR = 16
THRESHOLD = 1000
GPIO.setmode(GPIO.BCM)
GPIO.setup(Motor1a,GPIO.OUT)
GPIO.setup(Motor1b,GPIO.OUT)
GPIO.setup(Buzzer,GPIO.OUT)
GPIO.setup(FSR,GPIO.IN)
adc = Adafruit_ADS1x15.ADS1015()
GAIN = 1
channel = 0
adc.start_adc(channel, gain=GAIN)
while True:
 M = datetime.datetime.now().strftime('%M')
 if (H == 12 or H==16 or H==20) && M == 00 :
 value = adc.get_last_result()
 while value < THRESHOLD:
 GPIO.output(BUZZER,1)
 GPIO.output(MOTOR1a,1)
 GPIO.output(MOTOR1b,0)
 GPIO.output(MOTOR1a,0)
 GPIO.output(MOTOR1b,1)
 GPIO.output(Buzzer,0)
 time.sleep(5)
 GPIO.output(MOTOR1b,0)
 adc.stop_adc()
```

Now let's see what we have done!

```
Motor1a =   21
Motor1b = 20
Buzzer = 14
FSR = 16
THRESHOLD = 1000
```

Here, we are declaring the pins connected for the motor, buzzer, and **Force Sensitive Resistor (FSR)**. Also, we are assigning the value to a variable named THRESHOLD; this will determine the amount of food that will be dispensed. Here, we have kept an arbitrary value as 1000. In your code, you must put the value that you have calculated in the previous code.

Now that most of the code is easily understandable, let's jump to the part where the main show is happening:

```
'   H = datetime.datetime.now().strftime('%H')
    M = datetime.datetime.now().strftime('%M')

  if (H == 12 or H==20) && M == 00 :

      value = adc.get_last_result()

      while value < THRESHOLD:
          GPIO.output(BUZZER,1)
          GPIO.output(MOTOR1a,1)
          GPIO.output(MOTOR1b,0)
```

In the first line using the function `datetime.dateime.now().strftime('%H')`, we are deriving the value of hours at that moment, and using the function `M = datetime.datetime.now().strftime('%M')`, we are deriving the minutes. Once this is done, then using the condition `if (H == 12 or H ==20) && M == 00`, we are checking whether the time is 12 noon or 20:00 hours in the evening. Once any of these condition are true, then the value of `M` is also getting checked. If `M == 00`, then the value of ADC would be checked using the function `adc.get_last_result()`. The function stores the value in a variable named `value`. Once the value is checked, it is checked by `while value< THRESHOLD:`. If the condition is true, then `BUZZER` and `MOTOR1a` are set to high. This means that the buzzer will ring and the motor will turn in one direction. As we have an end-stop at both directions, the motor will stop whenever it reaches that position:

```
GPIO.output(MOTOR1a,0)
GPIO.output(MOTOR1b,1)
GPIO.output(Buzzer,0)

time.sleep(5)

GPIO.output(MOTOR1b,0)
```

Once the preceding condition is false, then the rest of code will come into action, which basically will turn the motor to the closing side and it will stop the buzzer from buzzing. The motor will try to retract to its closed position for 5 seconds, as after the condition `time.sleep(5)`, the motor will get a command `GPIO.output(MOTOR1b,0)`, which will stop the motor from turning.

Hence, in summary, the robot will dispense the food at certain times and in a very specific quantity that you decide.

Making the robot detect pets

The preceding code is good, and I'm sure it would be dispensing the food at set times. However, there can be a problem, as the robot would not be effective if the pet does not know whether the food had been fetched. Hence, we need to have an alarm that should inform the pets that the food is ready to be eaten.

Even in the previous program, we have used a buzzer that will inform the pet when the food is being dispensed, but, that was only for a very short period of time. However, what we are talking about here is an alarm system that will keep on ringing till the time the pet does not come and eat the food. To do this, connect the system as follows and mount the ultrasonic sensor in such a way that it notes the distance of the pet while he is eating the food.

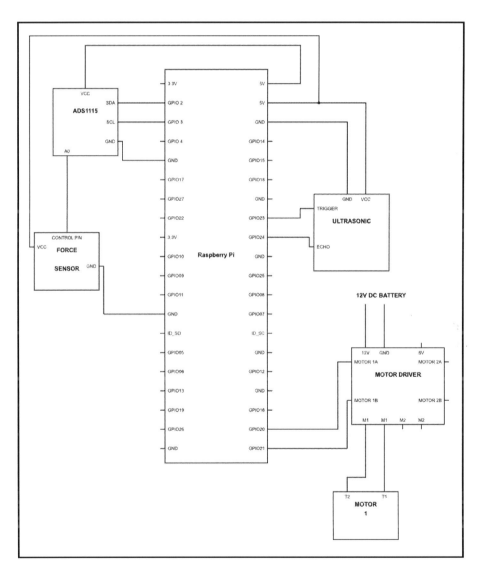

Now, to do that, you will need to upload the following code:

```
import time
import Adafruit_ADS1x15
import RPi.GPIO as GPIO

Motor1a =  21
Motor1b = 20
Buzzer = 14
FSR = 16

GPIO.setmode(GPIO.BCM)
GPIO.setup(Motor1a,GPIO.OUT)
GPIO.setup(Motor1b,GPIO.OUT)
GPIO.setup(Buzzer,GPIO.OUT)
GPIO.setup(FSR,GPIO.IN)

adc = Adafruit_ADS1x15.ADS1015()

GAIN = 1
channel = 0

adc.start_adc(channel, gain=GAIN)


def Distance():
    GPIO.output(23,GPIO.LOW)

    time.sleep(0.2)

    GPIO.output(23,GPIO.HIGH)

    time.sleep(0.000010)

    GPIO.output(23,GPIO.LOW)

    while GPIO.input(24)==0:
        pulse_start = time.time()

    while GPIO.input(24)==1:
        pulse_stop = time.time()

      duration = pulse_stop - pulse_start
      distance = duration*17150.0
     distance = round(distance,2)

    return distance
```

```
while True:
    H = datetime.datetime.now().strftime('%H')

    if H == 12 or H==16 or H==20:
     value = adc.get_last_result()

    while value < 100:
        GPIO.output(BUZZER,1)
        GPIO.output(MOTOR1a,1)
        GPIO.output(MOTOR1b,0)

time.sleep(5)

GPIO.output(MOTOR1a,0)
GPIO.output(MOTOR1b,0)

if Distance() <=2 :

    GPIO.output(Buzzer, 0)
    time.sleep(5)

  adc.stop_adc()
```

As you can see, most of the code is almost identical; however, there is an added feature that will keep ringing the buzzer till the time the pet does not come and eat the food. To do this, we input the following:

```
def Distance():
    GPIO.output(23,GPIO.LOW)

    time.sleep(0.2)

    GPIO.output(23,GPIO.HIGH)

    time.sleep(0.000010)

    GPIO.output(23,GPIO.LOW)

    while GPIO.input(24)==0:
        pulse_start = time.time()

    while GPIO.input(24)==1:
        pulse_stop = time.time()

      duration = pulse_stop - pulse_start
      distance = duration*17150.0
      distance = round(distance,2)
```

```
        return distance
```

We have defined a function that notes down the distance taken from the ultrasonic sensor. You may recollect this code form the previous chapters. So, now, whenever this function is called, the distance will be noted down:

```
    while value < 100:
        GPIO.output(BUZZER,1)
        GPIO.output(MOTOR1a,1)
        GPIO.output(MOTOR1b,0)

time.sleep(5)

GPIO.output(MOTOR1a,0)
GPIO.output(MOTOR1b,0)
```

As you can see, the buzzer is getting switched on in the while loop just like last time; however, after 5 in the previous code after 5 second of wait the buzzer was switched off. However, in this code, we are not doing so. Hence, the buzzer will stay active till the time some part of our code does not turn it off. Now, to turn on the buzzer, we are calculating the distance at the end of the code:

```
if Distance() <=2 && value < 50:

    GPIO.output(Buzzer, 0)
    time.sleep(5)
```

This part of code is checking whether distance is less than 2 centimeters and the weight value of the food container is less than 50. This means the pet approaches the food container and eats at least half of the food. If he does not eat the food properly, then the buzzer will keep on buzzing.

Summary

So readers, I think you understood the basics of motor integration with logic of time and force sensor to make a robot that does some of your work on a daily basis. These kinds of robots are available on the market for hundreds of dollars, but see how easily and at such low cost you made one for yourself. Moving forward, in the next chapter, we will be building a Bluetooth controlled robotic car.

6

Bluetooth-Controlled Robotic Car

We have come a long way; now it's time to go ahead and make something even better. The world is going all gaga over the inception of autonomous cars and within this decade this will become the new normal. There is so much going on in these vehicles. Multiple sensors, GPS, and telemetry are all calculated in real time to make sure that the car is on the right course and is being driven by the system safely on the road, so making a robotic vehicle proves to be an ideal way to learn robotics and future technologies. In this book, we will always try to make technologies that are not only as good as the present technologies but in some ways even better. So, let's go ahead and get to making this autonomous vehicle one step at a time.

This chapter will cover the following topics:

- Basics of the vehicle
- Getting the vehicle ready
- Controlling the vehicle by Bluetooth

Basics of the vehicle

You must be thinking: what can we possibly learn about the vehicle that we don't already know? This may be true, but there are a few that we must make sure we understand before taking on this chapter. So, let's get started.

First is the chassis, which we will be using: it's is a four-wheel drive chassis and all the four wheels are independently controlled by a dedicated motor. Hence, we can change the speed of every single wheels as per our needs. We have chosen a four-wheel drive drivetrain as it is harder for it to get stuck on carpets and uneven surfaces. You can also opt for a two-wheel drive drivetrain if you want to do so, as it won't make a huge difference.

Now, once you assemble the chassis you might see that it does not have a steering mechanism. Does this mean that the car will only go straight? Well, obviously not. There are many ways by which we can steer the direction of a car while making small vehicles. The best one is called differential turning.

In conventional cars, there is one engine and that engine powers up the wheels; hence in principal all the wheels turn at the same speed. Now this works fine when we are going straight but whenever the car wants to turn there comes a new problem. Refer to the following diagram:

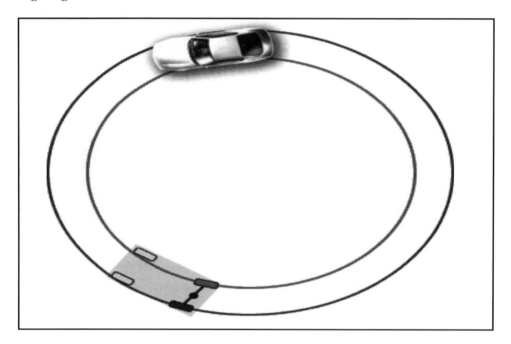

You will see that the wheels, which are on the inner curve, have a smaller diameter and the one on the outer edge has a larger diameter. You may remember a fact from elementary school: the larger the diameter the more the circumference, and vice a versa. Hence, the wheel towards the inner edge will be covering a shorter distance compared to the wheels on the outer edge at the same time, or in simple words, the inner wheels will be spinning slower and the outer wheels will be spinning faster.

This problem leads to the discovery of differentials in cars, which is a round lump at the center of the axle of the car. What this does is that it varies the rate at which the wheels are spinning based on the turning radius. Genius, isn't it? Now, you must be thinking: this is all right, but why are you telling me all this? Well, because we will do the exact opposite to turn the robot. If we change the speed of the motors on the inner and outer edge of the turning circle, then the car will try to turn towards inside and similarly if we do it for the other end then it will try to turn in the other direction. While making wheeled robot this strategy is not new at all. Steering mechanisms are complicated and implementing them on small robot is simply a challenge. Hence this is a far simpler and easy way to turn your vehicle around.

Not only is this way simple but it is a very efficient and simple strategy that requires minimal components. It is also better as the turning radius of the vehicle is also reduced. In fact, if we spin the opposite sides of the wheels in the opposite direction at the same speed then the vehicle will turn completely on its own axis, making the turning radius entirely zero. this type of configuration is called skid-steer drive. For a robot that is wheeled and works indoors, this is a killer feature.

To know more about it read more
here: https://groups.csail.mit.edu/drl/courses/cs54-2001s/skidsteer.html

Getting the vehicle ready

Now is the time to go ahead and make the robotic vehicle a reality. So let's unbox the vehicle chassis and screw every part together. The assembly manual generally comes along with the kit, so it won't take long for you to complete it.

Once you have completed building the kit, go ahead and segregate the wires for each of the motors. This is going to be a very important part of making the vehicle ready. So, once you have all the wires coming out of the vehicle, take a cell and power up each of the wheels. Notice the polarity of connection in which the wheels spin in the forward direction. All you have to do is to take a permanent marker or perhaps a nail paint and mark the wire which goes to the positive terminal when the motor is spinning in the forward direction. As all of these motors are entirely dependent on polarity for the direction, this step is key to ensure that whenever we power them up they always spin in the same direction. Trust me, this will save you a lot of headaches.

Now, once this is all done, connect the wires to the motor driver as shown in the following diagram (the wire marked by red is the wire that you marked earlier):

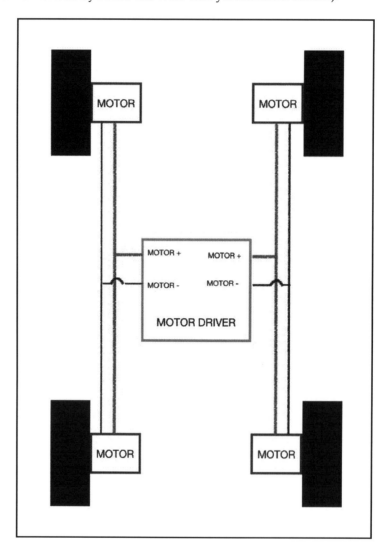

Perfect! Now everything seems sorted, except for the connection of the motor driver with the power source and Raspberry Pi. So let's see how we are going to do it:

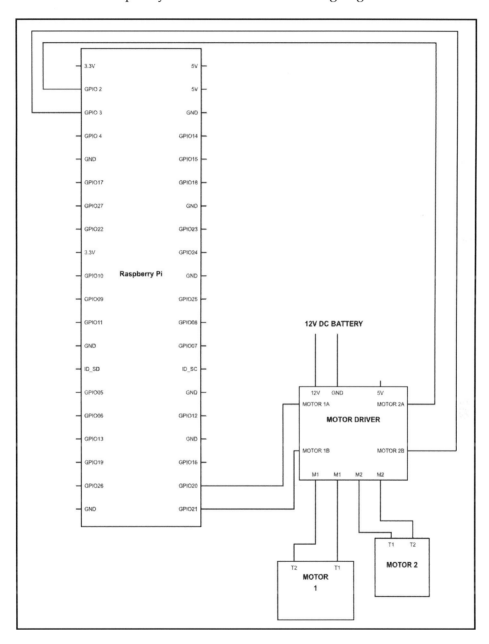

All right then! Time for the real deal! So the first thing we want to make sure is that all the connections are working exactly the way we planned them to. For this, we will start off with a dummy code which will simply switch all the motors on and in forward direction. So here is the code:

```
import RPi.GPIO as GPIO
import time
GPIO.setmode(GPIO.BCM)
Motor1a = 20
Motor1b = 21
Motor2a = 2
Motor2b = 3
GPIO.setup(Motor1a,GPIO.OUT)
GPIO.setup(Motor1b,GPIO.OUT)
GPIO.setup(Motor2a,GPIO.OUT)
GPIO.setup(Motor2b,GPIO.OUT)
GPIO.output(Motor1a,1)
GPIO.output(Motor1b,0)
GPIO.output(Motor2a,1)
GPIO.output(Motor2b,0)
time.sleep(10)
GPIO.cleanup()
```

The program can't be more simple than this; all we are doing here is giving the motor driver the command to spin the motor in one single direction. There might be a chance that a set of motors will be rotating in the reverse direction, in which case you should change the polarity of connections on the motor driver. This should solve the problem. Some people might think that we can make a change to the code as well to do this, but as per my experience it starts getting complicated from there and would cause you trouble if you chose the other path.

All right then, everything is set and all is working well. Go ahead, try some other output permutations and combinations and see what happens to the car. Don't worry, whatever you do, you won't be able to damage the car unless it runs off the roof!

Controlling the vehicle by Bluetooth

Had some fun trying those combinations? Now is the time that we take this journey a step ahead and see what else is possible. We have all played with remote-controlled cars and I'm sure everyone will have had fun with those zippy little toys. We are going to do something similar but in a much more sophisticated way.

We all are aware of Bluetooth: this is one of the best ways to communicate with devices in close proximity. Bluetooth communication is a medium data rate, low power communication method. This is almost omnipresent in mobile devices, hence it is an ideal way to start. What we will be doing in this chapter is controlling the car via your mobile phone using Bluetooth. Now let's see how we can do it.

The first thing we want to do is pair up the smartphone to the robotic vehicle, and to do so we need to open the terminal on Raspberry Pi and perform the following steps:

1. Type in the command `~ $ bluetoothctl`; this is a Bluetooth agent which allows two Bluetooth devices to communicate. Without the Bluetooth agent, the two devices will not be able to communicate with each other in the first place.

2. The `[Bluetooth] # power on` command simply powers up the Bluetooth on board the Raspberry.

3. The `[Bluetooth] # agent on` command starts up the agent which can then initiate the connection for us.

4. The `[Bluetooth] # discoverable on` command makes Raspberry Pi's Bluetooth discoverable. The Bluetooth might be on, but we must make it discoverable to make sure that the other device can find it and connect to it.

5. The `[Bluetooth] # pairable on` command makes the device pairable. If the Bluetooth is on, this doesn't mean your device will be able to connect, hence we need to make it pairable and this command does exactly that.

6. The `[Bluetooth] # scan on` command starts scanning for nearby Bluetooth devices. The output of this command will be a couple of MAC addresses along with the Bluetooth name. The MAC address is a physical address of the device; this is a unique address, hence it will never ever be the same for two devices.

7. The `[Bluetooth] # pair 94:65:2D:94:9B:D3` command helps you to pair up with the device you want. You simply need to type the mentioned command with the MAC address.

Just to be clear, this what your screen should look like:

Once you have done this process, you should be able to connect Raspberry Pi to your mobile devices. Now that you are connected, it's time to go ahead and write the code through which we will be able to control the Bluetooth car just using our mobile devices. So here is the code. Go ahead, have a look, then we will get to the explanation:

```
import bluetooth
import time
import RPi.GPIO as GPIO
Motor1a = 20
Motor1b = 21
Motor2a = 2
Motor2b = 3
GPIO.setmode(GPIO.BCM)
GPIO.setwarnings(False)
GPIO.setup(Motor1a,GPIO.OUT)
GPIO.setup(Motor1b,GPIO.OUT)
GPIO.setup(Motor2a,GPIO.OUT)
GPIO.setup(Motor2b,GPIO.OUT)
server_socket=bluetooth.BluetoothSocket( bluetooth.RFCOMM )
port = 1
server_socket.bind(("",port))
server_socket.listen(1)
client_socket,address = server_socket.accept()
print ("Accepted connection from "+str(address))
def stop_car():
  GPIO.output(Motor1a,0)
  GPIO.output(Motor1b,0)
  GPIO.output(Motor2a,0)
  GPIO.output(Motor2b,0)

while True:
  data = client_socket.recv(1024)
  if (data == "B" or data== "b"):
    GPIO.output(Motor1a,1)
    GPIO.output(Motor1b,0)
    GPIO.output(Motor2a,1)
    GPIO.output(Motor2b,0)
    time.sleep(1)
    stop_car()

  if (data == "F" or data == "f"):
    GPIO.output(Motor1a,0)
    GPIO.output(Motor1b,1)
    GPIO.output(Motor2a,0)
    GPIO.output(Motor2b,1)
    time.sleep(1)
    stop_car()
```

```
if (data == "R" or data == "r"):
  GPIO.output(Motor1a,0)
  GPIO.output(Motor1b,1)
  GPIO.output(Motor2a,1)
  GPIO.output(Motor2b,0)
  time.sleep(1)
  stop_car()

if (data == "L" or data == "l"):
  GPIO.output(Motor1a,1)
  GPIO.output(Motor1b,0)
  GPIO.output(Motor2a,0)
  GPIO.output(Motor2b,1)
  time.sleep(1)
  stop_car()

if (data == "Q" or data =="q"):
  stop_car()
if (data =='Z' or data == "z"):
  client_socket.close()
  server_socket.close()
```

Now let's see what this code is actually doing:

```
import bluetooth
```

We will be using some generic functions of Bluetooth during this program, hence we are calling the library `bluetooth` so that we are able to call those methods:

```
server_socket=bluetooth.BluetoothSocket( bluetooth.RFCOMM )
```

Now, whenever we connect two Bluetooth devices, we have various methods of communication; the easiest among them is radio frequency communication, herein referred to as RFCOMM. Now, in this line, we are using the `BluetoothSocket` method of the `bluetooth` library to define what communication protocol we are using in our program, which by now you know is RFCOMM. We are further storing this data in a variable called `server_socket` so that we don't have to repeat this step over and over again. Rather, whenever we need this data it will already be stored in the variable called `server_socket`:

```
port = 1
```

Now, Bluetooth has multiple ports; this is a very useful concept as through one single Bluetooth connection we can have various streams of data being transferred to various devices and programs. This avoids the clash of data and also makes sure that the data is securely communicated to exactly the right receiver. The program which we are using right now is extremely simple and we do not need multiple ports for data communication. Hence, we can use any of the 1 to 60 ports available to us for the communication. In this part of the program, you can write any port and your program will run just fine:

```
server_socket.bind(("",port))
```

Now, whenever we are connecting two devices we need to make sure that they stay connected throughout the communication. Hence, here we are writing this command: `server_socket.bind`. What this will do is that it will make sure that your Bluetooth connection is maintained during the entire communication.

As you can see, the first parameter inside the argument is empty. Here, we generally write the MAC address which it has to be bound with. However, as we have set this as empty it will automatically bind to the MAC address we are already paired with. The second argument we have is the port on which it has to be connected. As we know, the value of the `port` variable is set to be 1. Hence, it will automatically connect to port number 1:

```
server_socket.listen(1)
```

This is a very interesting line. As we know, we might not be the only person trying to connect to the Bluetooth device of Raspberry, hence what should Raspberry do when it receives another connection request?

In this line, we are defining just that: we are calling a method called `listen(1)`. In this function, we have defined the value of argument as 1. What it means is that it will be connected to one device only. Any other device that tries to connect will not get through. If we change this argument to 2 then it will be connected to two devices, however it would stay in the queue and hence it is called **queue connection**:

```
client_socket,address = server_socket.accept()
```

Now that most of the things for the connection have been done, we also need to know if we are connected to the right address. What the method `server_socket.accept()` does is that it returns the socket number and the address it is serving to. Hence, we are storing it within two variables called `client_socket` and `address`. However, as we know, the socket will remain only as 1, hence we will not be using it any further:

```
print ("Accepted connection from "+str(address))
```

In this line we are simply telling the user that the connection has been made successfully with the sue of the function `str(address)` we are printing the value of the address to which it is connected to. This way we can be double sure that the connection has been made to the right device.

```
data = client_socket.recv(1024)
```

In this line, we are receiving the data from the client; also, we are defining how long that data will be. Hence, in the method `client_socket.recv(1024)` we have passed on a parameter in the argument as `1024` which basically denotes that the maximum length of the data packet will be `1024` bytes. Once the data is received, it is then passed on to the variable `data` for further use.

After this, the rest of the program is pretty simple. We simply need to compare the value received by the mobile device and make the car do whatever we want to do. Here, we have made the car go in all four directions, that is, forward, backward, right, and left. You may also add specific conditions as per your needs:

```
client_socket.close()
```

In this line, we are closing the connection of the client socket so that the client can be disconnected and the data transfer can be terminated:

```
server_socket.close()
```

In the preceding line, we are closing the connection of the server socket so that the server connection can be disconnected.

Summary

This chapter taught us to automate and control a car using Bluetooth interfacing via data grabbing and sharing. Next up, we will develop what we have learned so far to interface IR sensors for obstacle avoidance and patch planning.

Sensor Interface for Obstacle Avoidance 7

To make a robotic vehicle that drives itself, we need to first understand how humans drive a vehicle. When we drive a car, we constantly analyze the space and the distance to other objects. Thereafter, we make a decision if we can go through it or not. This happens constantly with our brain – eye coordination. Similarly, a robot would have to do the same sort of thing.

In our previous chapters, you learned that we can find the proximity of objects around us, using sensors. These sensors can tell us how far an object is, and based on it, we can make decisions. We have done using an ultrasonic sensor primarily because it is extremely cheap. However, as you remember, it was slightly cumbersome to attach ultrasonic sensors and to run its code. It's time that we take a much simpler sensor and attach it to the car.

This chapter will cover the following topics:

- Infrared proximity sensor
- Autonomous emergency braking
- Giving it self-steering capabilities
- Making it fully autonomous

Infrared proximity sensor

The following photo depicts an infrared proximity sensor:

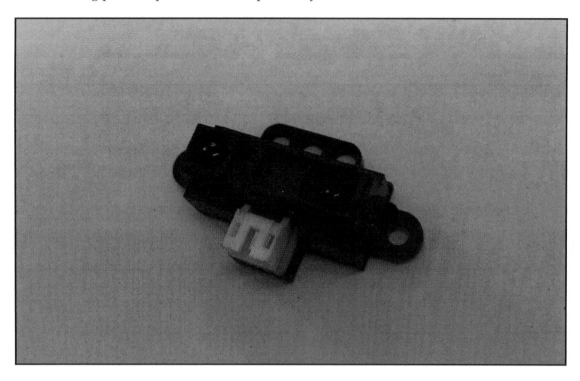

It consists of two major parts—the sensor and the transmitter. The transmitter emits IR waves; these **Infrared** (**IR**) waves then hit the object and come back to the sensor, as depicted in the following diagram..

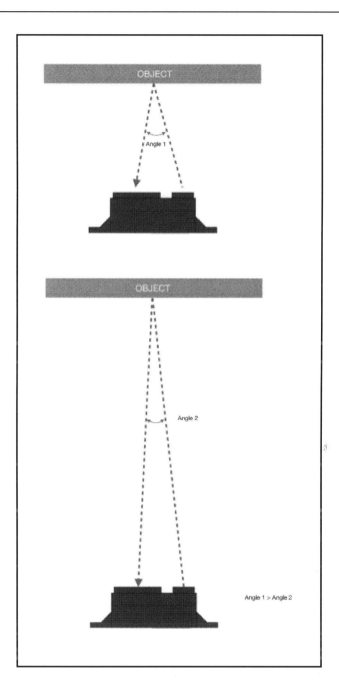

Now, as you can see in the preceding diagram, the emitted IR waves bounces back from a surface at a different distance from the sensor, then they makes an angular approach to the sensor. Now, because the distance between the transmitter and the sensor is fixed at all points of time, the angle corresponding to reflected IR waves would be proportional to the distance it has traveled before bouncing off. There are ultraprecise sensors in the IR proximity sensors that are capable of sensing the angle at which the IR waves approach it. By this angle, it gives the user a value of distance corresponding to it. This method of finding distance is named **triangulation**, and it has been used widely in the industry. One more thing we need to keep in mind is that we are all surrounded by IR radiation as we mentioned earlier in the chapters; any object above absolute zero temperature would have corresponding waves emitted to it. Also, the sunlight around us is having ample amount of IR radiations. Hence, these sensors have a built-in circuitry to compensate for it; however, there is only so much it can do. That's why, this solution might have some trouble when dealing with direct sunlight.

Now, enough of the theory, let's see how the car actually works. The IR proximity sensor we are using in this example is an analog sensor by Sharp with part code GP2D12. It has an effective sensing range of 1000-800 mm. The range is also dependent on the reflectivity of the surface of the object in question. The darker the object, the shorter the range. This sensor has three pins. As you might have guessed, there is one for VCC, another for ground, and the last for the signal. This is an analog sensor; hence, the distance reading would be given based on the voltage. Generally with most analog sensors you would get a graph which will depict the various voltages at various sensing ranges. The output is basically depending on the internal hardware of the sensor and its construction so it can be vastly different. Below is a graph for our sensor and its output :

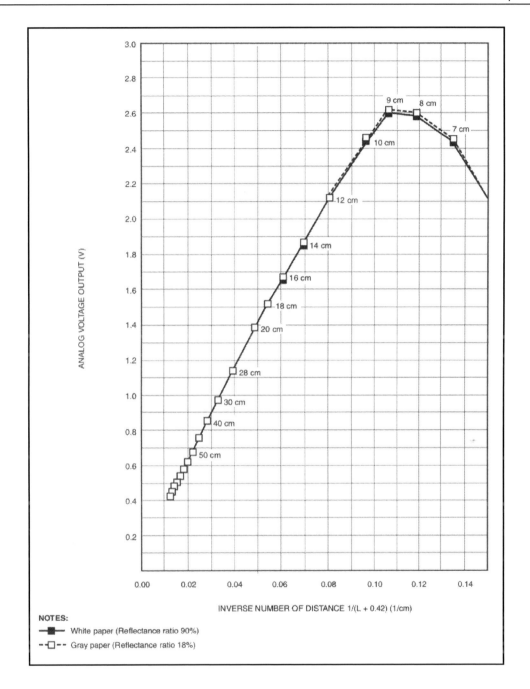

NOTES:

White paper (Reflectance ratio 90%)

Gray paper (Reflectance ratio 18%)

Okay then, so far so good. As we know that Raspberry Pi does not accept analog input; hence, we will go ahead and use what we have used earlier as well, an ADC. We will be using the same ADC we have used before.

Autonomous emergency braking

There is a new technology that newer cars are equipped with. It's called **autonomous emergency braking**; no matter how serious we are while driving, we do get distractions, such as Facebook or WhatsApp notifications, which tempt us to look away from the road onto the screen of our phones. This can be a leading cause of road accidents; hence, car manufacturers are using autonomous braking technology. This generally relies on long range and short range radars and it detects the proximity of other objects around the car, and in the case of an eminent collision, it applies the brakes to the car autonomously preventing them from colliding from other cars or pedestrians. This is a really cool technology, but what's interesting is that we would be making it today with our own bare hands.

To make this, we will be using the IR proximity sensor to sense the proximity of objects around it. Now go ahead, grab a double-sided tape, and attach the IR distance sensor at the front of the car. Once this is done, connect the circuit as shown here:

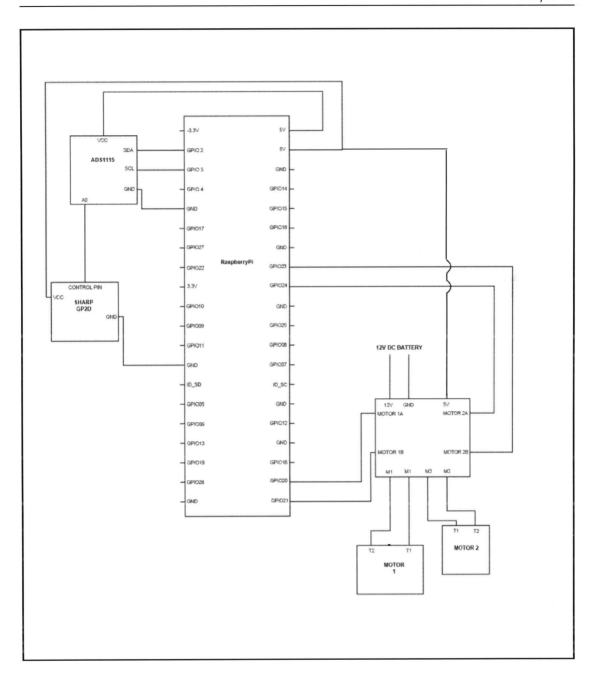

All right then, we are all set up to code it up. The following is the code, and just copy it into your Pi:

```python
import RPi.GPIO as GPIO
import time
GPIO.setmode(GPIO.BCM)

import Adafruit_ADS1x15
adc0 = Adafruit_ADS1x15.ADS1115()

GAIN = 1

adc0.start_adc(0, gain=GAIN)

Motor1a = 20
Motor1b = 21
Motor2b = 23
Motor2a = 24

GPIO.setup(Motor1a,GPIO.OUT)
GPIO.setup(Motor1b,GPIO.OUT)
GPIO.setup(Motor2a,GPIO.OUT)
GPIO.setup(Motor2b,GPIO.OUT)

def forward():
        GPIO.output(Motor1a,0)
        GPIO.output(Motor1b,1)
        GPIO.output(Motor2a,0)
        GPIO.output(Motor2b,1)

def stop():
        GPIO.output(Motor1a,0)
        GPIO.output(Motor1b,0)
        GPIO.output(Motor2a,0)
        GPIO.output(Motor2b,0)

while True:
    F_value = adc0.get_last_result()
    F =    (1.0 / (F_value / 13.15)) - 0.35
    forward()

    min_dist = 20
    if F < min_dist:
        stop()
```

Now, let's see what's actually happening in this code. Everything is very much elementary; the IR proximity sensor is sensing the proximity of objects in front of it and gives the corresponding distance value in the form of analog signals. These signals are then taken by the ADC, and they are converted into digital values. These digital values are finally transferred to Raspberry Pi via the I2C protocol.

So far, so good. But you must be wondering what this line is doing?

```
F =     (1.0 / (F_value / 13.15)) - 0.35
```

There is not much we are doing here, we are simply taking the digital values given by ADC, and using this formula, we are covering that digital value to understandable distance values in the unit of centimeters. This calculation is provided by the manufacturer, and we really don't have to get our head into this. Most of the sensors have these calculations provided. However, if you want to go and understand how and why we are using this formula, then I would recommend you go through the data sheet of the sensor. The data sheet is available easily online on the following link: https://engineering.purdue.edu/ME588/SpecSheets/sharp_gp2d12.pdf.

Moving on, the main part of the code is as follows:

```
min_dist = 20
If F < min_dist:
    stop()
```

It is again very simple. We have entered a distance value, which in this program, we have set to 20. So, whenever the value of F (the distance accrued by IR proximity sensor) is smaller than 20, then a stop() function is called. The stop function simply stalls the car and stops it from colliding with anything.

Let's upload the code and see if it actually works! Make sure that you run this car indoors; otherwise, you would have a tough time trying to stop this car if it does not get any obstacles. Have fun!

Giving the car self-steering capabilities

I hope that you are having fun with this little zippy thing. It is interesting how simple the application of sensors can be and how much difference it can make. As you have learned the basics, it's now time to move ahead and give the car some more powers.

In the previous code, we just made the robot stop in front of the obstacles, why don't we make it steer around the car? It's going to be super simple yet super fun. All we need to do is to tweak the function `stop()` and make it able to turn. Obviously, we will also change the name of the function from `stop()` to `turn()` just for the sake of clarity. One thing to remember that you won't have to rewrite the code; all we need to do is some minor tweaking. So, let's see the code and then I will tell you what exactly has changed and why:

```
import RPi.GPIO as GPIO
import time
GPIO.setmode(GPIO.BCM)

import Adafruit_ADS1x15
adc0 = Adafruit_ADS1x15.ADS1115()

GAIN = 1

adc0.start_adc(0, gain=GAIN)

Motor1a = 20
Motor1b = 21
Motor2a = 23
Motor2b = 24

GPIO.setup(Motor1a,GPIO.OUT)
GPIO.setup(Motor1b,GPIO.OUT)
GPIO.setup(Motor2a,GPIO.OUT)
GPIO.setup(Motor2b,GPIO.OUT)

def forward():
        GPIO.output(Motor1a,0)
        GPIO.output(Motor1b,1)
        GPIO.output(Motor2a,0)
        GPIO.output(Motor2b,1)

def turn():
        GPIO.output(Motor1a,0)
        GPIO.output(Motor1b,1)
        GPIO.output(Motor2a,1)
        GPIO.output(Motor2b,0)
)
```

```
while True:
   forward()

   F_value = adc0.get_last_result()
   F =    (1.0 / (F_value / 13.15)) - 0.35

   min_dist = 20

   while F < min_dist:
       turn()
```

As you would have noted, everything remains pretty much the same except for the following:

```
def turn():
        GPIO.output(Motor1a,0)
        GPIO.output(Motor1b,1)
        GPIO.output(Motor2a,1)
        GPIO.output(Motor2b,0)
```

This part of the code is defining the turn() function in which the opposite side wheels of the vehicles would be spinning in the opposite direction; hence, making the car turn on its own axis:

```
   min_dist = 20

   while F < min_dist:
       turn()
```

Now this is the main part of the program; in this part, we are defining what the car would do if it encounters any sort of obstacle in front of it. In our previous programs, we were primarily just telling the robot to stop as soon as it encounters any obstacle; however, now we are chaining the stop function with a turn function, which we have defined previously in the program.

We simply put in a condition as follows:

```
min_dist = 20
If F < min_dist:
    turn()
```

Then, it would turn just for a fraction of seconds, as the microcontroller would parse through the code and execute it and get out of the condition. To do this, our Raspberry Pi would hardly take a couple of microseconds. So, we might not even able to see what has happened. Hence, in our program, we have used a `while` loop. This essentially keeps the loops running till the time condition is fulfilled. Our condition is `while F < min_dist:`, so till the time the robot is detecting an object in front of it, it will keep executing the function inside it, which in our case is, the `turn()` function. So in simple words, till the time it has not turned enough to avoid the obstacle, the vehicle would keep turning and then once the loop is executed, it will again jump back to the main program and keep going straight.

Simple isn't it? That's the beauty about programming!

Making it fully autonomous

Now, you must have understood the basics of autonomous driving using a simple proximity sensor. Now is the time when we make it fully autonomous. To make it fully autonomous, we must understand and map our surroundings rather than to just turn the vehicle till the time it encounters an obstacle. We basically need to divide this whole activity in the following two basic parts:

- Scanning the environment
- Deciding what to do with the perceived data

Now, let's first write the code and then see what we need to do:

```
import RPi.GPIO as GPIO
import time

GPIO.setmode(GPIO.BCM)

import Adafruit_ADS1x15
adc0 = Adafruit_ADS1x15.ADS1115()

GAIN = 1
adc0.start_adc(0, gain=GAIN)

Motor1a = 20
Motor1b = 21
Motor2a = 23
Motor2b = 24

GPIO.setup(Motor1a,GPIO.OUT)
```

```
GPIO.setup(Motor1b,GPIO.OUT)
GPIO.setup(Motor2a,GPIO.OUT)
GPIO.setup(Motor2b,GPIO.OUT)

def forward():
        GPIO.output(Motor1a,0)
        GPIO.output(Motor1b,1)
        GPIO.output(Motor2a,0)
        GPIO.output(Motor2b,1)

def right():
        GPIO.output(Motor1a,0)
        GPIO.output(Motor1b,1)
        GPIO.output(Motor2a,1)
        GPIO.output(Motor2b,0)

def left():
        GPIO.output(Motor1a,1)
        GPIO.output(Motor1b,0)
        GPIO.output(Motor2a,0)
        GPIO.output(Motor2b,1)

def stop():
        GPIO.output(Motor1a,0)
        GPIO.output(Motor1b,0)
        GPIO.output(Motor2a,0)
        GPIO.output(Motor2b,0)

while True:

    forward()

    F_value = adc0.get_last_result()
    F =    (1.0 / (F_value / 13.15)) - 0.35

    min_dist = 20
    if F< min_dist:

        stop()

     right()
     time.sleep(1)

     F_value = adc0.get_last_result()
     F =    (1.0 / (F_value / 13.15)) - 0.35
     R = F

     left()
```

```
    time.sleep(2)

    F_value = adc0.get_last_result()
    F =    (1.0 / (F_value / 13.15)) - 0.3

    L = F

    if L < R:
        right()
        time.sleep(2)

    else:
        forward()
```

Now most of the program is just like all of our previous programs; in this program, we have defined the following functions:

- `forward()`
- `right()`
- `left()`
- `stop()`

There is not much I need to tell you about defining the functions, so let's move ahead and see what else do we have in stock for us.

The main action is going on in our infinite loop `while True:`. Let's see what exactly is happening:

```
while True:

    forward()

    F_value = adc0.get_last_result()
    F =    (1.0 / (F_value / 13.15)) - 0.35

    min_dist = 20
    if F< min_dist:

        stop()
```

Let's see what this part of code is doing:

- The first thing that is executed as soon as our program enters the infinite loop is the `forward()` function; that is, as soon as the infinite loop is executed, the vehicle will start to go forward
- Thereafter, `F_value = adc.get_last_result()` is taking the reading from ADC and storing it in a variable named `F_value`
- `F = (1.0/(F-value/13.15))-0.35` is calculating the distance into understandable metric distance value
- `min_dist = 20`, we have simply defined the minimum distance that we will be using later

Once this part of code is done, then the `if` statement will check whether `F < min_dist:`. If it is so, then the code that is under the `if` statement will start to execute. The first line of this will be the `stop()` function. So whenever the vehicle encounters any obstacle in front of it, the first thing it will do is stop.

Now, as I mentioned, the first part of our code is to understand the environment, so let's go ahead and see how we do it :

```
right()
    time.sleep(1)

    F_value = adc0.get_last_result()
    F =    (1.0 / (F_value / 13.15)) - 0.35
    R = F

    left()
    time.sleep(2)

    F_value = adc0.get_last_result()
    F =    (1.0 / (F_value / 13.15)) - 0.35

    L = F
```

After the vehicle has stopped, it will immediately turn right. As you can see, the next line of code is `time.sleep(1)`, so for another 1 second, the vehicle will keep turning right. We have randomly picked a time of 1 second, you can tweak it later.

Once it has turned right, it will again take the reading from the proximity sensor, and in using this code `R=F`, we are storing that value in a variable named `R`.

After it has done that, the car will turn to the other side, that is, toward left side using the `left()` function, and it will keep turning left for 2 seconds as we have `time.sleep(2)`. This will turn the car toward left of the obstacle. Once it has turned left, it will again take in the value of proximity sensor and store the value in a variable L using the code `L = F`.

So essentially what we have done is that we have scanned the areas around us. In the center, we have an obstacle. It will first turn right and take the distance value of the right side; thereafter, we will turn left and take the distance value of the left side. So we essentially know the environment around the obstacle.

Now we come to the part where we have to make a decision, in which direction we have to go forward. Let's see how we will do it:

```
if L < R:
      right()
      time.sleep(2)

  else:
      forward()
```

Using an `if` statement, we are comparing the values of the proximity sensor for the right and left of the obstacle by this code `if L < R:`. If L is smaller than R, then the vehicle will turn right for 2 seconds. If the condition is not true, then the `else:` statement would come into action, which will in turn make the vehicle go forward.

Now if we see the code in a larger picture, the following things are happening:

- The vehicle would go forward until it encounters an obstacle
- Upon encountering an obstacle, the robot will stop
- It will first turn right and measure the distance to objects in front of it
- Then, it will turn left and measure the distance to objects in front of it
- After this, it will compare the distance of both left and right and choose which direction it has to go in
- If it has to go right, it will turn right and then go forward
- If it has to go left, then it would already be in the left turned orientation, so it simply has to go straight

Let's upload the code and see whether things happen according to plan or not. Remember this, though every environment is different and every vehicle is different, so you may have to tweak the code to make it work smoothly.

Now I will leave you with a problem. What if in both case the reading of the sensor is infinity or the maximum possible value that it can give? What will the robot do?

Go ahead, do some brainstorming and see what we can do to solve this problem!

Summary

In this chapter, using all basics that you learned so far and also by introducing IR proximity sensor, we were able to take an advanced step of developing our robotic car to detect obstacles and accordingly change the directions. In the next chapter, we will study how to make our own area scanner—see you there!

8

Making Your Own Area Scanner

Motors are amazing things; they come in all shapes and sizes. Primarily, they can be considered the backbone of most robots. However, nothing is perfect in this world. There must be some drawbacks to these motors as well. By now, you might have figured out some by yourself. In the previous chapter, when we made the car turn, you might have seen that the angle of turn was never really the same. Also when the vehicle was given the command to go straight, it really would not do so. Rather it would try to run slight, toward one side.

Say hello to the first problem—precision. The motors are exceptionally simple to control, but the problem with these motors come when we have to rotate the motors only till a specific angle. If you need to rotate the motor of your robotic vehicle only by 90 degrees, then how would you do it? The first and foremost thing that might come to your mind would be to fiddle with the timings of the motors. You might be right here. But still, it would be impossible to make sure that it is exactly 90 degrees every single time.

But when we talk about robots, accuracy of even 1 degree may not be enough. Roboticists these days are looking forward to accuracy within the magnitude of two decimal digits. So, the precision we are talking about is close to 0.01 degrees. What do you think now? How do we achieve this level of accuracy with motors?

The answers to all these questions will be answered in this chapter through the following topics:

- Servo motor
- Lists
- LIDAR

Servo motor

So, let me introduce you to *servo motor*. Servo motor is basically a motor with a few added components. Now to understand what those added components, let's first go through this example. Let's say that you want to go to London. Now to see how you have to go there and what would be the route to reach London, the first thing you need to know is that where exactly you are now. If you don't know where you are currently, it is impossible to calculate a route. Similarly, if we want to reach a certain position of motor, we need to know where the shaft of the motor is standing right now. To do this, we use a **potentiometer**. A potentiometer is basically a variable resistor that essentially has a shaft that when rotated changes the value of resistance. A variable resistor looks like this:

When the value of resistor change, then the output voltage from the resistor will also change. The interesting thing is that if the input voltage to the potentiometer is well known, then the output voltage from it can be used to infer where the shaft is. Let's see how:

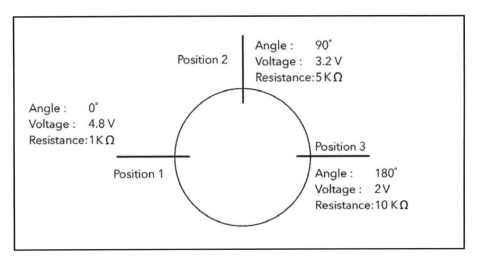

Now, let's say at a position of 0 degrees, the output voltage for the potentiometer is 4.8V; when we move it up to 90 degrees, the value changes to around 3.2V, and upon turning entirely 180 degrees, the voltage reduces to a mere 2V due to the change in resistance.

Without really looking at the shaft of the potentiometer, we can easily derive that if the voltage output from the resistor is 4.8V, then the shaft must be at a position of 0 degrees. Similarly, we can say that it is at 90 degrees if the voltage is 3.2V and at 180 degrees when the voltage is 2V.

Here, we have just plotted three points, but for any given point on the potentiometer, there would be a very specific resistance corresponding to it. Through this we can precisely calculate where the shaft of the potentiometer would be. Now, let's put it in an interesting combination:

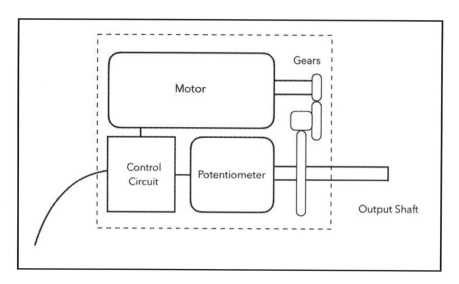

Now what we have is a motor coupled with potentiometer through multiple reducing gears that will reduce the speed of the motor and increase the torque. Further at the final gear, a shaft is mounted outward to the body coupled with a potentiometer.

So as you learned, the potentiometer will be able to sense at which angle the output shaft is pointing. The potentiometer is then connected to a control circuit that takes the reading from the potentiometer and further guides the motor on how much more to move to reach the goal position. Due to this closed loop arrangement in which the control circuit knows where the shaft is, it could calculate how much it has to move the motor to reach the goal position. Hence, this arrangement is able to turn the output shaft to any given position precisely.

This arrangement is typically known as a **servo motor**. Throughout the robotics industry, it is one of the most widely used hardware to control precise movements. Essentially, there are three wires going into the control circuit—VCC, ground, and signal. The signal line will receive the data from our Raspberry Pi, and upon receiving, it will do the necessary motor movement to make the shaft reach the desired position. An image of a servo motor is as follows:

These can start from being extremely inexpensive, around $4 to $5, but they can go up to thousands of dollars. But what really decides the pricing of these servo motors? There are several factors that we need to keep in mind while choosing a servo motor, but the most important of it is **torque**.

Torque is a basically a turning force by which a motor can turn the output shaft. This is measured usually in kg·cm or N·m. Now what does this actually mean? Let's see the following diagram:

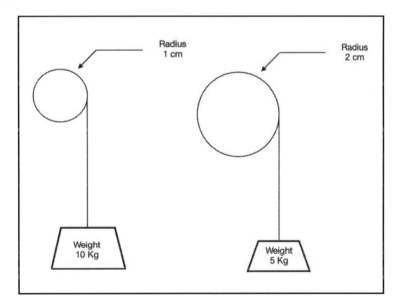

Let's say in the preceding diagram, we have a motor that has a torque of 10 kg·cm and the rotor attached to it is of 1 cm. So, it should be able to pull up a weight of 10 kg perpendicularly up from the ground. However, when we change the radius of the rotor to 2 cm, then the weight that can be lifted gets halved. Similarly, if the radius increases to 10 cm, then the weight that can be lifted would only reduce to 1 kg. So basically, the weight that can be lifted would be torque/radius.

But for most of our purposes, we would not be using a mechanism as shown previously, so let's look at the next diagram to see how the calculations can be made:

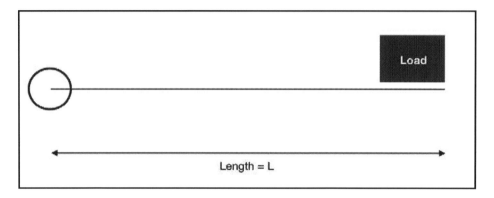

Now, let's say we have a shaft of length **L** and a load at the extreme edge of the shaft. For ease of calculation purposes, we would consider the weight of shaft to be negligible. Now if the servo is having a torque of 100 kg·cm and the length of shaft (**L**) is 10 cm, then by simple calculation, the load that we can pick up would be 100/10 = 10 kg. Similarly, if the length increases to 100 cm, the load that can be lifted would reduce to a mere 1 kg.

OK then; we have had a good amount of exposure to servo motors. Now the question is how do we control a servo motor? As I mentioned, there are different types of servo motors that are available that can be addressed by various means. However, the most common one used for hobby purposes is a digital servo motor. These servo motors require **PWM**, and based on the duty cycle of PWM, the angle of the shaft changes. So, let's see how it happens.

Typically, most of these servos have a frequency of 50 Hz. So basically the length of every pulse would be 1/50 = 0.02 seconds or in other words 20 ms. Further, the duty cycle that can be given to theses servo motors can be 2.5% to 12.5%, which basically means pulse width of 0.5 ms to 2.5 ms. Now let's see how it works:

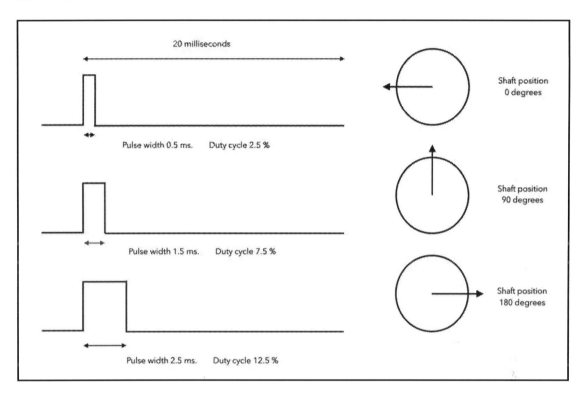

As you can see, when given a duty cycle of 2.5%, the shaft gets down to the minimum position of 0 degrees, and when the duty cycle is increased to 7.5%, the shaft goes to the middle position of 90 degrees. Finally, when the duty cycle is increased to 12.5%, the shaft goes to the maximum position of 180 degrees. If you want any position in between, then you can simply choose the PWM corresponding to it, and it will change the position of servo to the desired angle.

But you may be thinking what if we want to take it beyond 180 degrees? Well, good question, but most of the digital servos only come with a range of 180 degrees of rotation. There are servos that can rotate completely its axis, that is, 360 degrees; however, their addressing is slightly different. After this chapter, you can pretty much go ahead check out any digital servo motor's data sheet and control it the way you want.

All right, enough of theory; it's time to do some fun. So, let's go ahead and set up the hardware and control a servo by our bare hands! Connect the servo to Raspberry Pi as follows:

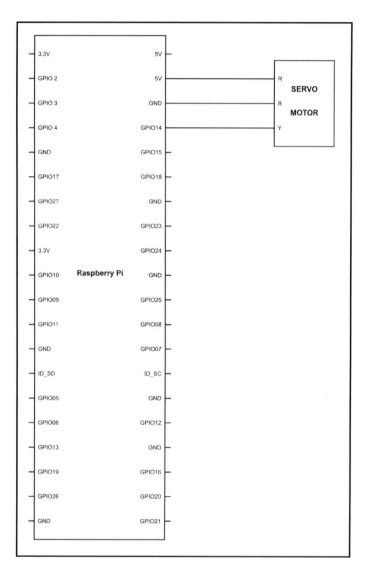

The color coding of the wires is as follows:

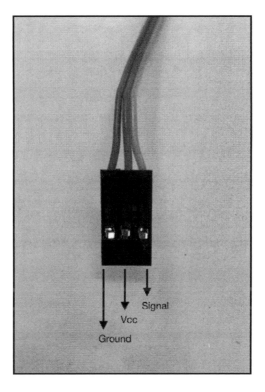

Next, we need to upload the following code and see what happens:

```
import RPi.GPIO as GPIO
import time

GPIO.setmode(GPIO.BCM)
GPIO.setup(14,GPIO.OUT)

pwm = GPIO.PWM(14, 50)
pwm.start(0)

while 1:

        pwm.ChangeDutyCycle(2.5)
        time.sleep(2)

        pwm.ChangeDutyCycle(5)
        time.sleep(2)
```

```
pwm.ChangeDutyCycle(7.5)
time.sleep(2)

pwm.ChangeDutyCycle(10)
time.sleep(2)

pwm.ChangeDutyCycle(12.5)
time.sleep(2)
```

As soon as you run this program, you will see the shaft of the servo moving from left to right, making steps at 0 degrees, 45 degrees, 90 degrees, 135 degrees, and finally 180 degrees.

Let's see what we have done in the program to achieve it:

```
pwm = GPIO.PWM(14, 50)
pwm.start(0)
```

With the line `pwm = GPIO.PWM(14, 50)`, we have defined that GPIO pin number `14` will be used for PWM and the frequency of PWM will be `50`. We have used the line `pwm.start(0)` in earlier chapters as well. It basically sets the PWM pin to `0` that is no duty cycle:

```
pwm.ChangeDutyCycle(2.5)
time.sleep(2)

pwm.ChangeDutyCycle(5)
time.sleep(2)

pwm.ChangeDutyCycle(7.5)
time.sleep(2)

pwm.ChangeDutyCycle(10)
time.sleep(2)

pwm.ChangeDutyCycle(12.5)
time.sleep(2)
```

No all the earlier program is in the `while` loop, that is, it will be executed over and over until the program is forced to quit. Now the line `pwm.ChangeDutyCycle(2.5)` sends a PWM of 2.5% duty cycle to the servo motor. This will simply turn the servo motor to 0 degree angle. Next, we use the good old `time.sleep(2)`, which we all know would halt the program that line for two seconds.

The same cycle is being repeated with different PWM values of 5%, which would turn the shaft to 45 degrees, 7.5% for 90 degrees, 10% for 135 degrees, 12.5 % for 180 degrees. It's a very simple program that would clear out our basics of the servo motor.

So by now, you have learned how to control servo motor and move it in the direction in which we want. Now, let's go a step ahead and change the code slightly to make the servo run smoothly:

```
import RPi.GPIO as GPIO
import time

GPIO.setmode(GPIO.BCM)
GPIO.setup(14,GPIO.OUT)

pwm = GPIO.PWM(14, 50)
pwm.start(0)

i=2.5
j=12.5

while 1:
        while i<=12.5:
                pwm.ChangeDutyCycle(i)
                time.sleep(0.1)
                i = i + 0.1

        while j>=2.5:
                pwm.ChangeDutyCycle(j)
                time.sleep(0.1)
                j = j - 0.1
```

What happened when you uploaded this code in your Pi? You would have noted that the servo is swiping from left to right very smoothly and then right to left. We have done a very simple trick; let's see what it is:

```
        while i<=12.5:
                pwm.ChangeDutyCycle(i)
                time.sleep(0.1)
                i = i + 0.1
```

Here, we are running a loop that will run till the time the value of $i<=12.5$, as we have defined earlier in the program the value of i has been set to 2.5 as default in the starting of the program. Thereafter every time the code runs, the duty cycle is set to the value of I , the program halts for 0.1 seconds and then the value of i is incremented by a value of 0.1. This is increasing the duty cycle of the PWM. Once the value reaches 12.5, the loop exits.

The entire PWM range we have is 2.5% to 12.5%, so we have a space of 10% to play with. Now if we map it to the angular rotation of the servo motor, then every percent of PWM corresponds to a change of 180/10 = 18 degrees. Similarly, every 0.1% of the change would result in a change of 180/100 = 1.8 degrees. Hence, with every 0.1 seconds, we are adding duty cycle by 0.1%, or in other words, we are increasing the angle by 1.8 degrees. Hence, we find this action extremely smooth.

We are doing the similar thing in the next portion of the program; however, we are doing it for the reverse motion.

Lists

All right then, we are quite sure on how to use the servo and have a controlled motion as per our needs. Now it's time to move forward and understand another concept that we would be using greatly. It's named **arrays**. If you have programmed in any other language, you must be familiar with it. But we need to understand a few basics concepts of it, which will make our lives a lot easier. So, let's get started.

First things, first. Arrays in Python are not named arrays, rather it is named as **lists**. List is basically a data structure that can store multiple elements at the same time. The only limitation being is that the elements must be of the same data type. Such as if you are storing integers, then all the values should be `int`. Similarly, if you are storing a character, then every element of the list should be `char`. To define a list, all you need to do is name the list such as we have done by doing `myList`; the name of the list could be anything next we need to tell the compiler that it is actually a list. To do that, we need to put values inside square brackets. It would look like:

```
myList = [14,35,108,64,9]
```

One thing to keep in mind is that every value should be separated with commas. Whenever we want to address any single element of the list, we can simply use it by calling their index number. This is based on the position of the element in the list. The index value in Python list starts from 0. So as per the preceding declaration at the index 0, the value would be `14`, and at the address 4, the value would be `9`. Now when we need to print these elements in between our program, we need to write the following code:

```
print myList[2]
```

Once we write this, the program will print the value of the second value in the list. In our case, it would be 35.

Now, this is one way to access the elements of the list; we can however access it in reverse order as well. So, let's say you want to access the last item of the array. Then, we can write the following code:

```
print myList[-1]
```

This code will return the value of the last element of the array. Now whenever we use the negative values in the lists, then it would start the indexing in the reverse order. So, let's say if we type in `print myList[-2]`, this will give us the value of the second last value in the array. One thing to remember in this whole schematic is that the numbering would start from 0, whereas when we start it in the reverse order, then the numbering would start from -1.

Python is really interesting and quite simple if you know the right tools. The developers of Python have included some really helpful functions that can be used over lists. So, let's go and explore them a bit.

The first one is to add elements to the array. For this, we use a function named `append()`. What the `append()` function does is that it adds the value, which would want at the end of the array. So, write the following:

```
myList.append(45)
```

What this would do is that it would add the element 45 at the end of `myList`. So now the list would be as follows:

```
myList = [14,35,108,64,9, 45]
```

Easy, isn't it ? But what if you want to add an element in between the list? Obviously, the developer won't leave you dry. They have included a function for that as well; it's named `insert(index, element)`. Now whenever you are using this function, you need to make sure that you mention the index where you want this element to be and second, the element that you want to put. So it looks something like this:

```
myList.insert(3,23)
```

When you have used this function, the array will look as follows:

```
myList = [14,35,108,23,64,9,45]
```

Obviously, whenever the developer has given the function to add an element, then they would have certainly given a function to remove the elements as well. But the trick is that you can do it two ways. First, the common way. We simply select the index number and delete it. We are going to do it now:

```
del myList[2]
```

Now what this will do is that it would delete the second element of the array, so after doing this operation, the array will look like this:

```
myList = [14,35,108,64,9,45]
```

But now here comes the real trick; you can also delete the element by simply specifying the element. This is how it's done:

```
myList.remove(9)
```

Now the moment you do this, it will find wherever the element 9 is in your list and delete it from the positions. So you don't have to care about where the element is; this function will say, I will find you and I will kill you!

Looking around

Okay then enough of movie quotes. We can talk about many other functions that we can use over lists, but what we have done is enough for now. We will see the rest of them as the need arise. But for now let's take the things a step further in robotics. You might have seen a rotating object on top of many autonomous cars. The production cars generally don't tend to have primarily due to its high price, but research purpose cars are always loaded with it.

So what is this device? It's named **LIDAR**; it is an acronym for **Light Detection and Ranging**. I know bad acronym. There is a reason for LIDAR to be very common. It gives distance reading of the areas around it in a very precise way. However, buying it for our projects would slightly overkill as a good one would cost you close $500 to $10,000. If you still think that it's in your budget, then you would be very lucky! But for those who don't want to buy it. I have a good news for you. Today, we are going to build our own LIDAR scanner. So to make an area scanner, we need a servo over which we will mount our IR proximity sensor. Now to do this, we would need a slight makeshift arrangement. You can take a cardboard and fix it like we have done in the picture here, or otherwise, you can also use a right-angled aluminum and drill it to fix the components if you want it to do the pro way. The one thing to remember that the sensor must be facing exactly parallel to the ground and not up or down.

Once the mounting is done, then it's time to connect the rest of the hardware. So go ahead and connect the hardware, as shown in the following diagram:

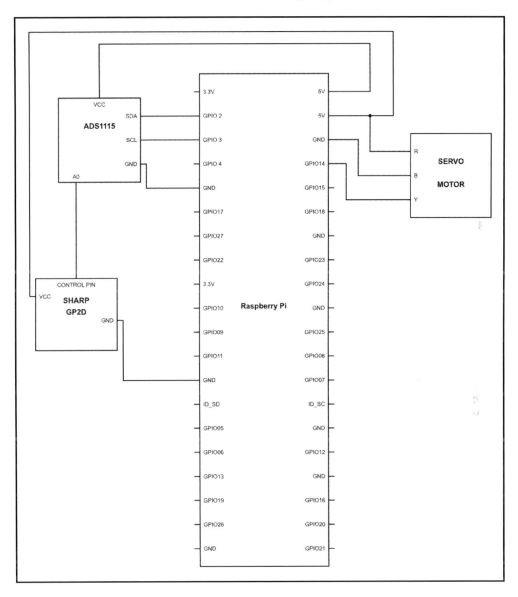

OK, so let's see what this thing can do, so get ready and upload this code:

```
import RPi.GPIO as GPIO
import time
import Adafruit_ADS1x15

adc = Adafruit_ADS1x15.ADS1115()
GAIN = 1

adc.start_adc(0, gain=GAIN)
GPIO.setmode(GPIO.BCM)
GPIO.setup(14,GPIO.OUT)
GPIO.setwarnings(False)

servo = GPIO.PWM(14, 50)

servo.start(0)

Def Distance():
    D_value = adc0.get_last_result()
    D =     (1.0 / (F_value / 13.15)) - 0.35
    Return D

j=12.5
k=2.5
i=0

distLR=[]
distRL=[]

while True:
        while k<=12.5:
                servo.ChangeDutyCycle(k)
                time.sleep(.1)
                distLR.insert(i,Distance())
                k = k + 2.5
                i = i + 1
        print distLR

        i=0
        k=0

        del distLR[:]

        while j>=2.5:
                servo.ChangeDutyCycle(j)
                time.sleep(.1)
                j = j - 2.5
```

```
                distRL.insert(i,Distance())
                i = i + 1

        print distRL

        i=0
        k=2.5
        j=12.5

        del distRL[:]
```

What did the code do? If it ran fine, then it should return you the scanned readings entire 180 degree broken down into 10 even steps. Go ahead—try it out and then return to see what actually is happening.

Now most of the code is elementary, and you must have also got an idea of what this code is actually doing. However, let's get deeper into it and see the specifics:

```
Def Distance():
    D_value = adc0.get_last_result()
    D =    (1.0 / (F_value / 13.15)) - 0.35
    Return D
```

In this part of the program, we have defined a function named `Distance()`. As you can see, it is simply getting the reading from the ADC in the step `D_value = adc0.get_last_result()`; thereafter, this is the value procured that is stored in a variable `D` is then computed in the line `D = (1.0/F-value/13.15)) - 0.35` to get the metric reading from the ADC reading. Finally, using the line `Return D`, we are returning the value `D` from the function:

```
distLR=[]
distRL=[]
```

We have declared two lists: `distLR`, namely for distance for left to right swipe of the servo and `distRL` for the distance received in right to left swipe of the servo. You might be wondering how is it that there is nothing inside these brackets. It is completely normal to have an empty array declared. There is no need for them to have value initially:

```
while k<=12.5:
        servo.ChangeDutyCycle(k)
        time.sleep(.1)
        distLR.insert(i,Distance())
        k = k + 1
        i = i + 1
    print distLR
```

Now this is where the real action is happening. The `while` loop will be executed only till the time the value of `k` is less than or equal to `12.5`. In the next line `servo.ChangeDutyCycle(k)`, the value of the duty cycle will be whatever the value of `k` would be. Initially, the value of `k` would be `2.5` as we have already defined in the beginning of the program. Now we add another line `time sleep(.1)`, which will make the program halt for `.1` second. This is necessary; otherwise, the program would parse through this loop within milliseconds and the servo would not be able to cope up with it. Hence, this is a short delay. In the next line, we have `distLR.insert(I,Distance())`. This line of program is doing a lot of things. First, as we have named a `Distance()` function inside this line. As we defined, it would calculate the distance using the ADC and the IR proximity sensor. Thereafter, it would insert that distance value inside an the list `distLR` at the position `I`. Previously in our program, we have already assigned the value i = 0; hence, the distance value would be put up in the first position in the array. Once this entire process is done, then we move forward and increment the value by one in this line `k = k + 1`; thereafter, we do the same thing in `I = I + 1`. Now finally, once this loop's executed, the values of the list is printed using the line `print distLR`:

```
i=0
k=0
```

In this line, we are simply resetting the values of `i = 0` and `k = 0` for the next loop:

```
del distLR[:]
```

This may be slightly new for you. Whenever we use a colon inside a bracket, that basically means that the entire elements of the array would be deleted:

```
while j>=2.5:
                servo.ChangeDutyCycle(j)
                time.sleep(.1)
                j = j - 2.5
                distRL.insert(i,Distance())
                i = i + 1

        print distRL
```

In this code, the same thing is happening that we did for the left to right swipe; the only difference being is that we are saving it a new list named `distRL`, and the swipe starts from 12.5% duty cycle and ends at 2.5%:

```
i=0
    k=2.5
    j=12.5

    del distRL[:]
```

When we have printed all the values, we again reset the values of `i = 1`, `k = 2.5`, and `j = 12.5` so that our first loop can start seamlessly further to it we are also making sure that there is nothing left inside the list `distRL`.

So this is how our code was working, straight and simple!

LIDAR on an autonomous vehicle

Remember the last time we made autonomous car. It was cool, and surely it might be something you can show off to your friends. However, now what we are about to make is surely cooler than anything we have ever done till now.

We are going to put this area scanner over our robotic vehicle. But wait, didn't we scan the area earlier using the same sensor and turning the car to other sides. We did it and it worked fine, almost fine. I bet sometimes it wasn't as accurate as you thought it would be. But that's not the real problem. The main problem is that it was not seamless. It has to stop in between check for spaces and then move in either direction. What we are going to do now is something that is a step ahead. So before doing any more explanation, let's go ahead and make this new robotic vehicle and then you be the judge to decide whether it is cooler.

So, to make it, you need to mount the area scanner on the vehicle. It's advisable that you set it up at the frontend of the vehicle and make sure that the arm of the servo is able to rotate 180 degrees. You can use the similar method that we did to fix the IR sensor on top of the servo. While you are doing all of this, try using cable ties to make sure the cables are not messy and also make sure to leave some slack for the movement of the shaft and the sensor on top of it. These cable ties can make your life really simple. Once we are all set up, you should connect the IR proximity using an ADS1115 to the Raspberry Pi and then connect the motor driver, as shown in the following diagram:

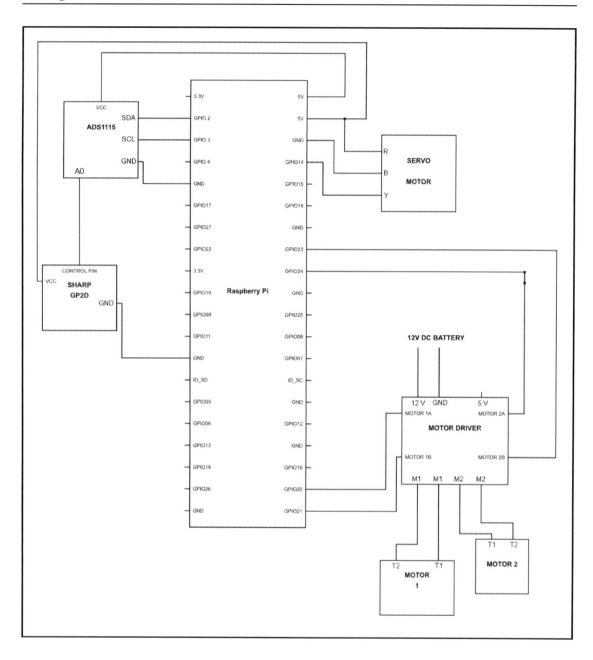

Once we are done go ahead and upload the following code:

```
import RPi.GPIO as GPIO
import time
import Adafruit_ADS1x15

adc0 = Adafruit_ADS1x15.ADS1115()
GAIN = 1
adc0.start_adc(0, gain=GAIN)

GPIO.setmode(GPIO.BCM)
GPIO.setup(14,GPIO.OUT)

servo = GPIO.PWM(14, 50)
servo.start(0)

def Distance():
    D_value = adc0.get_last_result()
    D =     (1.0 / (F_value / 13.15)) - 0.35
    Return D

GPIO.setup(20,GPIO.OUT)
GPIO.setup(21,GPIO.OUT)
GPIO.setup(23,GPIO.OUT)
GPIO.setup(24,GPIO.OUT)

LForward = GPIO.PWM(20, 50)
LReverse = GPIO.PWM(21, 50)
RForward = GPIO.PWM(23,50)
RReverse = GPIO.PWM(24,50)

def stop():
    LForward.changeDutyCycle(0)
    LReverse.changeDutyCycle(0)
    RForward.changeDutyCycle(0)
    RReverse.changeDutyCycle(0)


def direction(index):

  if index == 0 :
    LForward.changeDutyCycle(0)
    LReverse.changeDutyCycle(30)
    RForward.changeDutyCycle(30)
    RReverse.changeDutyCycle(0)

elif index == 1
```

```
            LForward.changeDutyCycle(20)
            LReverse.changeDutyCycle(0)
            RForward.changeDutyCycle(50)
            RReverse.changeDutyCycle(0)

    elif index == 2 :

            LForward.changeDutyCycle(50)
            LReverse.changeDutyCycle(0)
            RForward.changeDutyCycle(50)
            RReverse.changeDutyCycle(0)

   elif index == 3 :

            LForward.changeDutyCycle(50)
            LReverse.changeDutyCycle(0)
            RForward.changeDutyCycle(20)
            RReverse.changeDutyCycle(0)


    elif index == 4 :

            LForward.changeDutyCycle(20)
            LReverse.changeDutyCycle(0)
            RForward.changeDutyCycle(0)
            RReverse.changeDutyCycle(20)

    else:
    stop()

j=12.5
k=2.5
i=0

dist1=[]
dist2=[]

while True:

        while k<=12.5:
        servo.ChangeDutyCycle(k)
        time.sleep(.2)
        dist1.insert(i,Distance())
        k = k + 2.5
        i = i + 1

    print dist1
```

```
i=0
k=2

max_dist1 = max(dist1)
max_dist1_index = dist1.index(max_dist1)

direction(max_dist1_index)

del dist1[:]

print max_dist1
print max_dist1_index

while j>=2.5:
    servo.ChangeDutyCycle(j)
    time.sleep(.2)
     j = j - 2.5
     dist2.insert(i,Distance())
     i = i + 1

print dist2

i=0
j=12

max_dist2 = max(dist2)
max_dist2_index = dist2.index(max_dist2)

direction(max_dist2_index)

del dist2[:]

print max_dist2
print max_dist2_index
```

Phew! That was long wasn't it? But trust me it might be long, but not tough. So let's see what this code is doing:

```
LForward = GPIO.PWM(20, 50)
LReverse = GPIO.PWM(21, 50)
RForward = GPIO.PWM(23,50)
RReverse = GPIO.PWM(24,50)
```

This stuff might look pretty new to you. Though it isn't. What we are doing is that we are defining which pin number will be operating at what PWM frequency. Also, we have named every GPIO pins that is being used for motor control. OK then, it is fine that we are doing all this, but why have we suddenly started to give PWM to motor drivers. Were we not happy giving a simple high pulse?

The answer is very straightforward. With the use of PWM, we were able to change the brightness of an LED in previous chapters. Similarly, by changing the PWM output to the control pins of the motor driver, you cannot only define which direction to spin in. But also the speed at which it can spin. This is all done with PWM. So let's say pin number 20 is getting a PWM at 50% duty cycle. So it basically means that the motor which is attached to it will get half the input voltage that the motor driver is receiving. So now we can not only control which direction we want the motor to spin but also at what speed we can do so:

```
def direction(index):

  if index == 0 :
     LForward.changeDutyCycle(0)
     LReverse.changeDutyCycle(30)
     RForward.changeDutyCycle(30)
     RReverse.changeDutyCycle(0)

  elif index == 1
     LForward.changeDutyCycle(20)
     LReverse.changeDutyCycle(0)
     RForward.changeDutyCycle(50)
     RReverse.changeDutyCycle(0)
```

In this statement, we have defined a function `direction(index)`. What this does is that it compares the value of index and based on it. The power will be given to the motors. So lets say that the index is 0. In this case the wheel on the left side would move in reverse direction whereas the right wheel would move in the reverse direction this will turn the robot on its axis.

In the next statement, we have written an `elif` statement, so if the `else` statement is not true, then it will check for the rest `else if` statement in the body. There are four `elif` statements in the entire definition of `direction(index)`, which basically means that it will check for each one of it and do either of the activities based on the value of the argument. In this case, it is the index. Further, there is a final `else` statement, which would be done if none of the cases are true. So according to the statement, it will call a function of stop. That would stop the vehicle:

```
max_dist1 = max(dist1)
```

This line is pretty interesting as we are using another fun part of the lists that we have used. So, with the `max()` method, we can find the largest value inside a list. So, in this line, we are simply finding the max value and putting it in a variable named `max_dist1`:

```
max_dist1_index = dist1.index(max_dist1)
```

The beauty of lists just doesn't seem to end. In this line, we are using another method named `index()`; this method gives us the index of the value inside the list. So, we can know where the value exists in the list. Hence, in this line, we are proving the value of `max_dist1`. The method `index()` searches the index number and stores that value down into a variable named `max_dist1_index`:

```
direction(max_dist1_index)
```

As we have already defined the function `Direction()`, now all we are doing is calling the function to decide which direction to go in. Prefect then, power up your vehicles and see how well they are driving and do not forget to shoot a video and post it online.

Have fun!

Summary

Professional laser scanners are super expensive, so, in this chapter, we went on to build an alternative by ourselves and mounted it on our vehicle. In the next chapter, we will cover topics such as vision processing, and object detection, object tracking, which will enable us to do basic vision processing and to make the car move in the direction of a specific object such as a ball.

Vision Processing 9

It's really amazing what we can do using a simple combination of sensors and actuators. After all, these are the things that make robots what they are known for. There is a vast numbers of sensors available on the market today that we can use. We can put hundreds of sensors over a robot, but there is one thing that subsides the power of all other sensors. It's the camera. Sensors give us data about our physical environment, whereas the camera lets us see it. So, it is quite an important sensor to consider. In this chapter, we will go ahead and see how we can couple a camera to our Raspberry Pi and start computing with the image data that we get.

The following topics will be covered in this chapter:

- The basics of images
- Preparing Raspberry Pi for vision processing application
- Installing OpenCV
- Image recognition

The basics of images

When we say camera, we don't necessarily think of it as a sensor, even tough it is one. However, it is slightly different from all the sensors that we have studied until now. Most of the sensors are consisting of one sensing element such as proximity sensing, temperature sensing, or passive IR sensing. With a camera, what we are doing is capturing light; now, rather than having one light sensor, we have multiple, in fact an array of millions of these sensors grouped together on a single chip. But the story does not end here, and these sensors not only capture just light, but also different intensities of light; they can sense the color spectrum and its relative brightness. Every sensing element that does this functionality is named a **pixel**. Most of these pixels generate an RGB value, which is nothing but the intensity of red, green, and blue color. Why RGB, you might think? These are primary colors, and mixing these colors up in the right quantities results in making different shades of colors.

So, if we have a value of these colors, we can recreate the colors that we want. As we earlier understood, there are millions of these pixels in any camera, making up the length and the breadth of the image-sensing chip. The data from these image-sensing elements makes up the image. So far so good. But why are we talking about this? The reason is, this is how a camera sees the world and just to not how we see it. Biological vision is entirely a different story. So, we need to understand how the camera works and what the raw data that it gives is to go ahead and do the vision processing.

Now, let's get back to the pixels and their data. As there are millions of these pixels, there must be millions of readings of these pixels, and these readings would be in the form of RGB values. Now, this data must be arranged in a specific form so as to understand which pixel data we are dealing with. If it is not arranged, then none of this data would make any sense.

As you learned previously, an array/list is the best way to store large, structured data, and if you look at the data from the image, then it is nothing but the values of RGB for individual structured pixels. Perfect! So, now we know what we are dealing with and how we have to deal with it. Or do we?

As you may recollect, the images we are talking about here are made by millions of pixels. So, the pixel data would also be in the magnitude of millions as well. This data is extremely huge, as we are not just talking about millions of pixels but each RGB value. In other words, every single pixel will give us three values, that is, the value of red, green, and blue. In other words, it's a lot of data. Normal lists cannot handle this much of data; hence, we have to install a special library named **NumPy** to take care of this vast arrays. In this chapter, there are multiple dependencies that we will have to install and update in order for the Raspberry Pi to go ahead and do vision processing. We will see how we will install it.

Now moving forward, we have the data of every single pixel in a very structured way, but what are we exactly going to do with it? Well as you have learned in the previous chapters, when we have data in a structured form, then we can go ahead and do multiple operations as we have done in the previous chapter of lists. The data we are dealing with here is somewhat in a specific domain. That is, we know that the data we would be receiving would be image data. Hence, there are certain very specific libraries that has been made to do the tasks with ease. One of the most commonly used vision processing algorithm is OpenCV. It is widely used, and there are multiple functions in this library that are very specific to dealing with image data itself. So with a single command, you should be able to capture image, and with another command, we would be able to put filters over the image. No not the Instagram filters, but the filters that will segregate a specific type of object in the image from others.

Finally, we would also be able to output the data in the desired image format. So, it is quite interesting on what all we can do with OpenCV. But do keep in mind that this is an introductory lesson. OpenCV itself can be a topic for an entire book, but here, I'm trying to give you all a heads-up regarding the vision processing. You would be learning the basic commands and how to use it to make out projects.

Now it is time to stop talking and start doing stuff. So, let's see what all we have to do.

Preparing Raspberry Pi for vision processing application

The first thing you need to do is to make sure that you have ample time on your side and perhaps some popcorn to pass on the time. Because what we are about to start can be slightly long. How long, perhaps a few hours. If you have a slow internet connection, then you might even be spending an entire day. Also, one thing to note is that with time, there are various new updates that might come along on both the software and hardware end. This might mean that some of the commands might not work or might need some modification. A bit of Google might help in that situation. So, don't get worried if something doesn't work at the first go. Having said this, let's start by making your Raspberry Pi ready and make sure that we have all the prerequisites for the vision processing. First, we need to prepare our Raspberry Pi for vision processing application. To start it off, ensure that you are always connected to the internet at all times once that box is checked, then go ahead and fire up the terminal on your Raspberry Pi. Once you are on it, you need to type the following commands:

```
sudo apt-get update
sudo apt-get upgrade
```

```
pi@raspberrypi:~ $ sudo apt-get update
Get:1 http://archive.raspberrypi.org/debian stretch InRelease [25.3 kB]
Get:2 http://raspbian.raspberrypi.org/raspbian stretch InRelease [15.0 kB]
Get:3 http://raspbian.raspberrypi.org/raspbian stretch/main armhf Packages [11.7 MB]
Get:4 http://archive.raspberrypi.org/debian stretch/main armhf Packages [159 kB]
Get:5 http://archive.raspberrypi.org/debian stretch/ui armhf Packages [30.8 kB]
Fetched 11.9 MB in 11s (1,030 kB/s)
Reading package lists... Done
pi@raspberrypi:~ $ sudo apt-get upgrade
Reading package lists... Done
Building dependency tree
Reading state information... Done
Calculating upgrade... Done
The following packages were automatically installed and are no longer required:
  lxkeymap python-cairo python-gobject python-gobject-2 python-gtk2 python-xklavier
Use 'sudo apt autoremove' to remove them.
The following packages have been kept back:
  chromium-browser rpi-chromium-mods
```

Therefore, the first command downloads the updates for the operating system of your Raspberry Pi, and the second line will go ahead and download the upgrades for the OS of your Raspberry Pi. Did you get what I am saying? No? Let me tell you a bit more detail.

Your Raspberry Pi's OS has multiple packages that are used to do different activities. Now over the time, these packages get added functionalities, so when you update OS, you basically update the functionalities of the packages on your OS. This being one thing, sometimes new packages are also added to your Raspberry Pi's OS. They can be for various added functionalities. So an upgrade adds the new packages on to your operating system.

You must be asking why is all this necessary? Good question. There are multiple libraries that we will be using to make our code work. Now, the developer who made these would want his libraries to be better than ever and to do that he uses the latest packages of the Raspberry Pi. So now when you are trying to use the developer's libraries, then there is a good chance that it might need the latest packages and updates for it to run. Hence, it's always a good idea to update and upgrade your OS every few weeks.

Until now, we have only downloaded those updates and upgrades. We haven't really installed them. So to install them, we need to type the following command:

```
sudo rpi-update
```

Once you do this, you might like to restart your Raspberry Pi so that everything is up and running smoothly. To do this, you can go ahead and restart it manually, or you can take the pro way by wiring this command:

```
sudo reboot
```

```
pi@raspberrypi:~ $ sudo rpi-update
 *** Raspberry Pi firmware updater by Hexxeh, enhanced by AndrewS and Dom
 *** Performing self-update
  % Total    % Received % Xferd  Average Speed   Time    Time     Time  Current
                                 Dload  Upload   Total   Spent    Left  Speed
100 13403  100 13403    0     0  16743      0 --:--:-- --:--:-- --:--:-- 16732
 *** Relaunching after update
 *** Raspberry Pi firmware updater by Hexxeh, enhanced by AndrewS and Dom
 *** We're running for the first time
 *** Backing up files (this will take a few minutes)
 *** Backing up firmware
 *** Backing up modules 4.14.34-v7+
############################################################
This update bumps to rpi-4.14.y linux tree
Be aware there could be compatibility issues with some drivers
Discussion here:
https://www.raspberrypi.org/forums/viewtopic.php?f=29&t=197689
############################################################
 *** Downloading specific firmware revision (this will take a few minutes)
  % Total    % Received % Xferd  Average Speed   Time    Time     Time  Current
                                 Dload  Upload   Total   Spent    Left  Speed
100   168    0   168    0     0    170      0 --:--:-- --:--:-- --:--:--   170
100 55.6M  100 55.6M    0     0  1865k      0  0:00:30  0:00:30 --:--:-- 1464k
 *** Updating firmware
 *** Updating kernel modules
 *** depmod 4.14.39+
 *** depmod 4.14.39-v7+
 *** Updating VideoCore libraries
 *** Using HardFP libraries
 *** Updating SDK
 *** Running ldconfig
 *** Storing current firmware revision
 *** Deleting downloaded files
 *** Syncing changes to disk
 *** If no errors appeared, your firmware was successfully updated to 3b0fb6409c69c37502341bd8c9978e763527b281
 *** A reboot is needed to activate the new firmware
pi@raspberrypi:~ $
```

Perfect, so now our system is up to date. Now we need to install some more packages that are specific to image processing. Without these packages, it would be very hard to do any vision processing . These individual commands can take some time to go through, but just be patient and download it and then I'll explain what all of these are doing. So without much delay, let's go ahead and install these one by one:

```
sudo apt-get install build-essential git cmake pkg-config
```

```
pi@raspberrypi:~ $ sudo apt-get install build-essential git cmake pkg-config
Reading package lists... Done
Building dependency tree
Reading state information... Done
build-essential is already the newest version (12.3).
git is already the newest version (1:2.11.0-3+deb9u2).
pkg-config is already the newest version (0.29-4).
The following additional packages will be installed:
  cmake-data libjsoncpp1
```

```
sudo apt-get install libavcodec-dev libavformat-dev libswscale-dev libv4l-
dev
sudo apt-get install libxvidcore-dev libx264-dev
```

```
pi@raspberrypi:~ $ sudo apt-get install libxvidcore-dev libx264-dev
Reading package lists... Done
Building dependency tree
Reading state information... Done
The following packages were automatically installed and are no longer required:
  libjpeg8 libpng-tools
Use 'sudo apt autoremove' to remove them.
The following NEW packages will be installed:
  libx264-dev libxvidcore-dev
0 upgraded, 2 newly installed, 0 to remove and 1 not upgraded.
```

```
sudo apt-get install libjpeg8-dev
```

```
pi@raspberrypi:~ $ sudo apt-get install libjpeg8-dev
Reading package lists... Done
Building dependency tree
Reading state information... Done
The following additional packages will be installed:
  libjpeg8
The following NEW packages will be installed:
  libjpeg8 libjpeg8-dev
```

```
sudo apt-get install libtiff5-dev
```

```
pi@raspberrypi:~ $ sudo apt-get install libtiff5-dev
Reading package lists... Done
Building dependency tree
Reading state information... Done
The following package was automatically installed and is no longer required:
  libjpeg8
Use 'sudo apt autoremove' to remove it.
The following additional packages will be installed:
  libjbig-dev libjpeg-dev libjpeg62-turbo-dev liblzma-dev libtiffxx5
Suggested packages:
  liblzma-doc
The following packages will be REMOVED:
  libjpeg8-dev
```

```
sudo apt-get install libjasper-dev
```

```
pi@raspberrypi:~ $ sudo apt-get install libjasper-dev
Reading package lists... Done
Building dependency tree
Reading state information... Done
The following packages were automatically installed and are no longer required:
  libjpeg8 python-cairo python-gobject python-gobject-2 python-gtk2 python-xklavier
Use 'sudo apt autoremove' to remove them.
The following additional packages will be installed:
  libjasper1
```

```
sudo apt-get install libpng12-dev
```

```
pi@raspberrypi:~ $ sudo apt-get install libpng12-dev
Reading package lists... Done
Building dependency tree
Reading state information... Done
The following packages were automatically installed and are no longer required:
  libjpeg8 libpng-tools lxkeymap python-cairo python-gobject python-gobject-2 python-gtk2 python-xklavier
Use 'sudo apt autoremove' to remove them.
The following packages will be REMOVED:
  libfreetype6-dev libpng-dev
The following NEW packages will be installed:
  libpng12-dev
```

```
sudo apt-get install libgtk2.0-dev
```

```
pi@raspberrypi:~ $ sudo apt-get install libgtk-3-dev
Reading package lists... Done
Building dependency tree
Reading state information... Done
The following package was automatically installed and is no longer required:
  libjpeg8
Use 'sudo apt autoremove' to remove it.
```

```
sudo apt-get install libatlas-base-dev gfortran
```

```
pi@raspberrypi:~ $ sudo apt-get install libatlas-base-dev gfortran
Reading package lists... Done
Building dependency tree
Reading state information... Done
The following packages were automatically installed and are no longer required:
  libjpeg8 lxkeymap python-cairo python-gobject python-gobject-2 python-gtk2 python-xklavier
Use 'sudo apt autoremove' to remove them.
The following additional packages will be installed:
  gfortran-6 libatlas-dev libatlas3-base libblas-dev libgfortran-6-dev
```

```
sudo apt-get install python2.7-dev python3-dev
```

```
pi@raspberrypi:~ $ sudo apt-get install python2.7-dev python3-dev
Reading package lists... Done
Building dependency tree
Reading state information... Done
python2.7-dev is already the newest version (2.7.13-2+deb9u2).
python3-dev is already the newest version (3.5.3-1).
The following packages were automatically installed and are no longer required:
  libjpeg8 lxkeymap python-cairo python-gobject python-gobject-2 python-gtk2
  python-xklavier
Use 'sudo apt autoremove' to remove them.
0 upgraded, 0 newly installed, 0 to remove and 2 not upgraded.
pi@raspberrypi:~ $
```

Once done, your system will be ready with all the prerequisites required by the OS to do vision processing. Now, let's understand what each one of them is doing:

- `sudo apt-get install build-essential git cmake pkg-config`: This line is installing all the developer tools that you might need.

- `sudo apt-get install libavcodec-dev libavformat-dev libswscale-dev libv4l-dev` and `sudo apt-get install libxvidcore-dev libx264-dev`: In this line, we are installing video packages and codecs. This will make sure that the system is ready with I/O as the videos that we might be throwing at it later.

- `sudo apt-get install libjpeg8-dev libtiff5-dev libjasper-dev libpng12-dev`: As we installed the packages for videos, we are doing the same for the images as well.

- `sudo apt-get install libgtk2.0-dev`: We are installing a subpackage named the `gkt` development library. It is obvious that whenever we are processing some images, then we might also like to output it, perhaps in the form of images and simple GUI, and this library tells us to do exactly the same.

- `sudo apt-get install libatlas-base-dev gfortran`: Vision processing is a CPU-intensive task and when we are dealing with something that is not as powerful as a supercomputer, we must make sure that we are not wasting any CPU horsepower. To do this, we need to optimize the entire process, and this library helps us do that.

- `sudo apt-get install python2.7-dev python3-dev`: Now in this line, we are installing Python 2.7 and Python 3 header files. This necessary as without them, we would not be able to compile our code.

Now, in all the preceding commands, we installed the dependencies of vision processing or in other words, the dependencies of OpenCV that we will be using to do the vision processing. Now it is time to prepare the environment of the Python so that we can run OpenCV. Go ahead, open the terminal, and type the following command:

```
cd ~
wget -O opencv.zip https://github.com/Itseez/opencv/archive/3.4.0.zip
```

```
pi@raspberrypi:~ $ cd ~
pi@raspberrypi:~ $ wget -O opencv.zip https://github.com/Itseez/opencv/archive/3.4.0.zip
--2018-03-20 08:47:43--  https://github.com/Itseez/opencv/archive/3.4.0.zip
Resolving github.com (github.com)... 192.30.253.112, 192.30.253.113
Connecting to github.com (github.com)|192.30.253.112|:443... connected.
HTTP request sent, awaiting response... 301 Moved Permanently
Location: https://github.com/opencv/opencv/archive/3.4.0.zip [following]
--2018-03-20 08:47:44--  https://github.com/opencv/opencv/archive/3.4.0.zip
Reusing existing connection to github.com:443.
HTTP request sent, awaiting response... 302 Found
```

```
unzip opencv.zip
```

```
pi@raspberrypi:~ $ unzip opencv.zip    pi@raspberrypi:~ $ unzip opencv.zip
```

```
wget -O opencv_contrib.zip
https://github.com/Itseez/opencv_contrib/archive/3.4.0.zip
```

```
pi@raspberrypi:~ $ wget -O opencv_contrib.zip https://github.com/Itseez/opencv_contrib/archive/3.4.0.zip
--2018-03-20 09:15:16--  https://github.com/Itseez/opencv_contrib/archive/3.4.0.zip
Resolving github.com (github.com)... 192.30.253.112, 192.30.253.113
Connecting to github.com (github.com)|192.30.253.112|:443... connected.
HTTP request sent, awaiting response... 301 Moved Permanently
Location: https://github.com/opencv/opencv_contrib/archive/3.4.0.zip [following]
--2018-03-20 09:15:17--  https://github.com/opencv/opencv_contrib/archive/3.4.0.zip
Reusing existing connection to github.com:443.
HTTP request sent, awaiting response... 302 Found
```

```
unzip opencv_contrib.zip
```

```
pi@raspberrypi:~ $ unzip opencv_contrib.zip
```

Now, let's see what we have done:

- cd~: **cd** stands for **change of directory**, and the ~ sign stands for the main directory. So basically, we are switching to the main directory and the things that will be doing from here on will be done in the main directory itself.

- `wget -O opencv.zip`
  `https://github.com/Itseez/opencv/archive/3.4.0.zip`: This is pretty straightforward; we are downloading the OpenCV files from GitHub.
- `unzip opencv.zip`: Once we have downloaded all the files, we need to unzip those in order to use it.
- `wget -O opencv_contrib.zip`
  `https://github.com/Itseez/opencv_contrib/archive/3.4.0`: Now we are downloading `contrib` files. That is, these are added extra functionalities that have been developed for the OpenCV over and above the functionalities it already has.
- `unzip opencv_contrib.zip`: Now this is a no-brainer. We are unzipping the `contrib` files that we have just downloaded.

Perfect! I know it's taking a long time, and it's slightly a task. But this is something that is undeniably necessary and without this, we would not be able to go ahead and do the vision processing on our system. So now that we have done all of the preceding tasks, we need to then set up the Python. Let's go ahead and do it, then we will see why this is necessary:

```
wget https://bootstrap.pypa.io/get-pip.py
```

```
pi@raspberrypi:~ $ cd ~
pi@raspberrypi:~ $ wget https://bootstrap.pypa.io/get-pip.py
--2018-03-20 09:19:54--  https://bootstrap.pypa.io/get-pip.py
Resolving bootstrap.pypa.io (bootstrap.pypa.io)... 151.101.8.175
Connecting to bootstrap.pypa.io (bootstrap.pypa.io)|151.101.8.175|:443...
HTTP request sent, awaiting response... 200 OK
Length: 1780410 (1.7M) [text/x-python]
Saving to: 'get-pip.py'
```

```
sudo python get-pip.py
sudo pip install virtualenv virtualenvwrapper
```

```
pi@raspberrypi:~ $ sudo python get-pip.py
Collecting pip
  Downloading pip-9.0.2-py2.py3-none-any.whl (1.4MB)
    100% |████████████████████████████████| 1.4MB 64kB/s
Installing collected packages: pip
  Found existing installation: pip 9.0.1
    Uninstalling pip-9.0.1:
      Successfully uninstalled pip-9.0.1
Successfully installed pip-9.0.2
pi@raspberrypi:~ $ sudo pip install virtualenv virtualenvwrapper
```

```
sudo rm -rf ~/.cache/pip
```

```
pi@raspberrypi:~ $ sudo rm -rf ~/get-pip.py ~/.cache/pip
```

Now, let's see what this is all about:

- `wget https://bootstrap.pypa.io/get-pip.py`: Now we are getting the `pip` package. The basic work of PIP is to manage the packages over the Python system.
- `sudo python get-pip.py`: Now once we have got the package, it is time to run it and to do that we simply need to write the command.
- `sudo pip install virtualenv virtualenvwrapper`: This command is really interesting. What this is doing is installing something named `virtualenwrapper`. Now, this is an extension that lets us use the programs in a virtual environment. Why is this necessary? Well, it is a lifesaver when we talk about running various programs, which has various prerequisites. So, this helps us keeping all the programs running just fine by making a virtual environment where we have all the prerequisites already ready.
- `sudo rm -rf ~/.cache/pip`: We are simply using this command to clear the cache.

Now, after we are done with this. We would have to open the `.profile` file. To do this, we need to type the `sudo nano ~/.profile` command. This command will open the profile and then once it is open, copy following commands at the end of the files:

```
export WORKON_HOME=$HOME/.virtualenvs
source /usr/local/bin/virtualenvwrapper.sh
```

```
# virtualenv and virtualenvwrapper
export WORKON_HOME=$HOME/.virtualenvs
source /usr/local/bin/virtualenvwrapper.sh
```

Why did we do this? Basically, the terminal needs to know where the virtual environment is, and by doing this, the terminal will get to know it. Now, again, fire up the terminal; we have to load a few more things. So, this is what we need to do:

```
source ~/.profile
mkvirtualenv cv
source ~/.profile
workon cv
pip install numpy
```

Now after you are done with all of these commands, let's see what they means :

- `source ~/.profile`: This is to make sure that everything is set up
- `mkvirtualenv cv`: This is making a new environment named `cv`, and this is where we will be running all of the programs
- `source ~/.profile`: Now as we have made a new virtual environment, we need to again make sure that everything is set up, and to do that, we need to type this line again
- `workon cv`: This command will tell the system that we are working on the virtual environment that we have just created by the name of `cv`
- `pip install numpy`: This is a very important step; `numpy` is a library that helps us manage huge multidimensional arrays

After you have performed all the preceding commands, the time has finally come to install the OpenCV, and we need to use the following commands:

```
workon cv
cd ~/opencv-3.4.0/
mkdir build
cd build
cmake -D CMAKE_BUILD_TYPE=RELEASE \
    -D CMAKE_INSTALL_PREFIX=/usr/local \
    -D INSTALL_C_EXAMPLES=ON \
    -D INSTALL_PYTHON_EXAMPLES=ON \
    -D OPENCV_EXTRA_MODULES_PATH=~/opencv_contrib-3.4i.0/modules \
    -D BUILD_EXAMPLES=ON ..
```

OK, so what did we do here? Let's see:

- The `workon cv` command is simple; we are telling Python that we have to work on a virtual environment by the name of `cv`.
- Using the `cd ~/opencv-3.4.0/` command, we are changing the directory and moving inside the folder of the installed OpenCV.
- In the `mkdir build` command, we are making a new folder named `build`.
- In the `cd build` command, again we are using the basic `cd` command. This is changing the directory to which we have just made by the name `build`.
- The next command is `cmake`. What this does is compile whatever it is told to. So, in the entire next command, we are installing various settings onto our Python.

We have started compiling various settings, and now the next command is fairly important. Let's see what it is:

```
make -j4
```

Now, this command tells the Raspberry Pi how many cores it has to do while vision processing. Essentially, Raspberry Pi has four cores in total, so by giving a command of -j4, we are telling the Pi that we would be using all the four cores. Obviously, you would be thinking that it is always a good idea to use all the horsepower that we have. But that's certainly not the case. As, if we use all the cores, then it might not be able to do any other tasks. Not even take commands from the user. So, if you want to do some simultaneous task that let's say takes the vision processing data and applies it to do something else, then it might not be possible as you would have exhausted all the CPU compute power in the processing itself. However, for now, it is not the case. Hence, for the sake of time, we will be using all the cores.

Now finally, the time has come at last that we install the OpenCV. So let's see how we have to do that:

```
sudo make install
sudo ldconfig
```

As you would have guessed, `sudo make install` is compiling OpenCV, and `sudo ldconfig` creates cache and links to the important and recently shared libraries.

OK, so you think we are done. Well no, we need to finish the installation process, but there are a few additional steps. This is the last step, so just be patient for a little bit longer, and we should be there without any problems. Here are the steps that you need to do:

```
ls -l /usr/local/lib/python2.7/site-packages/
```

As you have installed all the preceding steps, now OpenCV should be installed in this part of the directory. We are using an `ls` command, which is used to list the directories in the certain location. Once you are done with this, the system will revert back with the output shown in the following screenshot:

```
cv) pi@raspberrypi:~/opencv-3.4.0/build $ sudo ldconfig
cv) pi@raspberrypi:~/opencv-3.4.0/build $ ls -l /usr/local/lib/python2.7/site-packages/
total 4432
-rw-r--r-- 1 root staff 4534312 Mar 21 04:40 cv2.so
cv) pi@raspberrypi:~/opencv-3.4.0/build $ cd ~/.virtualenvs/cv/lib/python2.7/site-packages/
cv) pi@raspberrypi:~/.virtualenvs/cv/lib/python2.7/site-packages $ ln -s /usr/local/lib/python2.7/site-packages/cv2.so cv2.so
cv) pi@raspberrypi:~/.virtualenvs/cv/lib/python2.7/site-packages $
```

Finally, once this step is done, then we need to verify that everything we have done till now has been completed successfully. So, to do that, we simply need to run these commands:

```
workon cv
python
```

The `workon cv` command will be used every time we need to work on OpenCV, so once that command is done, then the command `python` will open the Python library. If in any case the Python library is not installed properly, then it will revert with some errors, which means that the steps were not successful in which case you would have to install the OpenCV again. If everything is fine, then it will return the details, as shown in the following screenshot:

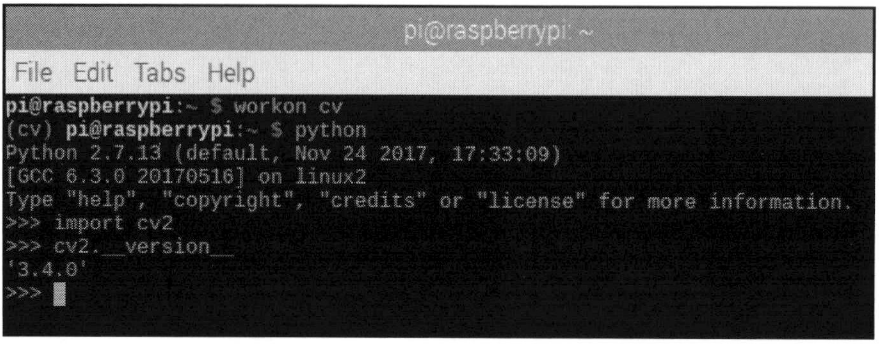

Wo-hoo! At last, we have completed the installation. Now we are all set and ready to do vision processing over Raspberry Pi.

Image recognition

Now, to go ahead and start doing vision processing, let's connect the camera to Raspberry Pi. Once you have done that, you need to write the following code:

```
import cv2
import numpy as np
cap = cv2.VideoCapture(0)

while True:
        _, image = cap.read()
        cv2.imshow("Frame", image)
        hsv = cv2.cvtColor(image, cv2.COLOR_BGR2HSV)
```

```
        lowerGreen = np.array([80,50,50])
        upperGreen = np.array([130,255,255])

        mask = cv2.inRange(hsv, lowerGreen, upperGreen)
        res = cv2.bitwise_and(image, image, mask=mask)
        cv2.imshow('mask',mask)
        cv2.imshow('result',res)
        key = cv2.waitKey(1) & 0xFF


        if key == ord('q'):
                break
   cv2.destroyAllWindows()
   cap.release()
```

Before you actually compile this code, let me tell you what exactly we are doing:

```
import numpy as np
```

In the preceding line, we are importing the library numpy as np, or in other words, we have imported the library, and every time we need to call is we simply need to write np:

```
cap = cv2.VideoCapture(0)
```

In the preceding line, we are telling Raspberry Pi to capture the video from a specific port. Now you must be thinking that how do we know which port it is connected to?

The thing with ports is that, unlike GPIOs, they are not hardware dependent rather they are software allocated. So, if your camera is the first device to be connected to the USB port, then it is very likely to be connected to port 0.

In this example, a USB camera is the only piece of hardware that we are adding; hence, we can be very sure that it will be at port 0 only.

Now the command is not only for port selection. The primary work for it is to capture the video from the camera. Now, every time we need to call it by our given name cap rather than the entire function itself:

```
_, image = cap.read()
```

In the preceding line, we are using the function `cv.VideoCapture(0)` by the name of `cap`. We are also using a function named `read()`. Now, what this will do is that it will return two things. First, it will return a Boolean value, or in another words, a true or a false. That is, whether the image has been captured successfully or not. The second reading, which we are more concerned with, is entire frame read from the image. This whole data would be stored in form of an array:

```
cv2.imshow("Frame", image)
```

In this line, we are using the library `cv2` and a function of the library named `imshow()`. What this does is that it shows the image that has been captured by the camera. Now going ahead, we have two arguments that are being passed, that is, `"Frame"` and `image`. Frame is the name of the window that would show us the captured image. Further to this, we have the second argument `image`. Now as we remember, we have stored the image in the variable named `image`. So, it will directly show what we have already stored in the previous line:

```
hsv = cv2.cvtColor(image, cv2.COLOR_BGR2HSV)
```

In this line, we are doing something amazing. The `cvtColour()` function is a converter. What does it convert? As we know, the image is made of an array of two-dimensional pixels. What this function does is convert the values that our camera gives into the desired value of the user.

Let me explain this in a bit more detail. The camera that we are using gives us RGB image. So whatever we can see is a mix of carried brightness of these three colors. Now for our detection, we would like to convert it into hue, saturation, and value. Why are we doing that you may as, first it makes the task pretty easy for us. So to understand this, let's see what this hue, saturation, and value is.

Hue basically represents the color we are talking about. Every hue value represents a specific color, and the saturation is the color intensity. So the more the saturation, the deeper it is, and the lower the saturation, the more faint the color is. Finally, value—this term can be confusing; this basically means how much black is there in the images. So let me give you a rough example:

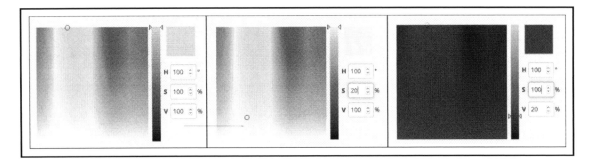

Now the first image shows you the hue: 100, saturation: 100, and value: 100. Hence, black is zero, the color is green, and saturation is 100%. In the subsequent picture, you can see the color has faded when the saturation is kept on a lower percentage. Finally, when value is reduced in the next image, then the color gets really dark.

So now coming back to the point, why hue saturation value? So now to detect any color, we simply need one unit instead of three different unit forming that color hence making the job simpler. There are various other reasons to do so as well. But at this time, it is not a concern for us.

Now moving forward, we have passed on two arguments—image, which is where the converting algorithm will take the raw data from, second is cv.Colour_BGR2HSV, which basically tells us the algorithm to use during the conversion. So as we have already discussed, we have to convert the RGB values to **hue saturation values (HSV)**. Finally, these values will be returned to a variable named hsv:

```
lowerGreen = np.array([40,50,50])
upperGreen = np.array([80,255,255])
```

In this line, we are giving the upper and lower range values, which needs to be detected. As you can see, we are detecting a green color; hence, we would be providing the upper and lower values for both the ends. If you want to change the color that you want to detect, then you simply need to change this value and the job will be done:

```
mask = cv2.inRange(hsv, lowerGreen, upperGreen)
```

Now, we are segregating the objects that are falling in this color range and giving the value to an array. This is done by a section function named `inRange()`. So, there are three arguments that we need to pass. First, which image does it need to work on, what is the lower range value that it needs to detect, and the upper range value that we have provided as `hsv`, `lowerGreen`, `upperGreen`. The result of this would be an array that would have the value of the image that has all color to be blacked out and only the color that lies in the specific color range to be shown in a plain white color:

```
res = cv2.bitwise_and(image, image, mask=mask)
```

`bitwise_and` is a function of `cv2` library; what it does is simply logical and of the two values of the array. The arguments that we are passing are `image` and the image with `mask`, or in other words, we are passing two images—one being the raw and the other being the `mask`. With this function, we are ending those two images. The result of this would an image that has a black background all around and the object that lies in the specific color range will be shown in a proper color image:

```
cv2.imshow('mask',mask)
```

We have previously used a function named `cv2.inRange`, and what it did was to filter out the specific color ranges that we had defined. Now, that function gave us a new array by the name of `mask`. What it had is an array that has all the value as null, except for those who fall into the specific color range. The image in the range would be the only one to be shown here. This would result in an image that is black all around except for the points wherein the color is in the specified range resulting in a white image. In our program, we are using `cv2.inRange` and storing the value into a variable named `mask`.

The `cv2.imshow()` function is something that we used before as well. This simply shows the resultant image of the array. Hence, we have given the command `cv2.imshow('mask',mask);` hence, it would open a window by the name of `'mask'`, and thereafter in that window, it would show the resulting image stored in the `mask` variable:

```
cv2.imshow('result',res)
```

We are doing a similar thing here. In the previous lines, we have used the function named `cv2.bitwise_and()`. This was used to do the logical and of two image arrays, that is, `image` and `mask`, the result of which was `res`; hence, it would show us the image corresponding to it. Now that we have done the logical part of `image` and `mask`, the output will be an image that would be black all around, but the portion falling into our chosen category to be shown in their original color:

```
key = cv2.waitKey(1) & 0xFF
```

Now this is interesting. The `cv2.waitKey()` function gives us the value of the key pressed. But the problem is that it returns a 32-bit integer value. However, when we talk about ASCII, it returns only 8 bit of data. Hence, we would have to only look for this 8 bits out of the 32-bit integer value returned by the `waitKey()` function. Now to do that, we are doing a logical `and` of the value received by the `waitKey()` and a hexadecimal number `0xFF` what this hexadecimal translates to is `11111111` in decimal. So when we add the 32-bit int to the hexadecimal number, we would only be left with the last 8-bit value, which is also the only relevant part for us. Hence, the value of key would a 8-bit ASCII value:

```
if key == ord('q'):
        break
```

Now we are taking a simple `if` statement and comparing the value of key to `ord('q')`. What the `ord` function does is that it takes in the argument and converts it into the ASCII value. So, in this function, if *q* key is pressed, then the loop would break and the program would come out of it:

```
cv2.destroyAllWindows()
```

This is a very simple command. It will close all the windows that we have opened using `cv2.imshow()`.

```
cap.release()
```

Using this function, we are releasing the camera. Hence, making this resource free and ready to be used by any other program.

Summary

In this chapter, you learned how to compute image data that we got from coupling the image to Raspberry Pi. In the next chapter, you will learn how to make a guard robot that can perform facial recognition.

10
Making a Guard Robot

I am sure you must have seen the movie *I, Robot* or *Chappie*. After watching the movie, a lot of people would be intrigued by the idea of making a robot that would work to protect and guard you. However, the security systems that are the state of the art can hardly be classified as a robot. In this chapter, we will take a step ahead in the lane of vision processing and make a guard robot. Its purpose would be to guard your gate and if an unknown person comes over to the gate it would start to trigger an alarm. However, the interesting thing is that the robot would not trigger any alarm if a known person comes home. What's more is that it would clear the way and get out of the door area to let you in. Once you are inside, it will automatically be back in its position to guard and get back to work yet again.

How cool would that be? So let's get going and make this robot a reality.

Face detection

Now, before we go ahead and detect faces, we need to tell the robot what a face is and what it looks like. Raspberry Pi does not know how exactly to classify a face from a pumpkin. So firstly, we would be using a dataset to tell the robot what our face looks like; thereafter, we will start recognizing the faces as we go. So let's go ahead and see how to do it.

Firstly, you need to install a dependency called Haar-cascade. This is a cascade-dependent algorithm that is used to detect objects rapidly. To do this, go ahead and run the following syntax on your terminal:

```
git clone https://github.com/opencv/opencv/tree/master/data/haarcascades
```

This will save the `haarcascades` file onto your Raspberry Pi and you will be ready to use it. Once you are done, see the following code but write it over your Raspberry only after you have seen the following explanation line by line:

```
import cv2
import numpy as np

face_cascade = cv2.CascadeClassifier('haarcascade_frontalface_default.xml')

cap = cv2.VideoCapture(0)

while True:

        ret, img = cap.read()
        gray = cv2.cvtColor(img, cv2.COLOR_BGR2GRAY)
        faces = face_cascade.detectMultiScale(gray)
        for (x,y,w,h) in faces:
            cv2.rectangle(img, (x,y), (x+w, y+h), (255,0,0), 2)

        cv2.imshow('img',img)

        k = cv2.waitKey(1) & 0xff
        if k == ord('q'):
                break

cap.release()
cv2.destroyAllWindows()
```

Now, this might look like something out of our world and pretty much every thing is new, so let's understand what we are doing here:

```
face_cascade = cv2.CascadeClassifier('haarcascade_frontalface_default.xml')
```

Once we have installed Haar-cascade, we are basically taking in the data which is already trained onto our Raspberry Pi. In this line, we are opening a classifier, which is reading the data from a file named `haarcascade_frontalface_default.xml`. This is the file that will tell Raspberry Pi whether the image captured is a frontal face or not. This file has a trained dataset to enable the Raspberry to do so. Now, we are using a function of OpenCV called `CascadeClassifier()`, which uses this learned data from the file mentioned and then classifies the images:

```
cap = cv2.VideoCapture(0)
```

This will capture the video from the camera with the port number 0. So whenever the data needs to be captured, the variable `cap` can be used instead of writing the whole program.

```
ret, img = cap.read()
```

We have understood this line in the previous chapter. It is simply capturing the image from the camera and saving it in the variable called `img` and then `ret` will return true if the capture is done or false if there is an error.

```
gray = cv2.cvtColor(img, cv2.COLOR_BGR2GRAY)
```

We have used this line previously as well. What it is doing is, it is simply converting the captured image using the `cv2.cvtColour()` function. The arguments passed in it are the following `img`, which will basically tell which image needs to be converted. Thereafter, `cv2.COLOR_BGR2GRAY` will tell from which image type it has to be converted into what.

```
faces = face_cascade.detectMultiScale(gray)
```

The `face_cascade.detectMultiScale()` function is a function of `face_cascade`. It detects the objects of various sizes and creates a rectangle of a similar size around it. The values returned to the variable faces would be the x and y coordinates of the object detected along with the width and height of the object as well. Hence, we need to define the size and position of the detected object.

```
for (x,y,w,h) in faces:
    cv2.rectangle(img, (x,y), (x+w, y+h), (255,0,0), 2)
```

In the previous line of code, we have taken the values of the position and the height of the rectangle. However, we still haven't drawn one in the actual picture. What this `for` loop will do is, it'll add a rectangle to the image using the `cv2.rectangle()` function. `img` is telling which image needs to be worked on. `(x,y)` is defining the starting coordinates of the position of the object. The value `(x+w, y+h)` is defining the end point of the rectangle. The value `(255,0,0)` is defining the color and argument 2 is defining the thickness of the line.

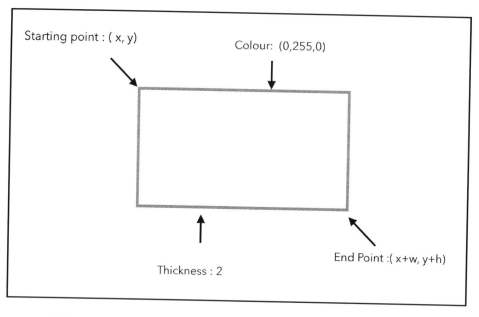

```
cv2.imshow('img',img)
```

In this line of code, we simply use the `imshow()` function to give the final output, which will have the image overlayed by the rectangle we just drew. This will indicate that we have successfully identified the image. The `'img'` argument will tell the name of the window and the second `img` will tell the function which image needs to be shown.

```
k = cv2.waitKey(1) & 0xff
if k == ord('q'):
        break
```

This line is simply waiting to take the key press of q. Whenever the user presses the q key, the `if` statement would become true, which will thereby break the infinite loop.

```
cap.release()
cv2.destroyAllWindows()
```

Finally, we are releasing the cameras using `cap.release()` and then closing all the windows using `cv2.destoryAllWindows()`.

Now, go ahead and run the code and see whether it is able to detect your face or not. Good luck!

Knowing the face

All right, we have detected the face by using a few lines of code, but I would not consider it to be a very big victory as we were fighting using the sword made by other developers. The learning set imported was a generic face learned set. However, in this chapter, we will go ahead and make our very own learning set to recognize a specific human face. This is really a cool thing and I'm sure you will love doing it.

So, let's get started. As you did earlier, go through the explanation first and then write the code so that you understand it very well.

Firstly, we are using the program to capture the images of the object that needs to be detected. In our case, this object will be a person and his face. So, let's see what we need to do:

```
import cv2
import numpy as np

faceDetect = cv2.CascadeClassifier('haarcascade_frontalface_default.xml')
cam = cv2.VideoCapture(0)

sampleNum = 0

id = raw_input('enter user id')

while True:
        ret,img = cam.read()
        gray = cv2.cvtColor(img, cv2.COLOR_BGR2GRAY)
        faces = faceDetect.detectMultiScale(gray,1.3,5)

        for (x,y,w,h) in faces:
                sampleNum = sampleNum + 1
```

```
cv2.imwrite("dataSet/User."+str(id)+"."+str(sampleNum)+".jpg",   gray[y:y+h,
x:x+w])
```

```
                    cv2.rectangle(img,  (x,y),  (x+w,y+h),  (0,0,255),  2)
                    cv2.waitKey(100)
            cv2.imshow("Face",  img)
            cv2.waitKey(1)
            if sampleNum>20:

                    break
    cam.release()
    cv2.destroyAllWindows()
```

Here is the explanation:

```
faceDetect = cv2.CascadeClassifier('haarcascade_frontalface_default.xml')
cam = cv2.VideoCapture(0)
```

As you have seen earlier, we are using the preceding two lines of code to import the learned dataset and also to start the camera.

```
id = raw_input('enter user id')
```

As we will be training the system to learn a specific face, it is very important that the program knows who it is detecting either by name or ID. This will help us clarify who we have detected. So, to go ahead and detect a person by face, we need to provide his ID, which is being done in the following code:

```
ret,img = cam.read()
gray = cv2.cvtColor(img,  cv2.COLOR_BGR2GRAY)
```

This is exactly the same as we did in the previous section of code. Refer to it if you need explanation.

```
faces = faceDetect.detectMultiScale(gray,1.3,5)
```

Now, this line of code might also sound to you like a repetition; however, there is an addition to it. In this function, two arguments have been passed instead of one. The first is grey and the second is the minimum and maximum size of the object that can be detected. This is important to make sure that the object detected is big enough for the learning process to happen.

```
for (x,y,w,h) in faces:
            sampleNum = sampleNum + 1
    cv2.imwrite("dataSet/User."+str(id)+"."+str(sampleNum)+".jpg",   gray[y:y+h,
x:x+w])
```

Here, we are using the same `for` loop to perform the following condition. So the loop will only be true when the face is detected. Whenever it is detected, the `sampleNum` variable would be incremented by 1 by counting the number of faces detected. Further, to capture the images onto our system, we need the following line of code:

```
cv2.inwrite('dataSet/User."+str(id)+"."+str(sampleNum)+".jpg",gray[y:y+h,x:
x+w])
```

What it does is, it simply saves the image onto a folder by the name `dataSet/User`. It is very important to be able to make a folder by this name yourself. If you don't do this, then it would go haywire when it does not find the folder where it is supposed to save. `+str(id)` will save the name by the ID of the person and increment it with the number of samples counted using `+str(sampleNum)`. Furthermore, we have mentioned that the image would be saved by the format `.jpg` and finally `gray[y:y+h, x:x+w]` is selecting the part of the image that contains the face.

The rest of the program beyond this point is self explanatory and I suspect you can understand it on your own. In very simple English, this would save the images in a folder and will keep doing so, until it reaches 20 images.

Now that we have captured the images, it's time to make the system learn the images and understand how to recognize them. To do this, we need to install something called the `pillow` library. Installing it is easy. All you need to do is, write the following line in the terminal:

```
sudo -H pip install pillow
```

This `pillow` library would help us read the dataset. We will understand more in a moment. Once this is installed, let's go ahead and see how we are doing the learning part. So go ahead and understand the following code and then let's get going:

```
import os
import cv2
import numpy as np
from PIL import Image

recognizer = cv2.face.LBPHFaceRecognizer_create()

path = 'dataSet'

def getImageID(path):
    imagePaths = [os.path.join(path,f) for f in os.listdir(path)]

    faces=[]
    IDs=[]
```

```
for imagePath in imagePaths:
    faceImg = Image.open(imagePath).convert('L')

    faceNp = np.array(faceImg, 'unit8')

    ID = int(os.path.split(imagePath)[-1].split('.')[1])

    faces.append(faceNp)
    print ID
    IDs.append(ID)

return IDs, faces

Ids, faces = getImageID(path)
recognizer.train(faces, np.array(Ids))
recognizer.save('recognizer/trainningData.yml')

cv2.destroyAllWindows()
```

Alien might be the word which might come in your head after seeing this code, but it sure won't be alien after you have gone through this explanation. So let's see:

```
recognizer = cv2.face.LBPHFaceRecognizer_create()
```

It is creating a recognizer using the `cv2.face.LBPHFaceRecognizer_create()` function.

```
path = 'dataSet'
```

This line here tells where the captured data is stored in Raspberry Pi. We have already made a folder by this name and it contains the images that we have stored previously.

```
def getImageID(path):
    imagePaths = [os.path.join(path,f) for f in os.listdir(path)]
```

Here we are defining the function named `getImageID(path)`.

This join function will join the path with `f`. Now, `f` is a variable containing the filename as it loops through the list of files inside the folder defined as path using `os.listdir(path)`.

```
for imagePath in imagePaths:
    faceImg = Image.open(imagePath).convert('L')
```

The `for` loop in this line will be true for every image that we have and will run the code inside of it. What `Image.open(imagePath).convert('L')` does is, it simply covers the image in monochrome format. Using this line, every image that we are having would be converted into monochrome.

```
faceNp = np.array(faceImg, 'unit8')
```

OpenCV works with `numpy` array; hence, we need to convert the images to the desired format. To do this, we are using a `faceNp` variable to call the `np.array()` function. This function converts the images into `numpy` array of name `faceImg` and with 8-bit integer value, as we have passed the argument `unit8`.

```
ID = int(os.path.split(imagePath)[-1].split('.')[1])
```

In this line, we are using a variable to call the `int()` function, which will split the path name for the images being captured. Why are we doing this? This is done to extract the ID number from the actual filename. Hence, we are doing this using the following function:

```
faces.append(faceNp)
print ID
IDs.append(ID)
```

Here, using `faces.append(faceNp)`, we are adding the data into the array by the name of `faces` and the data being added is `faceNp`. Then, we are printing the `ID` of that image.

Once done, `IDs.append(ID)` will add the `ID` to the array `IDs`. This whole process is being done as the function that we would be using for training would only take in the values in the form of an array. So we have to convert the entire data in the form of an array and fetch it to the trainer.

So the entire explanation so far was defining the function named `getImageId(Path)`.

```
return IDs, faces
```

Now this line would return the values of `IDs` of the faces which will be further used to train the dataset.

```
Ids, faces = getImageID(path)
recognizer.train(faces, np.array(Ids))
recognizer.save('recognizer/trainningData.yml')
```

In the first line here, the `getImageID(path)` function would take in the path of the any image and return the `Ids` of the images. Then, `faces` would have the array data of the images.

Finally, in `recognizer.train(faces, np.array(Ids))`, we are using a function of `recognizer` called `train` to train the system based on their images. The arguments passed here are that `faces` has the array of the images. Furthermore, `np.array(Ids)` is the array, which is returned by the function defined by the name `getImageID()`.

Once the system is trained using the following program, we would save the trained data to a file. This is done using the `recognizer.save()` function. The argument passed in it is the name and the extension of the file saved.

It can be a little intense and sometimes confusing as well. However, it will seem easy once you do it. Now, it's time that you go ahead and make the system learn about your face and its data.

Recognizing the face

Now that we have learned how to make our system learn, it's time to use that learned data and recognize the face. So without much talking, let's go ahead and understand how this would be done:

```
import numpy as np
import cv2

faceDetect = cv2.CascadeClassifier('haarcascade_frontalface_default.xml')

cam = cv2.VideoCapture(0)
rec = cv2.face.LBPHFaceRecognizer_create()

rec.read("recognizer/trainningData.yml")
id = 0
font = cv2.FONT_HERSHEY_SIMPLEX

while True:

    ret, img = cam.read()
    gray=cv2.cvtColor(img,cv2.COLOR_BGR2GRAY)
    faces = faceDetect.detectMultiScale(gray,1.3,5)

    for (x,y,w,h) in faces:
        cv2.rectangle(img, (x,y), (x+w, y+h), (0,0,255), 2)
```

```
id, conf = rec.predict(gray[y:y+h, x:x+w])

if id==1:
    id = "BEN"
cv2.putText(img, str(id), (x,y+h),font,2, (255,0,0),1,)

cv2.imshow("face", img)

if cv2.waitKey(1)==ord('q'):
    break

cam.release()
cv2.destroyAllWindows()
```

In this code, there are not a lot of new things that you might encounter. It is very similar to the first code that we started with in this chapter. Essentially, it is also doing the same work. The only difference is that it recognizes the person by his ID. So, let's see what is different and how well it performs.

Now, most of the code is repetitive. So instead of going through all of it, I will only touch on the ones which are new. Here we go:

```
font = cv2.FONT_HERSHEY_SIMPLEX
```

Like last time, we were drawing a rectangle over an identified image. However, this time there are places where overlay has to be done with some text as well. So here we are choosing the font that we need to use in this program:

```
id, conf = rec.predict(gray[y:y+h, x:x+w])
```

With this line, the prediction is taking place using the function of the recognizer called `predict()`. This predicts the images and returns the `id` of the detected image.

```
if id==1:
    id = "BEN"
```

Now, finally, if the `id` is equal to 1, then the value of `id` would be changed to BEN.

```
cv2.putText(img, str(id), (x,y+h),font,2, (255,0,0),1,)
```

The `putText()` function will put a text on the detected object. The definition of each of the arguments is as follows:

- `img`: This is the image on which the text has to be put.
- `str(id)`: This is the string that needs to be printed, in our case it would print the ID of the person.
- `(x, y+h)`: This is the position where the text would be printed.
- `font`: This is the font of the printed text. In our case, it would be the value of the font defined earlier.
- `2`: This is the font scale, that is, how big the font would be. This can be similar to magnification.
- `(255,0,0)`: This is the color of the font.
- `1`: This is the thickness of the font.

With this program, we would be able to find out if the learning set is working as per our requirement. Once you have written the code, try identifying the people with it and see whether it works accurately. If the accuracy is not satisfactory, then you may want to take more than 20 samples for learning. Conduct a few trials and I am sure you would reach perfection very soon.

Making the guard robot

Now that we have understood how the learning works and how the learned data can be used to identify people, it's time to put it to use. As the name of the chapter suggests, we will be making a guard robot using this technology. Now, let's have a look at the following program. Before you start programming, take out the robotic vehicle you had and make the connection like we did before in Chapter 6, *Bluetooth-Controlled Robotic Car*. Attach the motor, motor driver, and Raspberry Pi. Once you have done that, then write the following code. This code is utilizing all the learning of the previous programs in the chapter and we would be able to distinguish between an intruder and a resident of the house based on vision processing. So let's get going:

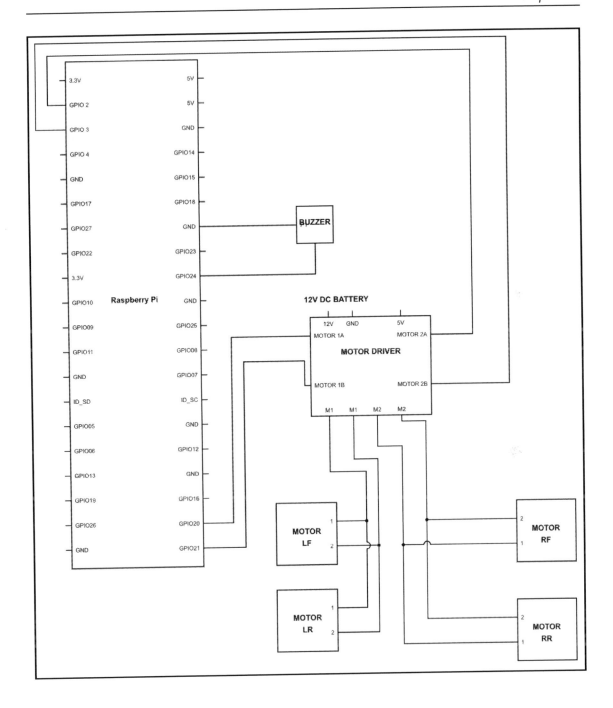

```
import numpy as np
import cv2
Import RPi.GPIO as GPIO

Motor1F = 20
Motor1R = 21
Motor2F = 2
Motor2R = 3
Buzzer = 24

GPIO.setmode(GPIO.BCM)
GPIO.setwarnings(False)
GPIO.setup(Motor1a,GPIO.OUT)
GPIO.setup(Motor1b,GPIO.OUT)
GPIO.setup(Motor2a,GPIO.OUT)
GPIO.setup(Motor2b,GPIO.OUT)
GPIO.setup(Buzzer, GPIO.OUT)

def forward():

        GPIO.output(Motor1F,1)
        GPIO.output(Motor1R,0)
        GPIO.output(Motor2F,1)
        GPIO.output(Motor2R,0)

def backward():

        GPIO.output(Motor1F,0)
        GPIO.output(Motor1R,1)
        GPIO.output(Motor2F,0)
        GPIO.output(Motor2R,1)

def stop():

        GPIO.output(Motor1F,0)
        GPIO.output(Motor1R,0)
        GPIO.output(Motor2F,0)
        GPIO.output(Motor2R,0)

faceDetect = cv2.CascadeClassifier('haarcascade_frontalface_default.xml')

cam = cv2.VideoCapture(0)
rec = cv2.face.LBPHFaceRecognizer_create()
rec.read("recognizer/trainningData.yml")

id = 0
font = cv2.FONT_HERSHEY_SIMPLEX
```

```
while True:

    ret, img = cam.read()
    gray=cv2.cvtColor(img,cv2.COLOR_BGR2GRAY)
    faces = faceDetect.detectMultiScale(gray,1.3,5)

    for (x,y,w,h) in faces:
        cv2.rectangle(img, (x,y), (x+w, y+h), (0,0,255), 2)
        id, conf = rec.predict(gray[y:y+h, x:x+w])

        if id==1:
            id = "BEN"

            forward()
            time.sleep(1)
            stop()
            time.sleep(5)
            backward()
            time.sleep(1)

        else :

            GPIO.output(Buzzer, 1)
            time.sleep(5)

        cv2.putText(img, str(id), (x,y+h),font,2, (255,0,0),1,cv2.LINE_AA)
        cv2.imshow("face", img)

    id = 0
    if cv2.waitKey(1)==ord('q'):
    break

cam.release()
cv2.destroyAllWindows()
```

As always, we will only be looking at the peculiar changes in the program, a lot of it will be carried over from the previous chapter. So we will try not to repeat the explanation unless necessary.

```
def forward():

        GPIO.output(Motor1a,0)
        GPIO.output(Motor1b,1)
        GPIO.output(Motor2a,0)
        GPIO.output(Motor2b,1)

def backward():
```

```
GPIO.output(Motor1a,1)
GPIO.output(Motor1b,0)
GPIO.output(Motor2a,1)
GPIO.output(Motor2b,0)

def stop():

    GPIO.output(Motor1a,0)
    GPIO.output(Motor1b,0)
    GPIO.output(Motor2a,0)
    GPIO.output(Motor2b,0)
```

Just as a recap, we are defining two functions, namely, `backwards`, `reverse`, and `stop`. These functions will help us move the vehicle in the direction in which we want.

```
faceDetect = cv2.CascadeClassifier('haarcascade_frontalface_default.xml')
```

This line is importing the previously learned dataset by the name of `harrcascade_frontalface_default.xml`. This will help us recognize any face that comes in front of the camera.

```
for (x,y,w,h) in faces:
    cv2.rectangle(img, (x,y), (x+w, y+h), (0,0,255), 2)
    id, conf = rec.predict(gray[y:y+h, x:x+w])

    if id==1:
        id = "BEN"

        forward()
        time.sleep(1)
        stop()
        time.sleep(5)
        backward()
        time.sleep(1)

    else :

        GPIO.output(Buzzer, 1)
        time.sleep(5)
```

In this piece of the code, we are identifying the face and taking decisions based on it. As we have done earlier, if the face is detected, then its corresponding ID would be given by the program. However, no ID would be given if the face is not detected by the previously learned dataset in which any face could be detected. Hence, according to the program, if the `id == 1`, then the robotic vehicle would move forward moving away from the path, thereafter it would stop for 5 seconds and get back to where it was earlier. In case the ID generated is anything except 1, then the Buzzer would be turned on for 5 seconds alerting the user.

By using this system, anyone who is identified can be let inside the premises; however, if the person is not identified, then the alarm would be triggered.

Summary

In this chapter, we have learned how to detect objects using a prelearned dataset. We also learned how to make our very own learned dataset for a specific object. Finally, we have used all of that learning to make a guard robot, who will guard our home using the power of vision processing.

11
Basic Switching

It must have been an epic journey so far! Recollect the time when you would have started reading this book, did you ever imagine that things could be this simple? It is worth noting that everything starts off very simple and, slowly and steadily, with the need for more sophisticated systems, the complexity of the technology also increases. Go back to the time when personal computing was not really a thing. It was only used in business and companies such as IBM were only servicing business clients. At that time, people who wanted a personal computer had only one option. They needed to build it from scratch, and to be honest, a lot of people used to do that. It really wasn't that hard either at least from my perspective. But, in contrast to that time, think about what they have become right now. Ever thought of building a computer at home? By building, I mean designing everything and not just assembly of the CPU. It is not very easy.

What I am trying to tell you here is that there was a time when computers were exotic; they were not very common, and they had very limited functionalities. However, with time and the brains of people, such as Steve Jobs, Bill Gates, and Hewlett and Packard, computers became more user-friendly, more easily available, and a desirable commodity. Think of the same thing with robots. They are expensive; for most people, there is not much they can do with them and also they are rare in the public space. But, as you have learned, it is not very hard to build a robot for our personal use, and with some tweaking here and there and with inventive minds such as yours, things can be taken in an altogether different direction. You could be the next Steve Jobs or Bill Gates. All we need is zeal, passion, and out-of-the-box thinking. You may be ridiculed for your vision. But do remember every inventor has been called mad at some point in time. So the next time someone calls you mad, you can be very sure that you are progressing!

Well, I'm quite sure that, if you are a robotic enthusiast, then you must have seen the movie *Iron Man*. If you haven't seen it yet, then take a break from reading this book and go ahead and open Netflix and see that movie.

Once I saw that movie, there were two main things that I wanted to build: one, the suit of Iron Man and other his personal assistant Jarvis, who takes care of all his needs. Though suits seem to be something that I may have to work on for a while, but, by that time, you can go ahead and build the personal assistant for yourself.

Imagine your home doing things for itself. How cool would it be? It knows what you like, what time you wake up, when you come back home, and, based on that, it automatically does things for you. Best of all, it would not be something you buy off the shelf, rather you would be making it with your own hands.

Before you do any of this, I must tell you that you will be dealing with high voltages and considerable currents. Electricity is no joke, and you must take care at all times and wear all the safety equipment. If you are not sure of it, then it would be a good idea to get an electrician to help you. Before you touch or open any of the electrical boards, make sure that you are wearing non-conductive shoes; also inspect whether the tools such as screwdrivers, pliers, nose pliers, cutters, and other tools are well insulated and in good condition. It is a good idea to wear gloves for added safety. If you are under 18, then you must have an adult with you all times to help you.

Now that that's said, let's get started and see what we have got here.

Making Jarvis wake you up

Now, this one is very interesting, as you all know our human body is programmed in a certain way. Hence, we react to different stimuli in a very known way. Like when it gets dark, our brain produces hormones that trigger sleep. Once the sunlight falls on our eyes, we tend to wake up. Well, at least this should be the case! In recent times, our lifestyle has changed enormously, which has started to defy this cycle. That's why, we are seeing more and more cases of insomnia. Waking up by an alarm is certainly not natural. Hence, you are never happy listening to an alarm in the morning, even if it has your favorite song as its tone. Our sleep cycle is supposed to be synchronized with the sunlight, but nowadays hardly anyone wakes up by this method. So, in this chapter, let's first make a smart alarm that will replicate the natural way we wake up.

Working with relay and PIR sensor

As we are dealing with high voltage and higher currents, we would be using a relay. To do this, connect the wires as follows:

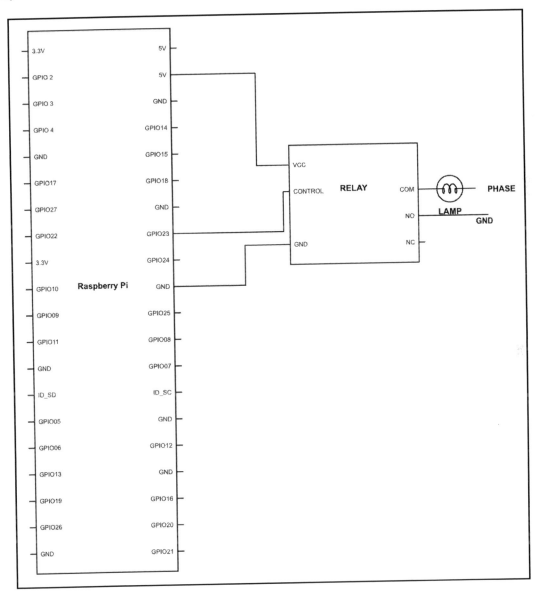

Once you are done connecting it, upload the following code and let's see what happens:

```
import RPi.GPIO as GPIO
import time

LIGHT = 23

GPIO.setmode(GPIO.BCM)
GPIO.setwarnings(False)
GPIO.setup(LIGHT,GPIO.OUT)

import datetime

H = datetime.datetime.now().strftime('%H')
M = datetime.datetime.now().strftime('%M')

while True:

    if H = '06'and M < 20 :
        GPIO.output(LIGHT,GPIO.HIGH)

    else:
        GPIO.output(LIGHT,GPIO.LOW)
```

OK, then it is a fairly simple code with not much explanation needed. We have done a very similar code before as well. Do you remember when? It was in the first few chapters when we were making a gardening robot where we had to fetch water to the plants at a certain time. All it is doing at this time is to check the time and whether the time is 06 hours and the minute is less than 20. That is, the light would be switched on between 07:00 hours to 07:19 hours. Thereafter, it would switch off.

Making the alarm irritating

But there is a problem. The problem is that the lights will be switched on and, no matter whether you get up, the light would automatically switch itself off within 20 minutes. That is a bit of problem because not every time will you wake up in just 20 minutes. So, in that case, what should we do? The first thing we need to do is to detect whether you have woken up. This is very simple and not much needs to be told here. If you wake up in the morning, it is very certain that you will move out of the bed. Once you do, we can detect the motion that can tell our automated system whether you have really woken up.

Now, what we can do here is something very simple. We can detect your motion, and based on that detection, we can be decisive on whether you have really woken up. This doesn't seem much of a task. All we need to do is to add a motion detection sensor. For this purpose, we can use a PIR sensor, which can tell us whether the motion has been detected. So, let's go ahead, add another layer of sensor on top of our system, and see what happens.

So, first, connect the circuit as follows. While mounting the PIR sensor, do make sure that it is facing the bed and detecting any motion on and around it. Once the PIR is set up, wire the sensors as shown in the following diagram and see what happens:

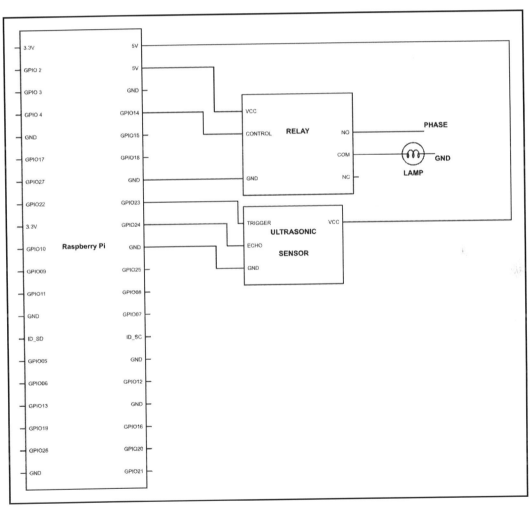

Once done, then go ahead and write the following code:

```
import RPi.GPIO as GPIO
import time

LIGHT = 23
PIR = 24
Irritation_flag = 3

GPIO.setmode(GPIO.BCM)
GPIO.setwarnings(False)

GPIO.setup(LIGHT,GPIO.OUT)
GPIO.setup(PIR, GPIO.IN)

import datetime

H = datetime.datetime.now().strftime('%H')
M = datetime.datetime.now().strftime('%M')


    while True:

        if H = '07' and M <= '15' and Iriitation_Flag > 0 and
GPIO.input(PIR) == 0:

            GPIO.output(LIGHT,GPIO.HIGH)


        if H = '07'and GPIO.input(PIR)==1:

            GPIO.output(LIGHT,GPIO.LOW)
            time.sleep(10)
            Irritation_Flag = Irritation_Flag - 1


        for H = '07'and M > '15' and Irritation_Flag > 0 and
GPIO.input(PIR) = 0:

            GPIO.output(LIGHT,GPIO.HIGH)
            time.sleep(5)
            GPIO.output(LIGHT,GPIO.LOW)
            time.sleep(5)

        if H != '07':
            Irritation_flag = 3
            GPIOP.output(LIGHT, GPIO.LOW)
```

OK, let's see what we have done. The code is extremely simple, but we had a small twist in it, that is, `Irritation_Flag`:

```
Irritation_flag = 3
```

Now this variable works something like a snooze button. As we know, when we wake up sometimes, or in fact, most of the time, we again go back to sleep only to wake up much later to realize that we are late. To prevent this, we have this `Irritation_flag`, and what this basically would be used for is to detect the number of times you have performed the action to stop the alarm. How it would be used we will see later:

```
if H = '07' and M <= '15' and Irritation_Flag > 0 and
GPIO.input (PIR)  == 0:

        GPIO.output (LIGHT, GPIO.HIGH)
```

In this line, we are simply comparing time values by hours and minutes. If the hours is 07 and minutes are fewer than or equal to 15, then the lights would be switched off. There is also a condition that says `Irritation_Flag > 0` as we have already declared in the beginning that the value of `Irritation_flag = 3`; hence, initially this condition will always be true. The last condition is `GPIO.input (PIR)  == 0;` which means that the condition will only be satisfied when the PIR has not detected any motion. In very simple words, the alarm will go off every time between 07:00 and 07:15 if the PIR does not detect any motion:

```
if H = '07'and GPIO.input (PIR)==1:

        GPIO.output (LIGHT, GPIO.LOW)
        time.sleep(10)
        Irritation_Flag = Irritation_Flag - 1
```

In this part of the program, the condition will only be true if the hours or H is equal to 7 and when the PIR is detecting some motion. Hence, every time when the time is between 07:00 and 07:59 and whenever the motion is detected, the condition will be true. Once true, the program will first switch off the light using the line `GPIO.output *LIGHT, GPIO.LOW`. Once it is turned off, it waits for 10 seconds using `time.sleep(10)`. Once the time is over, it will implement the following operation: `Irritation_Flag - Irritation_Flag - 1`. Now what it does is that it decrements the value of `Irritation_Flag` by 1 every time it detects a motion. So the first time a motion happens, the value of `Irritation_Flag` would be 2; thereafter, it would be 1, and finally, it would be 0.

If you look at the previous part of the code, you will be able to make out that the light would be switched on if the value of `Irritation_Flag` was greater than 0. So if you want to turn off the light, you would have to move at least three times. Why three times? Because then the code `Irritation_Flag = Irritation - 1` would be executed three times so as to make the value get down to 0, which obviously makes the condition `GPIO.input(PIR) > 0` false:

```
       for H = '07'and M > '15' and Irritation_Flag > 0 and
  GPIO.input(PIR) = 0:

           GPIO.output(LIGHT,GPIO.HIGH)
           time.sleep(5)
           GPIO.output(LIGHT,GPIO.LOW)
           time.sleep(5)
```

Now, let's say even after of all this, you still do not wake up. Then what should happen? We have something special for you here. Now, instead of an `if` condition, we have a `for` loop. What this will check for is that the time should be `07` hours, and minutes should be greater than 15, `Irritation_Flag > 0`, and obviously no motion is being detected. Till the time all of these are true, the light would be switched on thereafter for 5 seconds, it would be kept switched on using the `time.sleep(5)`. The lights would be again switched on. Now this will keep on happening till the time the conditions are true or in other words, till the time is between 07:15 and 07:59. `Irritation)_Flag > 0`, that is, the motion is not detected for three times and there is no motion detected. Till that time, the for loop would keep on the switch on and off of the light in action. Due to frequent biking of light, there is a very higher chance of you waking up. This may be very effective, but surely not the most convenient. Well, however inconvenient it is, it will still be better than the conventional alarm:

```
      if H != '07':
          Irritation_flag = 3
```

We have the entire light-based alarm ready for us to wake us up every morning. However, there is a problem. Once it is turned off, the value of `Irritation_Flag` will be 0. Once it is turned to 0, then no matter what the time is, the light would never start up. Hence, to make sure that the alarm is always operational at the same time every single day, we would need to set the value of the flag to any number more than 0.

Now in the preceding line, if `H != '07'`, then the `Irritation_flag` would be 3. That is whenever the time is anything other than 07 hours, then the value of `Irritation_Flag` would be 3.

It was simple, wasn't it? But I'm sure that it would do a good job to make sure you wake up on time.

Making it even more irritating

Can you completely rely on the preceding system? If you really have control over your morning emotions of not getting out of the bed, then, yes, sure you can. But for those who just love to be in bed and sleep again after hitting the snooze button, then I am sure you would be able to find a way to switch off the light without properly waking up. So as in the code, the light would switch off whenever the motion was detected three times. But the motion can be anything. You can simply wave your hand while still being in the bed, and the system would detect it as a motion, which would defy the whole purpose. So what should we do now?

We have a solution for it! We can use a way by which we can be sure that you have to get out of bed. For this very purpose, we will be using our IR proximity sensor, which we have used earlier in our projects, and based on the distance reading of the sensor, we can detect whether you have gone past any specific area. This can be really interesting as you can fit this sensor pointing away from the bed or maybe on the gate of the bathroom, and till the time, you do not cross that specific line. The system would not switch off the alarm. So let's see how we would do it. First, connect the hardware, as shown in the following diagram:

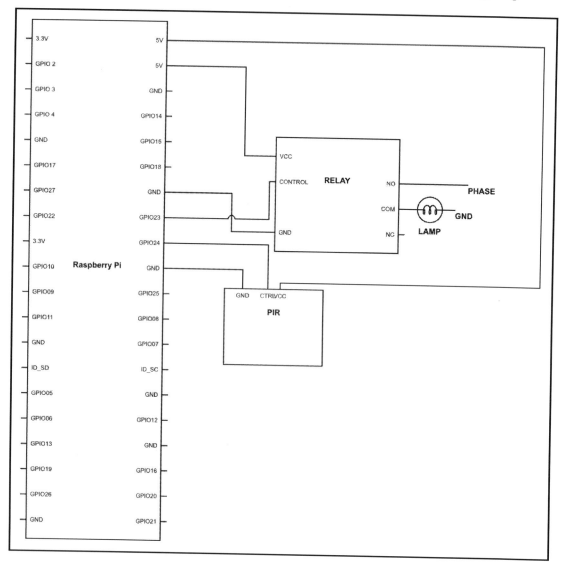

Once you are done with the diagram, go ahead and upload the following code:

```
import RPi.GPIO as GPIO
import time

import Adafruit_ADS1x15
adc0 = Adafruit_ADS1x15.ADS1115()

GAIN = 1

adc0.start_adc(0, gain=GAIN)

LIGHT = 23
PIR = 24
Irritation_flag = 1
IR = 2

GPIO.setmode(GPIO.BCM)
GPIO.setwarnings(False)

GPIO.setup(LIGHT,GPIO.OUT)
GPIO.setup(PIR, GPIO.IN)
GPIO.setup(IR. GPIO.IN)

import datetime

H = datetime.datetime.now().strftime('%H')
M = datetime.datetime.now().strftime('%M')


  while True:

  if H = '07' and M <= '15' and Iriitation_Flag > 0 and GPIO.input(PIR) ==
0:

     GPIO.output(LIGHT,GPIO.HIGH)


  if H = '07'and GPIO.input(PIR)==1:
   M_snooze = datetime.datetime.now().strftime('%M')
   M_snooze = M_snooze + 5
   for M <= M_snooze
     GPIO.output(LIGHT,GPIO.LOW)

     F_value = adc0.get_last_result()
     F1 =    (1.0 / (F_value / 13.15)) - 0.35
```

```
time.sleep(0.1)
F_value = adc0.get_last_result()
F2 =     (1.0 / (F_value / 13.15)) - 0.35

F_final = F1-F2

M = datetime.datetime.now().strftime('%M')

if F_final > 25

    Irritation_flag = 0



for H = '07'and M > '15' and Irritation_Flag > 0 and GPIO.input(PIR) = 0:

GPIO.output(LIGHT,GPIO.HIGH)
time.sleep(5)
GPIO.output(LIGHT,GPIO.LOW)
time.sleep(5)

if H != '07':

Irritation_flag = 1
```

Mind blown? This code seems quite complex, having conditions inside conditions and again some more conditions. Say hello to robotics! These conditions make up a lot of robot's programming. A robot has to see continuously what is happening around and make decisions according to it. It's also the way humans work, don't we?

So, that being said, let's see what we are actually doing here. Most of the code is pretty much the same as the last one. The main difference comes somewhere around the middle of the programming section:

```
if H = '07' and M <= '15' and Iriitation_Flag > 0 and GPIO.input(PIR) ==
0:

    GPIO.output(LIGHT,GPIO.HIGH)
```

We are switching on the lights as soon as the time is between 07:00 and 07:15:

```
if H = '07'and GPIO.input(PIR)==1:
  M_snooze = datetime.datetime.now().strftime('%M')
  M_snooze = M_snooze + 5
```

In the hour of 07 whenever the PIR sensor is triggered or in other words, the PIR sensor detects any motion, then it will do a set of activities inside the `if` condition, which includes noting down the time by the function `datetime.datetime.now().strftime('%M')` and then storing it down in a variable named M_snooze.

In the next line, we are taking the value of that minute stored in M_snooze and adding another 5 minutes to it. So the value of M_snooze is now incremented by 5:

```
for M <= M_snooze
```

Now, in the same `if` condition that we used previously, we have placed a `for` loop, which looks like this: `for M <= M_snooze`. But what does this mean? Here, what we are doing is pretty simple. The program inside the `for` loop will keep on running and will stay in the loop till the time the condition that we have stated is true. Now, the condition here states that till the time M is smaller or equal to M_snooze, the condition will stay true. As you have learned earlier, M is the current minute value and M_snooze is the value of M at the time of starting of this loop, which is incremented by 5. Hence, the loop would be true for 5 minutes from the time of starting:

```
GPIO.output(LIGHT,GPIO.LOW)

F_value = adc0.get_last_result()
F1 =    (1.0 / (F_value / 13.15)) - 0.35

time.sleep(0.1)
F_value = adc0.get_last_result()
F2 =    (1.0 / (F_value / 13.15)) - 0.35

F_final = F1-F2
```

Now, this is the most interesting part of the program. Till the time, the `for` loop `for M <= M_snooze` is true, the preceding lines of code will run. Let's see what it is doing. In the line, `F-value = adc0.get_last_result()`, it is taking the value of the IR proximity sensor and storing it in `F_value`. Thereafter, in the line `F1 = (1.0/(F_value/13.15))-0.35`, we are simply calculating the distance in centimeters. We have already studied how this is happening, so not much explanation needs to be done here. The value of distance is stored in a variable named `F1`. Thereafter, using the function `time.sleep(0.1)`, we are pausing the program for `0.1` seconds. Thereafter, we are again repeating the same task again; that is, we are again taking the value of distance. But this time, the distance value calculated is stored in an another variable named `F2`. Finally, after all of this is done, we are calculating `F_final`, which is `F_final = F1 - F2`. So we are simply calculating the difference in distance between the first and the second reading. But, you must be asking why are we doing this. What good does it do?

Well, as you remember, we have placed the IR proximity sensor in front of our bathroom gate. Now, if no one is passing in front of it, the value will remain fairly constant. But whenever a person passes through it, there will be a change in distance. So if there is a change in the overall distance from first to last reading, then we can say that someone has passed through the IR sensor.

That is pretty cool, but why don't we simply keep a threshold value like we have done previously? The answer to this is simple. That is because if you need to change the position of the sensor, then you again need to recalibrate the sensor according to the position. So this is a simple yet robust solution that can be used anywhere:

```
if F_final > 10
    Irritation_flag = 1
```

Now we have got the reading, which can tell us whether a person has passed in front of it. But this data will not be useful until we put it somewhere.

So, here in the condition `if F_final > 10`, whenever the distance change is more than `10` cm, then the condition would be true and the line `Irritation_flag` would be set to `1`.

If you go back to the previous lines, then you will be able to make out that the lights will only be on when the time is between 07:00 and 07:15 and the `Irritation_flag` must be `0`. As with this condition, we have set a part of the condition false by making the `Irritation_flag = 1`; hence, the program to switch on the lights will not work.

Now, let's look back and see what we have done so far:

- Whenever the time is 07:00–07:15, the lights would be switched on
- If a movement is detected, then the lights would be switched off
- A condition will be true for another five minutes, which will wait for detection of human motion through the IR proximity sensor
- If a person crosses that within five minutes, then the alarm would be deactivated or else the alarm will again start to switch on the light

Pretty cool, huh? That being said, let's add another added functionality from the previous program:

```
for H = '07'and M > '15' and Irritation_Flag = 0 and GPIO.input(PIR) = 0:

GPIO.output(LIGHT,GPIO.HIGH)
time.sleep(5)
GPIO.output(LIGHT,GPIO.LOW)
time.sleep(5)
```

You know what this does. If you do not move around in the first 15 minutes, that is from 07:00 to 07:15, then it will start blinking the lights every five seconds, forcing you to wake up:

```
if H != '07':
    Irritation_flag = 0
```

Finally, we use the condition `if H != '07':`. So, whenever the value of `H` is anything other than `07`, then the condition would be true, and this will reset the `Irritation_flag` to 0. By now, you know what turning `Irritation_flag` to 0 does.

Summary

So, finally, we have made our first mini Jarvis, which wakes you up in the morning and even irritates you if you don't wake up on time. I hope you have really enjoyed this chapter by learning about two-motion sensors and their application in automating the electrical appliance. So, go ahead and try one at home, modify the code according to your needs, and bring out some really cool stuff. Next up, we will make our Jarvis do some more cool stuff, and we will cover some more exciting stuff on human detection.

12
Recognizing Humans with Jarvis

By now we have understood in the last chapter how multiple layers of conditions can be clubbed together to get the functionality that is desired. We have just completed the first step in making Jarvis work for you. Now, it's time to make it even more capable.

In this chapter, we will make it control more electronics at your home, which can be controlled autonomously without you telling anything to the system. So without delay, let's get straight into it and see what we have in our bucket.

Turn on the light Jarvis

One of the basic functionalities of a smart home is to turn on the lights for you whenever you are around. It is one of the most basic things that any system can do for you. We will start off by turning on the light as soon as you come inside the room, thereafter, we will make the system more and more intelligent.

So, the first thing we need to do is recognize whether you are in a room or not. There are multiple ways to do that. One important characteristic of life is the presence of movement. You may say plants don't move, well they do; they grow, don't they? So detecting movement can be a key step in detecting whether someone is there or not!

This step will not be so difficult for you, as we have already interfaced this sensor previously. We are talking about the good old PIR sensor. So the sensor will sense any movement in the area. If there is any movement, then Jarvis will switch on the lights. I am sure this is something you can do by yourself by now. You can still refer to the code and the circuit diagram here:

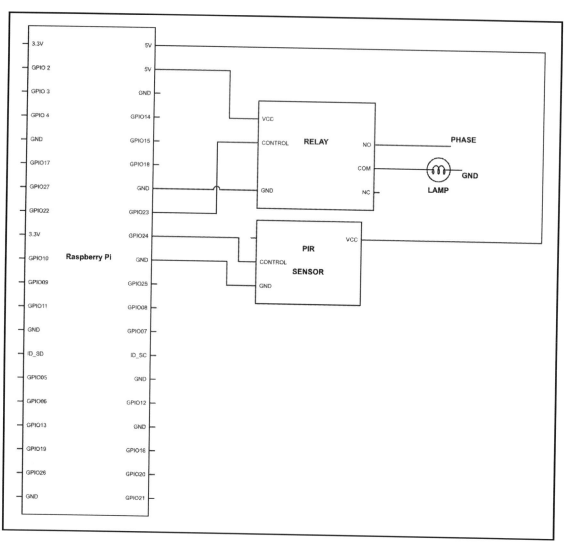

Now upload the following code:

```
import RPi.GPIO as GPIO
import time
```

```
GPIO.setmode(GPIO.BCM)
GPIO.setwarnings(False)
PIR = 24
LIGHT = 23
GPIO.setup(DOPPLER,GPIO.IN)
GPIO.setup(BUZZER,GPIO.OUT)
While True:
    if GPIO.input(PIR) == 1:
        GPIO.output(LIGHT,GPIO.HIGH)
    if GPIO.input(PIR) == 0:
        GPIO.output(LIGHT,GPIO.LOW)
```

In the preceding code, we are simply turning on the light as soon as the motion is detected, but the problem is that it will only switch on the light for the time the motion is there. What does that mean? Simple, while there is some movement, will keep the lights on and as soon as the movement stops, it will switch off the light.

This can be a very good code for a person who wants to lose weight, but for most of us, it will be annoying. So, let's include a small loop, which we have used in the previous chapter and make this a little better:

```
import RPi.GPIO as GPIO
import time

GPIO.setmode(GPIO.BCM)
GPIO.setwarnings(False)

PIR = 24
LIGHT = 23
TIME = 5

GPIO.setup(PIR,GPIO.IN)
GPIO.setup(BUZZER,GPIO.OUT)

While True:

    If GPIO.input(PIR) == 1:
        M = datetime.datetime.now().strftime('%M')
        M_final= M + TIME

        for M < M_final:

            GPIO.output(LIGHT,GPIO.HIGH)
            M = datetime.datetime.now().strftime('%M')

            if GPIO.input(PIR) == 1:
                M_final = M_final + 1
```

```
if GPIO.input(PIR) = 0:

        GPIO.output(LIGHT, GPIO.LOW)}
```

So, in this program, all we have done is we have added a `for` loop, which switches on the light for a set amount of time. How long that time will be can be toggled by changing the value of the variable `TIME`.

There is one more interesting part in that loop which is as follows:

```
if GPIO.input(PIR) == 1
    M_final = M_final + 1
```

Why did we do this you might wonder? Whenever the light will be switched on, it will remain on for 5 minutes. Then, it will switch off and wait for movement to occur. So, essentially, the problem with this code will be that if you are in the room and the light switches on, then for 5 minutes it will see if there is any motion detected or not. There is a chance that you will be in motion when it searches for the motion after 5 minutes. But for most of the time, it won't be the case. So we are detecting the movement using the PIR sensor. Whenever movement is detected, the value of `M_final` is incremented using the line `M_final = M_final + 1`, thereby increasing the time until which the light will be switched on.

Understanding motion

By now you must have figured that the PIR sensor is not the most idealistic sensor for us to switch the lights on or off. Mostly because, although the motion is one of the best indicators of presence, there can be times when you might not move at all, for example, while resting, reading a book, watching a movie, and so on.

What do we do now? Well, we can do a little trick. Remember in the last chapter we used our proximity sensor to sense whether a person has crossed a specific area or not? We will implant a similar logic here; but rather than just copy pasting the code, we will improve it and make it even better.

So rather than using one single IR proximity sensor, we will be using two of these things. The mounting will be as shown in the following diagram:

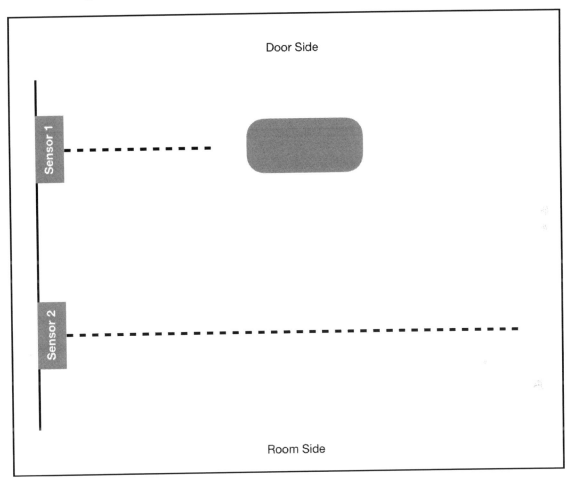

Now it is very evident that whenever a person walks in from the door side to the room side the **Sensor 1** will show a lower reading when detecting a body. Then, while he is walking towards the room side, **Sensor 2** will show a similar reading.

If first **Sensor 1** is triggered and thereafter **Sensor 2** is triggered, then we can safely assume that the person is travelling from the door side to the room side. Similarly, if the opposite is happening, then it is understood that the person is walking out of the room.

Now, this is fairly simple. But how do we implement it in a real-life situation? Firstly, we need to connect the circuit as follows:

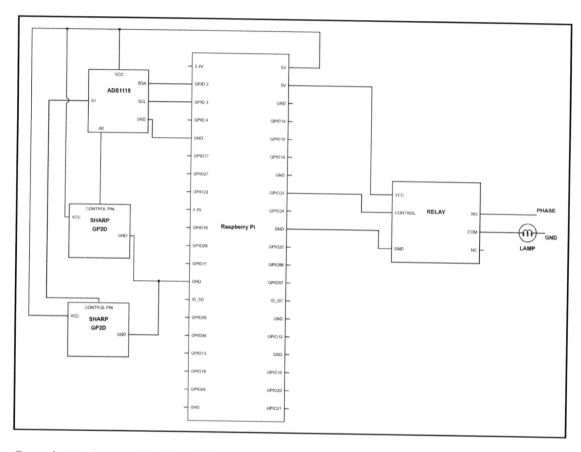

Once that is done, upload the following code:

```
import GPIO library
import RPi.GPIO as GPIO
import time

import Adafruit_ADS1x15
adc0 = Adafruit_ADS1x15.ADS1115()

GAIN = 1
LIGHT = 23

adc0.start_adc(0, gain=GAIN)
adc1.start_adc(1, gain=GAIN)
```

```
GPIO.setmode(GPIO.BCM)
GPIO.setwarnings(False)


while True:


   F_value = adc0.get_last_result()
   F1 =     (1.0 / (F_value / 13.15)) - 0.35

   time.sleep(0.1)

   F_value = adc0.get_last_result()
   F2 =     (1.0 / (F_value / 13.15)) - 0.35

   F0_final = F1-F2

   if F0 > 10 :
       Time0 =  time.time()


   F_value = adc1.get_last_result()
   F1 =     (1.0 / (F_value / 13.15)) - 0.35

   time.sleep(0.1)

   F_value = adc1.get_last_result()
   F2 =     (1.0 / (F_value / 13.15)) - 0.35

   F1_final = F1-F2

   if F1 > 10:

       Time1 =  time.time()

     if Time1 > Time0:

        GPIO.output(LIGHT,  GPIO.HIGH)


     if Time1 < Time0:

        GPIO.output(LIGHT,  GPIO.LOW)        }
```

Now, let's see what are we doing here. As always, most of the syntax is very simple and straightforward. The most important part is the logic. So, let's understand in proper steps as to what we are doing.

```
F_value = adc0.get_last_result()
F1 =    (1.0 / (F_value / 13.15)) - 0.35

time.sleep(0.1)


F_value = adc0.get_last_result()
F2 =    (1.0 / (F_value / 13.15)) - 0.35
```

In the preceding lines of code, we are taking the value of the IR proximity sensor and calculating the distance corresponding to it and storing that value in a variable called F1. Once that is done, we are stopping for a brief period of 0.1 seconds using the time.sleep(0.1) function. Thereafter, we are taking the reading from the same sensor again and storing the value in a variable called F2. Why are we doing this? We have already understood that in the previous chapters.

```
F0_final = F1-F2
```

Once the value of F1 and F0 is acquired, we will calculate the difference to find out whether someone has passed through it or not. If no one has passed, then the reading will almost be the same and the difference will not be considerable. However, if a person does pass, then the reading will be considerable and that value will be stored in a variable called F0_final.

```
if F0 > 10 :
        Time0 =  time.time()
```

If the value of the F0 or the difference in distance between the first and the second reading is more than 10 centimeters, then the if condition will be true. Once true, it will set the value of the Time0 variable as the current value of time. The time.time() function will make a note of the exact time.

```
F_value = adc1.get_last_result()
F1 =    (1.0 / (F_value / 13.15)) - 0.35

time.sleep(0.1)

F_value = adc1.get_last_result()
F2 =    (1.0 / (F_value / 13.15)) - 0.35

F1_final = F1-F2
```

```
if F1 > 10:

    Time1 =  time.time()
```

Now, we'll perform the exact same step for **Sensor 2** as well. There is nothing new to tell here; it's all self explanatory.

```
if Time1 > Time0:

    GPIO.output(LIGHT, GPIO.HIGH)
```

Once all of this is done, we compare `if Time1 > Time0`. Why are we comparing it? Because `Time0` is the time noted for **Sensor 1**. If the person is moving inside, then **Sensor 1** would be the first one to be triggered and then the **Sensor 2** would be triggered. Hence, the time noted would be greater for **Sensor 2** and relatively earlier for **Sensor 1**. If that happens, then we can assume that the person is coming inside. Well, if a person is coming inside, then we simply need to switch the light on, which is exactly what we are doing here.

```
if Time1 < Time0:

    GPIO.output(LIGHT, GPIO.LOW)
```

Similarly, when a person is going out, the first sensor to be triggered would be **Sensor 2**, thereafter **Sensor 1** will be triggered. Making the time noted for `Time1` earlier than `Time2`; hence, whenever this condition is true, we will know that the person is moving out of the room and the lights can be switched off.

Go ahead and mount it near the door and see how it reacts. I'm sure this will be way better than what we had done through PIR. Have fun with it and try to find any flaws that it might have.

Perfecting motion

Were you able to find any flaws in the previous code? They are not hard to find; the code works brilliantly when it's only a single person in the room. If this is installed somewhere where multiple people are coming and going, then it might be challenging. This is because whenever a person moves outside, the light will be turned off.

So now that the problem is evident, it's time to make the code even more better. To do this, the hardware will remain exactly the same; we simply need to make the code smarter. Let's see how we can do that:

```
import GPIO library
    import RPi.GPIO as GPIO
    import time
    import time
    import Adafruit_ADS1x15
    adc0 = Adafruit_ADS1x15.ADS1115()
GAIN = 1
 adc0.start_adc(0, gain=GAIN)
adc1.start_adc(1, gain=GAIN)
GPIO.setmode(GPIO.BCM)
GPIO.setwarnings(False)
PCount = 0
while True:
    F_value = adc0.get_last_result()
    F1 = (1.0 / (F_value / 13.15)) - 0.35
    time.sleep(0.1)
    F_value = adc0.get_last_result()
    F2 = (1.0 / (F_value / 13.15)) - 0.35
    F0_final = F1-F2
    if F0 > 10 :
        Time0 = time.time()
    F_value = adc1.get_last_result()
    F1 = (1.0 / (F_value / 13.15)) - 0.35
    time.sleep(0.1)
    F_value = adc1.get_last_result()
    F2 = (1.0 / (F_value / 13.15)) - 0.35
    F1_final = F1-F2
    if F1 > 10:
        Time1 = time.time()
    if Time1 > Time0:
        PCount = PCount + 1
    if Time1 < Time0:
        PCount = PCount - 1

if PCount > 0:

        GPIO.output(LIGHT, GPIO.HIGH)
    else if PCount = 0:
        GPIO.output(LIGHT, GPIO.LOW)
```

What we have done is something really basic. We have declared a variable called PCount. This variable is declared to count the number of people who are there inside a room or a home. As you can see in the first few lines of the code, we have declared the value of PCount as 0. We are assuming that once we start this, the number of people inside would be 0.

```
if Time1 > Time0:

    PCount = PCount + 1
```

Whenever the condition if Time1 > Time0: is satisfied, the PCount value is incremented by 1. As we all know, the condition will only be true when a person is walking inside the home.

```
if Time1 < Time0:
    PCount = PCount - 1
```

Similarly, when a person is walking outside, the condition if Time1 < Time0: is true; whenever that happens, the value of PCount is decremented by 1.

```
if PCount > 0:

    GPIO.output(LIGHT, GPIO.HIGH)
```

Now that we have started counting the number of people in the room, we are now applying the condition, which will turn on if the number of PCount is more than 0. Hence, the light will be on for the time when the number of people inside the home is more than 0.

```
else if PCount = 0:

    GPIO.output(LIGHT, GPIO.LOW)
```

In a very similar fashion, the lights will be turned off if the value of PCount or the number of people inside the home gets to 0.

Hence, nailed!

Controlling the intensity

We have controlled a lot of light now. It's time that we control our fans and other air circulation systems. Whenever we talk about fans or any other air circulation devices, then essentially we are talking about motors. As we have learned earlier, motors are simple devices, which can be controlled every easily using a motor driver. But as you know, back then we were controlling DC motors. DC motors are extremely simple devices. But when we talk about our household appliances, then most of these devices will be working on AC or alternating current. I am assuming that you must be aware of what that is and how it is different from DC.

Now that you know that the motors used in our households are working on AC, you must also think about the fact that their control mechanism will be much different to DC motors. You are right, if you thought so. However, the good thing about electronics is, nothing is really difficult or complicated. The basics are pretty much the same. So, let's see how we can control the speed of the motors in AC supply.

As we have seen earlier, we can simply have a PWM signal given to the DC motor and the motor will run at the speed of the average voltage as a result of the PWM signal. Now, you must be thinking that this can be applied to AC as well. The thing is, yes it can be done if you want to control a light or similar devices, which do not have any major change in the characteristics in case the wave form is distorted. However, when we are talking about any other component, then we come across a big problem. The AC wave form looks like this:

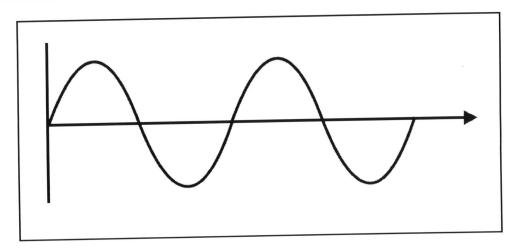

This basically means that the potential is changing periodically. In most of the households, this is 50 times per second. Now, imagine if we have a PWM-controlled device that is switching the circuit that only lets the power supply to pass at certain intervals. Then, the different parts of the sinusoidal waves would be passed on to the final output.

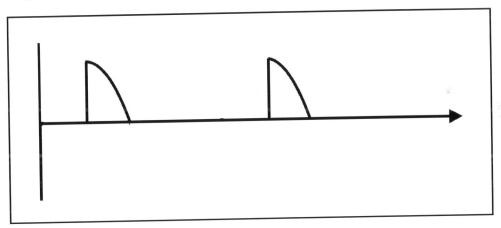

As you can see in the preceding PWM, fortunately the PWM signal has matched with the phase of the AC power; however, due to this, only the positive end of the phase is being transferred to the final output and not the negative end. This will cause a severe problem to our load and there is a very good chance that the appliance that is connected will not work.

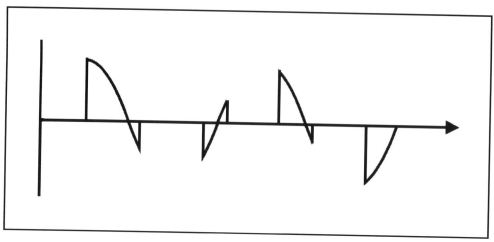

We have another example in which the PWM is random and it lets random parts of the wave pass by. In this, we can clearly see that randomly any part of the wave is being transferred and the positive and negative end voltage is not in sync, which again will be a huge problem. Hence, instead of using PWM, we use something really interesting.

The method that is most commonly used is called **phase fired control**. Sometimes it is also called phase angle control or phase cutting. What it essentially does is, it cuts the wave at certain parts of the phase letting the rest of the wave cross by. Confused? Let me show you here:

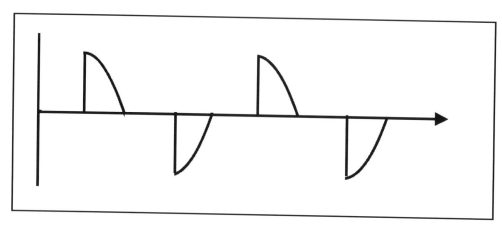

Now, as you can see the phase behind the second half of the AC wave is getting chopped and is not getting passed in the final output. This makes the final output to be only 50% of the overall input. What this technique does is, it maintains the AC nature of the power supply while still being able to reduce the overall resulting voltage. Likewise, as you can see in the next diagram, the wave is getting chopped after 75% of the wave has already passed. This results in the output being relatively lower:

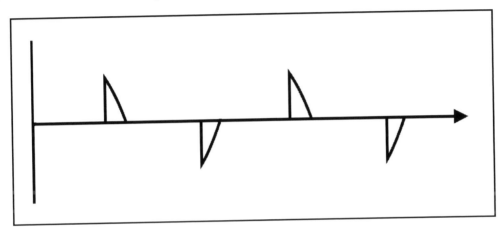

Now you must be asking, how did we actually go ahead and do this? It is done by a relatively complex circuit that detects the phase angle of the wave and then opens or controls a triac, which is a high power bi-directional semiconductor. This leads the power supply to pass or to be stopped at certain phases. We will leave the exact working of this circuit for the next time as it is fairly complex and will not be relevant to this book.

Now coming to the basic point, we know what phase cutting is, we also know that triac is the basic device that lets us do that. But how do we go ahead and do it using Raspberry Pi is the question.

So firstly, we will need an AC-dimmer module. This module already has all the components of phase detection and chopping. So all we need to do is simply control it using simple PWM.

Though I might not have to demonstrate how to connect the circuit or what the code should be, for the sake of understanding, let's connect a light bulb to our Arduino using this module and then control the bulb. Now, the first thing to remember is that the load should be a bulb and not anything else such as an LED light. So go ahead and connect the circuit as shown in the following figure:

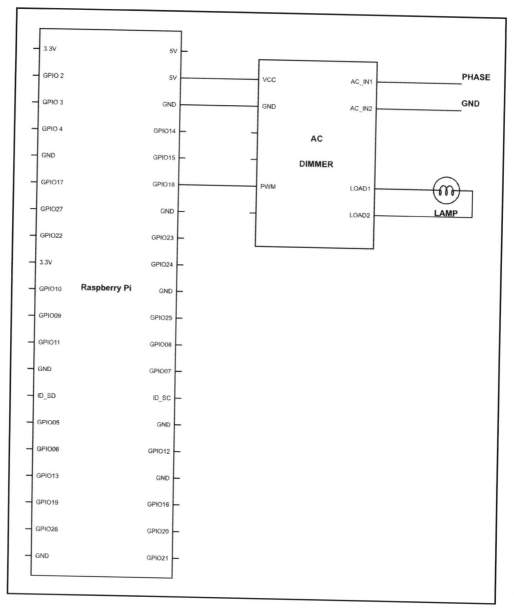

Once this is done, go ahead and upload the following code:

```
import RPi.GPIO as GPIO
import time
GPIO.setmode(GPIO.BCM)
GPIO.setup(18,GPIO.OUT)
I = 0
pwm= GPIO.PWM(18,50)

for I < 100:

    I = I+1
    pwm.start(I)
    time.sleep(0.1)


GPIO.cleanup()}
```

As expected, the attached light will start to glow very faintly first and will increase the intensity gradually until it reaches 100%. That is how simple it is to control such a complex process.

Intelligent temperature control

Now that the basics are done, let's go ahead and build something meaningful using this system. Isn't it difficult to set your air-conditioner to the perfect temperature? No matter what you do, you end up feeling not in the most comfortable spot. This happens due to physiological changes in the body temperature over the course of the day.

When you wake up, your body temperature is relatively low. It is as much as 1° F, which is lower than the normal body temperature. As the day progresses, the body temperature rises until the time you hit the bed. Once you sleep, again your body temperature starts to dip reaching its lowest point around 4:00-6:00 am in the morning. That's the reason why what might feel warm while you go to bed, can be pretty cold when you wake up. Modern air-conditioners have something called a sleep mode. What this does is, it simply increases the temperature through the night. So that you do not feel cold at any point. But then again, how well it works is also a question.

So, now that we know the robotics very well, we will go ahead and make a system of our own that will take care of everything.

In this part, we will connect both the air-conditioner and your fan together so that they can both work in tandem and make you sleep well. Now, before jumping straight into it, I would like you to see the ratings that are mentioned on the relay. As you can see, the relay can handle only 250V and 5 ampere. Now, if you go through the brochure of your air-conditioner, you will easily understand why I am showing all of this to you. The power consumption of the air-conditioner will be much higher than what your relays can handle. So, if you try to run your air conditioner using the normal relays, then you will surely end up blowing the relay. There might be a chance that your appliance will be of a lower current rating than your relay. But with any device that has motors in it just keep in mind that the initial power consumption of that device is much higher than the nominal power consumption. Hence, if your air-conditioner needs 10 ampere nominal, then the starting load may be as much as 15 ampere. You must be thinking, it's not a problem, why don't we just purchase a relay that has a higher rating. Well, correct! That's exactly what we will be doing. But the naming of electronics can be tricky at times. The devices that deal with a higher-power higher-voltage electro-mechanical switching is generally called contractor instead of relay. Technically, they have the same working principal; However, there are construction differences, which at this point would not be our concern. So we will be using a contractor for the air conditioner switching and a dimmer for the fan speed control. Now that this has been cleared up, let's go ahead and attach the hardware as shown in the following diagram:

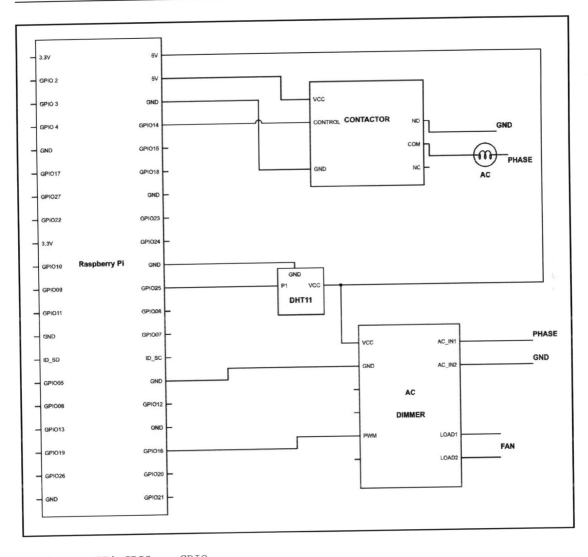

```
import RPi.GPIO as GPIO
import time
import Adafruit_DHT

GPIO.setmode(GPIO.BCM)

FAN = 18
AC = 17

pwm= GPIO.PWM(18,50)
GPIO.setup(FAN,GPIO.OUT)
```

```
GPIO.setup(AC, GPIO.OUT)

while True:

    humidity, temperature = Adafruit_DHT.read_retry(sensor, pin)

    if temperature =>20 && temperature <=30:

        Duty = 50 + ((temperature-25)*10)
        pwm.start(Duty)

    if temperature <22 :

        GPIO.output(AC, GPIO.LOW)

    if temperature >= 24

        GPIO.output(AC, GPIO.HIGH) }
```

The logic used here is pretty basic. Let's see what it is doing:

```
humidity, temperature = Adafruit_DHT.read_retry(sensor, pin)

if temperature =>20 && temperature <=30:

    Duty = 50 + ((temperature-25)*10)
    pwm.start(Duty)
```

Here we are taking the value of `humidity` and `temperature`. So far so good, but can we take it a step further and make it even more intelligent? The previous logic must have helped you sleep better, but can we make it just perfect for you?

There are multiple indicators in our body that give us an idea of what the state of the body is. For example, if you are tired, you will probably not be walking very fast or talking very loud. Instead, you would be doing the opposite! Similarly, there are multiple factors that indicate how our sleep cycle is going.

Some of these factors are: body temperature, respiration rate, REM sleep, and body movements. Measuring the exact body temperature or respiration rate and REM sleep is something of a challenge. But when we talk about body movements, I think we have already perfected it. So based on the body movements, we will be sensing how well we are sleeping and what kind of temperature adjustment is needed.

If you notice, whenever someone is sleeping and starts feeling cold, the body will go to a fetal position and will move much less. This happens automatically. However, when a person is comfortable, there are some inevitable movements such as changing sides and movement of arms or legs. This does not happen when a person is feeling cold. So with these movements we can figure out whether a person is feeling cold or not. Now that we have understood the physiological changes of the body, let's try to build a program around it and see what we can achieve.

To do this, firstly, we need to connect the circuit as follows:

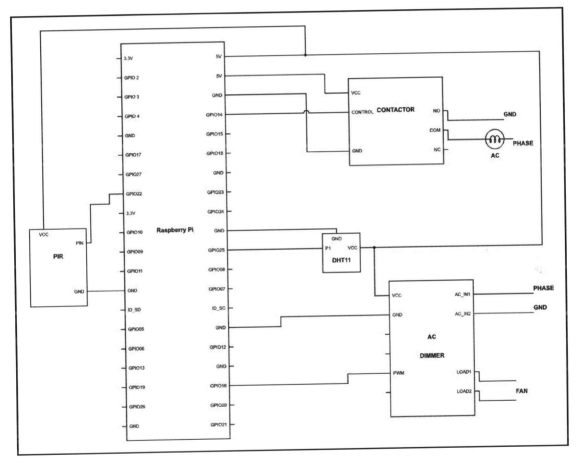

Once this is done, go ahead and write the following code:

```
import RPi.GPIO as GPIO
import time
import Adafruit_DHT

GPIO.setmode(GPIO.BCM)

FAN = 18
AC = 17
PIR = 22
PIN = 11
Sensor = 4

pwm= GPIO.PWM(18,50)
GPIO.setup(FAN,GPIO.OUT)
GPIO.setup(AC, GPIO.OUT)

while True:

    humidity, temperature = Adafruit_DHT.read_retry(sensor, pin)
    H = datetime.datetime.now().strftime('%H')
    M = datetime.datetime.now().strftime('%M')

    if H <= 6 && H <= 22:

        if M <=58 :

            M = datetime.datetime.now().strftime('%M')
            humidity, temperature = Adafruit_DHT.read_retry(sensor, pin)
            if GPIO.input(PIR) == 0 :
                Movement = Movement + 1
                time.sleep(10)

            if temperature < 28:
                if Movement > 5 :

                    Duty = Duty + 10
                    pwm.start(Duty)
                    Movement = 0

        if M = 59 :

            if Movement = 0 :

                Duty = Duty -10
                pwm.start(Duty)
```

```
        Movement = 0

    if temperature <22 :

        GPIO.output(AC, GPIO.LOW)

    if temperature >= 24 && H <= 6 && H >= 22:

        GPIO.output(AC, GPIO.HIGH)

    if temperature > 27

        pwm.start(100)

  for H > 7 && H < 20

      GPIO.output(AC, GPIO.LOW)

  if H = 20

      GPIO.output(AC,GPIO.HIGH)


 }
```

Let's have a look at what is going on under the hood:

```
    if H <= 6 && H <= 22:

      if M <=58 :

          M = datetime.datetime.now().strftime('%M')
          humidity, temperature = Adafruit_DHT.read_retry(sensor, pin)
```

The first thing you will see is that we have a condition: `if H,= 6 && H<= 22:`. This condition will only be true if the time frame is between 10 o'clock in the morning and 6 o'clock in the night. That is because this is the time when we generally sleep. Hence, the logic under this head will only work if it's time to sleep.

The second condition is `if M <= 58`, which will be true only when the time is between 0 and 58 minutes. So when the time is `M = 59`, then this condition will not work. We will see the reason for having this logic.

Thereafter, we are calculating the time and storing the value in a variable called M. We are also calculating the humidity and temperature values and storing it in variables called `temperature` and `humidity`:

```
if GPIO.input(PIR) == 0 :
    Movement = Movement + 1
    time.sleep(10)
```

Now, in this line, we are implementing a condition which will be true if the reading from the PIR is high. That is, there is some motion that will be detected. Whenever this happens, the `Movement` variable will be incremented by 1. Finally, we are using the `time.sleep(10)` function to wait for 10 seconds. This is done as the PIR might be high for a momentary period. In that case, the condition will be true over and over again which in turn will increment the value of `Movement` multiple times.

Our purpose of incrementing the value of `Movement` is to count the number of times the person has moved. Hence, incrementing it multiples times in one single time will defy the objective.

```
if temperature < 28:
    if Movement > 5 :

        Duty = Duty + 10
        pwm.start(Duty)
        Movement = 0
```

Now we have another condition, which says `if temperature < 28`. Not much explanation is needed for when the condition will be true. So whenever the condition is true and if the counted number of `Movement` is more than 5, the value of `Duty` will be incremented by 10. Therefore, we are sending the PWM to the AC dimmer, which in turn will increase the speed of the fan. Finally, we are resetting the value of `Movement` to 0.

So essentially, we are just counting the number of movements. This movement is counted only if the temperature is less than 28° C. If the movement is more than 5, then we will increase the speed of the fan by 10%.

```
if M = 59 :

    if Movement = 0 :

        Duty = Duty -10
        pwm.start(Duty)

    Movement = 0
```

In the previous section, the logic will only work when the time is between 0 and 58, that is, the time in which the counting will happen. When the value of M is 59, then the condition `if Movement = 0` will be checked, and if true, then the value of Duty will be decremented by 10. This in turn will reduce the speed of the fan by 10%. Also, once this condition is executed, the value of Movement will be reset to 0. So then a new cycle can start for the next hour.

Now what it basically means is that counting will happen on an hourly basis. If the Movement is more than 5 then immediately the value of the Duty would be increased. However, if that is not the case, then the program will wait until the minute approaches the value of 59 and whenever that happens, it will check whether there is any movement, in which case, the fan speed will be decreased.

```
if temperature <22 :

    GPIO.output(AC, GPIO.LOW)

if temperature >= 24 && H <= 6 && H >= 22:

    GPIO.output(AC, GPIO.HIGH)

if temperature > 27

    pwm.start(100)
```

All of this code is very straightforward. If the temperature is less than 22, then the AC will be switched off. Furthermore, if the temperature is equal to or more than 24, and time is between 10:00 p.m. and 6:00 a.m., then the AC will be turned on. Finally, if the temperature is more than 27, then the fan will be switch on to 100% speed.

```
for H > 7 && H < 20

    GPIO.output(AC, GPIO.LOW)

if H = 20

    GPIO.output(AC, GPIO.HIGH)
```

Finally, we are making sure by using the condition `for H > 7 && H <20` that during this time the AC is always switched off. Also, if H = 20, then the AC should be turned on so that the room is cooled before you are ready to sleep.

Adding more

As you would have understood by now, we can control any AC electrical appliances as per our needs. We have understood switching and have also perfected the way we can vary the intensity of light and the speed of fans. But did you notice one thing? Sooner or later as our system gets more and more complex, the number of GPIOs needed will increase. There will come a moment when you will want to have more and more devices connected to your Raspberry Pi; however, you will not be able to do so due to lack of physical ports.

This is a very common situation in electronics. As always, there is a solution for this problem as well. This solution is known as a multiplexer. The basic job of a multiplexer is to multiply the number of ports in any computer system. Now you must be thinking, how is it able to do so?

The concept is extremely simple. Let's first look at the diagram of a multiplexer here:

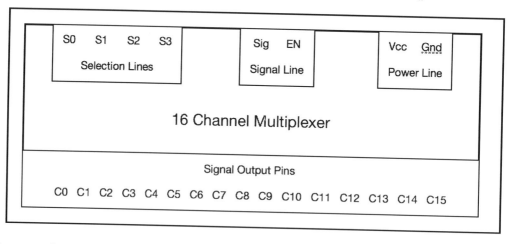

In the preceding diagram, you can see that there are two ends to the multiplexer—one being the signal output lines and the other opposite to it. The first thing we need to understand is that the multiplexer is a bidirectional device, that is, it sends the data from the multiplexer to the connected devices and also vice versa.

Now, firstly, we have the power line, which is pretty basic. It is there to power up the multiplexer itself. Then, we have **Signal Lines**, which have two ports, the **Sig** and **EN**. **EN** stands for enable, which means that until the time **EN** is not high, the data communication will not happen either way. Then we have something called **Sig**. This is the port that is connected to the GPIO of Raspberry Pi for data communication. Next we have the selection line. As you can see, we have four ports for it, namely, **S0**, **S1**, **S2**, and **S3**. The selection lines have a purpose of selecting a particular port that needs to be selected. The following is a table that will clarify what exactly is happening:

S0	S1	S3	S4	Selected output
0	0	0	0	C0
1	0	0	0	C1
0	1	0	0	C2
1	1	0	0	C3
0	0	1	0	C4
1	0	1	0	C5
0	1	1	0	C6
1	1	1	0	C7
0	0	0	1	C8
1	0	0	1	C9
0	1	0	1	C10
1	1	0	1	C11
0	0	1	1	C12
1	0	1	1	C13
0	1	1	1	C14
1	1	1	1	C15

In the preceding table, you can see that by using various logic combinations on the selection lines, various lines can be addressed. Let's say, for example, we have the following sequence on the selection pins—S0 = 1, S1 = 0, S2 = 1, S3 = 1. If this is the input on the selection pins from Raspberry Pi, then the pin number C13 will be selected. This basically means that now C13 can communicate the data to and from the pin **Sig** for the multiplexer. Also, we must remember that the enable pin must be high for the data transfer to happen.

In a similar fashion, we can go ahead and address all the 16 pins of the multiplexer. Hence, if we see it logically, then by using six pins of Raspberry Pi, we can go ahead and utilize 16 GPIOs. Now that we have understood the basics of multiplexing, let's go ahead and try using one of them.

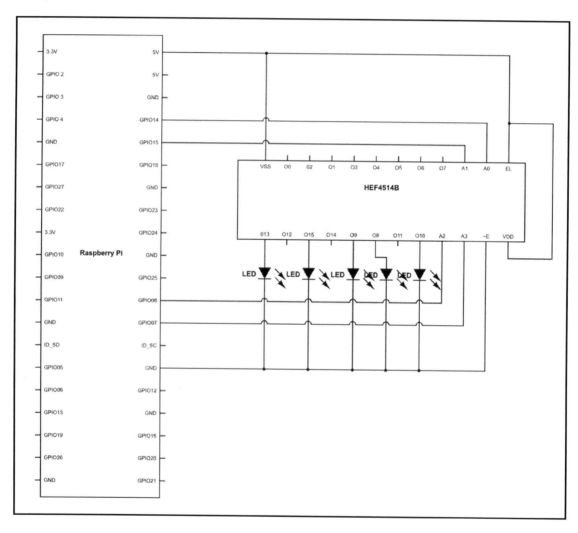

Once the hardware is connected, let's go ahead and upload the following code:

```python
import RPi.GPIO as GPIO
import time

GPIO.setmode(GPIO.BCM)
GPIO.setwarnings(False)

S0 = 21
S1 = 22
S2 = 23
S3 = 24

GPIO.setup(S0,GPIO.OUT)
GPIO.setup(S1,GPIO.OUT)
GPIO.setup(S2,GPIO.OUT)

While True:

    GPIO.output(S0,1)
    GPIO.output(S1,0)
    GPIO.output(S2,1)
    GPIO.output(S4,1)

    time.sleep(1)

    GPIO.output(S0,1)
    GPIO.output(S1,1)
    GPIO.output(S2,1)
    GPIO.output(S4,1)

    time.sleep(1)

    GPIO.output(S0,1)
    GPIO.output(S1,0)
    GPIO.output(S2,0)
    GPIO.output(S4,1)

    time.sleep(1)

    'GPIO.output(S0,0)
    GPIO.output(S1,0)
    GPIO.output(S2,0)
    GPIO.output(S4,1)

    time.sleep(1)

    GPIO.output(S0,0)
```

```
GPIO.output(S1,1)
GPIO.output(S2,0)
GPIO.output(S4,1)

time.sleep(1)  }
```

Here, what we are essentially doing is, triggering the selection lines one by one to address every single port where the LED is connected. Whenever that happens, the LED corresponding to it glows. Also, the reason it glows is because the signal port `Sig` is connected to 3.3V of Raspberry Pi. Hence, send a logic high to whichever port it is connected to.

This is one of the basic ways in which the multiplexer works. This can be incredibly useful when we will be using multiple devices and sensors.

Summary

In this chapter, we enabled Jarvis to automate your home appliances under different conditions, also applying various properties to the system. So go on and try many other scenarios under which you can enhance your home automation system.

In the next chapter, we will enable Jarvis IoT, thus controlling the appliances from your mobile phone using Wi-Fi and the internet.

13
Making Jarvis IoT Enabled

There was a time when we used to imagine controlling the world with our fingertips. Now, this imagination has become a reality. With the advent of smartphones, we have been doing stuff which one could have only imagined until a decade back. With mobile phones becoming smart, the industry and businesses have also tried their best to keep up with the disruptive change. However, there is one part that is still lagging behind. Which is that part? Your home!

Think about what you can control in your home using your smartphone? Not many things! There are some devices that can turn on or off a bunch of devices such as your AC. However, the list is exhaustive. So, with all the knowledge gained in the previous chapters and the powerful hardware in our hands, why don't we become the trendsetters and the disrupters and make something that is still just a part of our imagination.

The following topics will be covered in this chapter:

- Basics of **Internet of Things (IoT)**
- **Message Queuing Telemetry Transport (MQTT)** protocol
- Setting up MQTT broker
- Making an IoT-based intrusion detector
- Controlling the home

Basics of IoT

In this chapter, we will be controlling devices in our home using our smartphones, but before doing this, we should understand the basics of this technology. The first topic of this chapter is IoT—the overused jargon in the modern world. It is something that everyone wants to know about but no one does. IoT can be related to a technology, where your refrigerator will tell you what items are low in supply and will order it automatically for you. Poor thing! This technology has some time to invade our houses. But IoT does not mean this alone. IoT is a very wide term, something which can be applied to almost all the places for optimization. So what is IoT then?

Let's break this acronym, **Internet of Things** sometimes also known as cyber physical systems. Now, what is **Things**? Any electronic object that has the ability to collect or receive data without human intervention can be called a thing here. So this thing can be your mobile, a pacemaker, a health monitoring device, and so on. The only *if* is that it should be connected to the internet and has the ability to collect and/or receive data. The second term is **Internet**; the internet refers to the internet, Duh! Now, all of these IoT devices send and receive data from a cloud or a central computer. The reason why it does that is because any IoT device, whether big or small, is considered a resource-constrained environment. That is, the resources such as computing power is much less. This is because the IoT devices have to be simple and cheap. Imagine you have to put IoT sensors on all of the street lights to monitor traffic. If the device costs $500, then it would be impractical to install this kind of device. However, if it could be made for $5-$10, then no one would bat an eye. That's the thing with IoT devices; they are extremely cheap. Now the flip side to this story is that they do not have a lot of computing power. Hence, to balance this equation, instead of computing the raw data on their own processors, they simply send this data to a cloud computing device or perhaps a server where this data is computed and the meaningful result is taken. So, this solves all our problems then. Well, no! The second problem with these devices are that they can be battery operated, use-and-throw devices as well. For example, where temperature sensors are installed all across the forests; in such situations, no one and absolutely no one will go and change the batteries every week. Hence, these devices are made in such a way that they consume little to almost no power, thereby making the programming very tricky.

Now that we have understood the IoT concepts, in this chapter, we'll be making our home IoT enabled. This means, we will be able to receive and collect data from the sensors from our home, see it on our mobile devices, and if needed, we can control the devices using your smartphones as well. There is one thing though, instead of computing it on cloud, we will simply be uploading all of our data onto the cloud and just accessing that data or sending our data to the cloud from where it can be accessed. We will be talking about the cloud computing aspect in a different book as this can be a whole new dimension and will be out of the scope of this book.

The MQTT protocol

MQTT is an ISO-certified protocol and is in use very widely. The interesting thing about this protocol is that it was developed by Andy Stanford and Arlen Nipper in 1999 for monitoring of an oil pipeline through the desert. As you can imagine, in middle of a desert, the protocol they developed had to be energy efficient and bandwidth efficient as well.

How this protocol works is quite interesting. It has a publish-subscribe architecture. This means, it has a central server, which we also call a broker. Any device can register with this broker and publish any meaningful data onto it. Now, the data that is being published should have a topic, for example, air temperature.

These topics are particularly important. Why, you may ask? To the broker, there can be one or many devices that can be connected. With the connection, they also need to subscribe to a topic. Let's say they are subscribed to the topic *Air*-Temperature. Now, whenever any new data comes, it gets published to the subscribed devices.

One important thing to know is that there need not be any request to gain the data from the broker like what we have in HTTP. Rather, whenever the data is received, it will be pushed to the device which is subscribed to that topic. It is very obvious that the TCP protocol will also be up and working during the whole time and the port related to the broker will always be connected for seamless data transmission. However, should there be any break in the data, the broker will buffer all the data and send it to the subscriber whenever the connection is resumed.

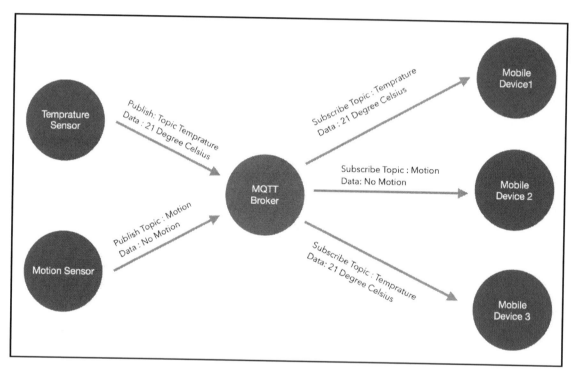

As you can see The motion sensor and the temperature sensors are giving the data to MQTT server by a specific topic namely **Temperature** and **Motion**. Those whose are subscribed to these topics would get the reading from this device. Hence there is no direct communication needed between the actual sensor and the mobile device.

The good thing about this whole architecture is that there can be limitless devices attached with this protocol and there need not be any scalability issues. Also, the protocol is relatively simple and easy to work with even a huge amount of data. Hence, this becomes the preferred protocol for IoT as it provides an easy, scalable, and seamless link between the data producer and the data receivers.

Setting up the MQTT broker

Remember the old boring update process of vision processing? How can you forget? We have to do the same here as well. But lucky for us, this time it's not very long. So, let's see what we have to do to set up this server. Open up your command line and type in these following lines:

```
sudo apt-get update
sudo apt-get upgrade
```

You know what this line does. If you don't have a clear memory of it, then refer to `Chapter 9`, *Vision Processing*. Once the update and upgrade processes are complete, go ahead and install the following packages:

```
sudo apt-get install mosquitto -y
```

This will install the Mosquitto broker onto your Raspberry Pi. This broker will take care of all the data transfer:

```
sudo apt-get install mosquitto-clients -y
```

Now, this line will install the client packages. As you can imagine, Raspberry Pi in itself will be a client to the broker. Hence, it will take care of the needful.

We have now installed the packages; yes exactly, it was that small. Now, all we need to do is configure the Mosquitto broker. To do this, you need to type in the following command:

```
sudo nano etc/mosquitto/mosquitto.conf
```

Now, this command will open the file where the Mosquitto file configuration is saved. To configure it, you need to get to the end of this file, where you will see the following:

```
include_dir/etc/mosquitto/conf.d
```

Now, you can comment out the the preceding line of code by simply adding # before the lines. Once done then go ahead and add the following lines:

```
allow_anonymous false
```

```
password_file /etc/mosquitto/pwfile
```

```
listener 1883
```

Let's see what we have done here. The `allow_anonymous false` line tells the broker that not everyone can access the data. The next line, `password_file /etc/mosquitto/pwfile` is telling the broker the location of password file, which is located at `/etc/mosquitto/pwfile`. Finally, we will define the port of this broker, which is `1883`, using the `listener 1883` command.

So finally, we have completed setting up the MQTT client in our Raspberry Pi. Now we are ready to go ahead and use it for the IoT-enabled home.

Making an IoT-based intrusion detector

Now that Raspberry Pi is set up and we are ready to make it IoT enabled let's see how we are going to connect the system to the internet and make things work. Firstly, we need to connect Raspberry Pi to the devices, which we want to control using the IoT technology. So go ahead and use the following diagram to make the connection:

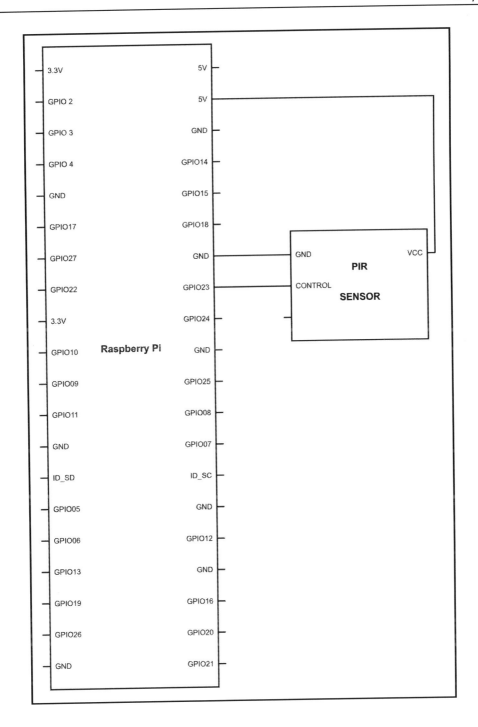

Once you have set up all the components, let's go ahead and upload the following code:

```
import time
import paho.mqtt.client as mqtt
import RPi.gpio as gpio
pir = 23
gpio.setmode(gpio.BCM)
gpio.setup(pir, gpio.IN)
client = mqtt.Client()
broker="broker.hivemq.com"
port = 1883
pub_topic = "IntruderDetector_Home"
def SendData():
  client.publish(pub_topic,"WARNING : SOMEONE DETECTED AT YOUR PLACE")

def on_connect(client, userdata, flag,rc):
  print("connection returned" + str(rc))
  SendData()
while True:
  client.connect(broker,port)
  client.on_connect = on_connect
  if gpio.output(pir) == gpio.HIGH :
    SendData()
  client.loop_forever()
```

This code, unlike the other chunks of code that we have seen so far, will be quite new to you. So I will be explaining every part of it except for a few obvious parts. So, let's see what we have here:

```
import paho.mqtt.client as mqtt
```

In this part, we are importing the `pho.mqtt.client` library as `mqtt`. So whenever this library needs to be accessed, we simply need to use the line `mqtt` instead of the entire name of the library.

```
client = mqtt.Client()
```

We are defining a client using the client method of the `mqtt` library. This can be called using the `client` variable.

```
broker="broker.hivemq.com"
```

So we are defining the broker in our program. For this program, we are using the broker as `broker.hivemq.com`, which is providing us the broker services.

```
port = 1883
```

Now as we have done earlier, we will once again define the port at which the protocol will be working, which in our case is `1883`.

```
pub_topic = "IntuderDetector_Home"
```

Here, we are defining the value of the variable called `pub_topic`, which is `IntruderDetector_Home`. This will be the final topic to which one can subscribe once the code is running.

```
def SendData():
    client.publish(pub.topic, "WARNING : SOMEONE DETECTED AT YOUR PLACE")
```

Here, we are defining a function called `SendData()`, will publish the data `Warning : SOMEONE DETECTED AT YOUR PLACE` to the broker with the topic which we had declared previously.

```
def on_message(client, userdata, message):

    print('message is : ')
    print(str(message.payload))
```

In this line, we are defining a function named `on_message()`, which will print a value `message is :` followed by whatever the data is. This will be done using the line `print(str(message.payload))`. What this is doing is, it is printing whatever is being passed on in the arguments of the function.

```
def on_connect(client, userdata, flag,rc):

    print("connection returned" + str(rc))
    SendData()
```

In this line, we are defining the `on_connect()` function, which will print the line `connection returned` followed by the value of `rc`. `rc` stands for return code. So, whenever the message is delivered, a code is generated, even if it is not, then the specific code will be returned notifying the error. So, consider this as an acknowledgement. After this is done, the `SendData()` function that we defined earlier will be used to send the data to the broker.

```
client.connect(broker,port)
```

`connect()` is a function of the MQTT library which connects the client to the broker. Doing this is very simple. All we need to do is pass on the arguments of the broker which we want to connect to and the port which would be used. In our case, `broker = broker.hivemq.com` and `port = 1883`. So when we call the function, Raspberry Pi gets connected to our broker.

```
client.on_connect = on_connect
```

This is the heart of the program. What the `client.on_connect` function is doing is that every time Raspberry Pi gets connected to the broker, it starts executing the `on_connect` function defined by us. This in-turn will send the data continuously to the broker after every 5 seconds, exactly the way in which we have defined in the function. This process is also called callback, which makes it event driven. That is, if it is not connected, it will not try to send the data to the broker.

```
if gpio.output(pir) == HIGH :
    sendData()
```

the sendData() function is called when the PIR sensor gets high or whenever the motion is detected the message is sent on the broker with the warning that someone is detected at your place.

```
client.loop_forever()
```

This is my favorite function, especially because of the lovely name it has. As you can expect, the `client.loop_forver()` function will keep looking for any event and whenever it is detected it will trigger the data to be sent to the broker. Now comes the part where we will see this data. For this, we'll have to download the *MyMQTT* app from App Store if you are running iOS or from Playstore if you are running android.

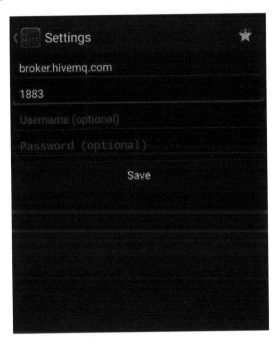

Once you start the app, you will be presented with the preceding screen. You need to fill in the name of the broker URL, which in our case is `broker.hivemq.com`. Then, fill in the port, which in our case is `1883`.

Once this is done, you will see a screen similar to the following:

Simply add the name of the subscription you need, which is `IntruderDetector_Home`. Once done, you'll see the magic!

You can also apply the same logic that we used in `Chapter 10`, *Making a Guard Robot*. So go ahead and play with it; I will leave you here.

In the next section, we will be controlling things based on IoT; see you then.

Controlling the home

Finally, using the following diagram, make the connections and upload the following code:

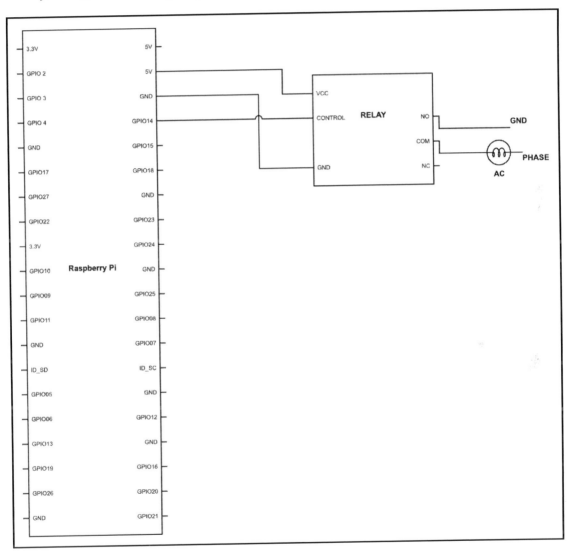

```
import time
import paho.mqtt.client as paho
import RPi.GPIO as GPIO
GPIO.setmode(GPIO.BCM)
GPIO.setup(14,GPIO.OUT)
```

```
broker="broker.hivemq.com"
sub_topic = light/control
client = paho.Client()
def on_message(client, userdata, message):
    print('message is : ')
    print(str(message.payload))
    data = str(message.payload)
    if data == "on":
        GPIO.output(3,GPIO.HIGH)
    elif data == "off":
        GPIO.output(3,GPIO.LOW)

def on_connect(client,userdata, flag, rc):
    print("connection returned" + str(rc))
    client.subscribe(sub_topic)
client.connect(broker,port)
client.on_connect = on_connect
client.on_message=on_message
client.loop_forever()
```

Now, there is not much I need to tell you in this code; it's pretty straightforward. We are sending the data just like we did last time. However, this time we are using a new function. So, let's see what this code is all about:

```
def on_message(client, userdata, message):

        print('message is : ')
        print(str(message.payload))
        data = str(message.payload)

        if data == "on":
            GPIO.output(3,GPIO.HIGH)

        elif data == "off":
            GPIO.output(3,GPIO.LOW)
```

Here we are defining what the on_message() function is doing. There are three arguments to the function over which the message would be working on. This includes client, which we have already declared previously; userdata, which we are not using right now; and finally, message, which we will be sending through our smartphones over the internet.

Once you look inside the program, this function will print the message using the lines print('message is : ') and print(str(message.payload)). Once this is done, the value of data will be set as the message sent by the subscriber.

This data will be evaluated by our conditions. If the data is kept on, then the GPIO port number 3 will be set to HIGH, and if the string is off, then the GPIO port number 3 will be set to LOW—in simple words, switching your device on or off your device.

```
def on_connect(client,userdata, flag, rc):
    print("connection returned" + str(rc))
    client.subscribe(sub_topic)
```

We have defined the on_connect() function previously as well. However, this time it is slightly different. Rather than just printing the connection returned with the value of rc, we are also using another function called client.subscribe(sub_topic), which will let us get connected to the broker on the specific topic that we have defined earlier in this program.

```
client.on_message=on_message
```

As we know that the entire algorithm is based on an event-driven system, this client.on_message function will keep waiting for a message to be received. Once received, it will then execute the on_message function. This will decide whether to turn the appliance on or off.

To use it, just go ahead and send the data based on the topic and it will be received by your Raspberry Pi.

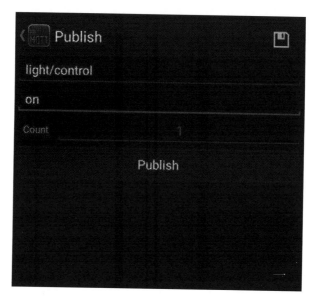

Once received, the decision-making function, `on_message()`, will decide what data is being received by the MyMQTT app. If the data received is `on`, then the lights will be turned on. If the data received is `off`, then the lights will be turned off. It's as simple as that.

Summary

In this chapter, we have understood the basics of IoT and how the MQTT server works. We also made an intruder detection system that will alert you whenever someone is in your home, no matter where you are in the world. Finally, we also created a system to switch on a device in your home using a simple mobile command. In the next chapter, we will let Jarvis enable to let you interact with the system based on your voices.

14
Giving Voice to Jarvis

Ever wondered whether using robots to get our work done is possible? Well yes! Certainly in some high-tech fiction or Marvel movies or even comic books. So, get your seat belt tight and get ready for this amazing chapter where you will actually be implementing what I just mentioned.

This chapter will cover the following topics:

- Basic installation
- Automatic delivery answering machine
- Making an interactive door answering robot
- Making Jarvis understand our voice

Basic installation

There are various ways and methods through which we can control our smart home Jarvis, some of which we have explored earlier such as controlling it through. So, to start with, we need to prepare our system to be able to do speech synthesis; to do that, let's perform the following process.

First, go to the terminal and enter the following command:

```
sudo apt-get install alsa-utils
```

What this will do is install the dependency `alsa-utils`. The `alsa-utils` package contains various utilities that are useful for controlling your sound drivers.

Once this is done, you need to edit the file. To do it, we need to open the file. Use the following command:

```
sudo nano /etc/modules
```

Once that is done, a file will open; at the bottom of that file, you need to add the following line:

```
snd_bcm2835
```

You don't need to get too much into why we are doing it. It's just there to set things up. I can give you an explanation; however, I do not wish to bore you at this exciting moment.

Also, if you are lucky, then sometimes, you might find the line to be already present. If that is the case, then let it be there and don't touch it.

Now, to play the sounds that we need the Jarvis to say, we need an audio player. No, not the one that you have at your home. We are talking about the software that would play it.

To install the player, we need to run the following commands:

```
sudo apt-get install mplayer
```

All right, we are done with audio player; let's see what we have next. Now, again, we need to edit the file of the media player. We will use the same steps to open the file and edit it:

```
sudo nano /etc/mplayer/mplayer.conf
```

This will open the file. As before, simply add the following line:

```
nolirc=yes
```

Finally, we need to give it some voice, so run the following command:

```
sudo apt-get install festvox-rablpc16k
```

This will install a 16 kHz, British, male, voice to Jarvis. We love British accents, don't we?

Perfect. Once we have done all of the steps mentioned previously, we would be good to go. To test the voice, simply connect a USB speaker to the Raspberry Pi and run the following code:

```
import os
from time import sleep
os.system('echo "hello! i am raspberry pi robot"|festival --tts ')
sleep(2)
os.system('echo "how are you?"| festival --tts ')
sleep(2)
os.system('echo "I am having fun."| festival --tts ')
sleep(2)
```

All right then, let's see what we have actually done:

```
import os
```

As you might have figured out, we are importing the library named os. This library provides a way of using operating-system-dependent functionality:

```
os.system('echo "Hello from the other side"|festival --tts ')
```

Here, we are using a method called `system()`; what this does is that it executes a shell command. You might be wondering what this is. A shell command is a command used by the user to access the functionality of a system to interact with it. So now that we want to convert our text to voice, we would be providing two arguments to this function. First, what is the text? In our case, it is Hello from the other side; the second argument that we have here is festival --tts. Now festival is a library, and tts stands for text to speech conversion. So when we pass it on to the argument, the system will know that the text passed on to the argument has to be converted from text to speech.

And that's it! Yes, that's it. That's all we have to do to make your Raspberry speak.

Automatic delivery answering machine

These days, we all order things online. Yet no matter how automated the process of Amazon is, when talking about 2018, we still have humans delivering the packages to our doorsteps. Sometimes, you want them to know a few things about where to leave the parcel. Now that we are becoming more and more automated, gone are the days when you might leave a note outside your gate. It's time to make something really interesting with our technology. To do that, we hardly need to do anything serious. All we need to do is to wire up the components as shown in the following diagram:

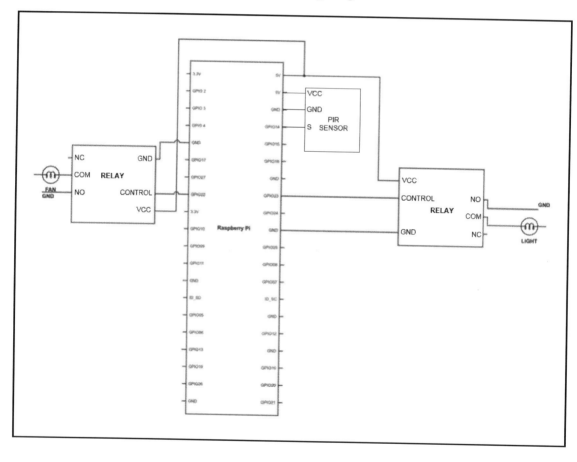

The PIR sensor must be placed so that it gives a logic high whenever there is movement around the gate.

Once that is done, go ahead and upload the following code:

```
import RPi.GPIO as GPIO
import time
Import os
GPIO.setmode(GPIO.BCM)
PIR = 13
GPIO.setup(PIR,GPIO.IN)
while True:

   if GPIO.input(PIR) == 1 :
       os.system('echo "Hello, welcome to my house"|festival --tts ')
       time.sleep(0.2)
       os.system('echo "If you are a delivery agent then please leave the
package here"|festival --tts ')
       time.sleep(0.2)
       os.system('echo "If you are a guest then I'm sorry I have to leave I
will be back after 7pm"|festival --tts ')
       time.sleep(0.2)
       os.system('echo "also Kindly don't step over the grass, its freshly
grown and needs some time"|festival --tts ')
       time.sleep(1)
       os.system('echo "Thank you !"|festival --tts ')
```

Now what we have done is very simple. As soon as the PIR sensor gives a logic high, a certain instruction is spoken. There is no need of an explanation. You can refer to the previous code if you need any clarification.

Making an interactive door – answering robot

In the previous chapter we have used a PIR sensor to sense any human activity, however the problem with the sensor is, that no matter who comes or leaves it would deliver the same message. That basically means that even when you come home after a long day, it would end up asking the same question. Pretty dumb huh?

So in this chapter we would use the previous repository and integrate the vision and the voice together to make an amazing duo. In this, the camera would identify who is on the gate and would recognize if it is a human and a stranger, if so then, it would deliver the message you intend to give. On the other hand if its you then it would simply let you pass with a simple greeting. However if the face is detected but not recognized then it would give a set of instructions to the person standing in-front of the camera.

To implement it all you need to do is to set up a camera on the gate of your door along with the PIR. The PIR is basically to activate the camera. In other words the camera would not get activated till the time no movement is detected. This set up is very straight forward and does not need any GPIO to be used. Simply fix the camera and PIR and upload the following code:

```
import RPi.GPIO as GPIO
import time
Import os
import cv2
import numpy as np
import cv2

faceDetect = cv2.CascadeClassifier('haarcascade_frontalface_default.xml')
cam = cv2.VideoCapture(0)
rec = cv2.face.LBPHFaceRecognizer_create()
rec.read("recognizer/trainningData.yml")
id = 0

while True:

  GPIO.setmode(GPIO.BCM)
PIR = 13
GPIO.setup(PIR, GPIO.IN)

if GPIO.input(PIR) == 1:

  ret, img = cam.read()
gray = cv2.cvtColor(img, cv2.COLOR_BGR2GRAY)
```

```
faces = faceDetect.detectMultiScale(gray, 1.3, 5)
for (x, y, w, h) in faces:
   cv2.rectangle(img, (x, y), (x + w, y + h), (0, 0, 255), 2)
id, conf = rec.predict(gray[y: y + h, x: x + w])

if id == 1:
   id = "BEN"
os.system('echo "Hello, welcome to the house BEN"|festival --tts ')
time, sleep(0.2)

else :

   os.system('echo "If you are a delivery agent then please leave the
package here"|festival --tts ')
time, sleep(0.2)

os.system('echo "If you are a guest then I'
     m sorry I have to leave I will be back after 7 pm "|festival --tts ')
     time, sleep(0.2)

     os.system('echo "also Kindly don'
        t step over the grass, its freshly grown and needs some time
"|festival --tts ')
        time.sleep(1)

        os.system('echo "Thank you !"|festival --tts ') cv2.imshow("face",
img) if cv2.waitKey(1) == ord('q'):
        break cam.release()

        cv2.destroyAllWindows()

faceDetect = cv2.CascadeClassifier('haarcascade_frontalface_default.xml')
```

In the preceding code, we are creating a cascade classifier using the method `CascadeClassifier` so that faces can be detected by the camera.

```
cam = cv2.VideoCapture(0)
rec = cv2.face.LBPHFaceRecognizer_create()
```

In the preceding code, we are reading the frames from the camera using `VideoCapture(0)` method of `cv2`. Also, the face recognizer is being created to recognize a particular face.

```
ret, img = cam.read()
```

Now read the data from the camera using `cam.read()` as done in the previous code.

```
gray = cv2.cvtColor(img,cv2.COLOR_BGR2GRAY)
faces = faceDetect.detectMultiScale(gray,1.3,5)
```

The images are converted into gray color. Then, `faceDetect.detectMultiScale()` will be using the gray color-converted images.

```
for (x,y,w,h) in faces:
    cv2.rectangle(img, (x,y), (x+w, y+h), (0,0,255), 2)
    id, conf = rec.predict(gray[y:y+h, x:x+w])
    if id==1:
        id = "BEN"
        os.system('echo "Hello, welcome to my house BEN"|festival --tts ')
        time, sleep(0.2)
```

As the face is detected, the part of the image containing the face will be converted into gray and passed to a predict function. This method will tell if the face is known or not, it also returns the ID if the face is identified. Suppose the person is BEN, then Jarvis would say `Hello, welcome to my house BEN`. Now BEN can tell the Jarvis to turn on the lights, and the Jarvis would respond as the wake word Jarvis gets activated. And if the person is not recognized, then maybe it was a delivery boy. Then, the following commands get executed:

```
os.system('echo "If you are a delivery agent then please leave the package
here"|festival --tts ')
time, sleep(0.2)


os.system('echo "If you are a guest then I'm sorry I have to leave I will
be back after 7pm"|festival --tts ')
 time, sleep(0.2)


os.system('echo "also Kindly don't step over the grass, its freshly grown
and needs some time"|festival --tts ')
time.sleep(1)


os.system('echo "Thank you !"|festival --tts ')
```

Making Jarvis understand our voice

Voice is an essence of communication. It helps us transfer huge amounts of data in a very short period of time. It is certainly faster and easier than typing. Hence, more and more companies are working toward making systems that understands human voice and language and work according to them. It is certainly not easy because of the huge variations that are present in the language; however, we have come a considerable distance. So without much time, let's make our system get ready to recognize our voice.

So here, we would be using an API from Google Voice. As you may know, Google is really good at understanding what you say. Like, very literally. So it makes sense to use their API. Now, the way it works is very simple. We capture the voice, and we convert it into the text. Then, we compare if the text is similar to something we have defined in the configuration file. If it matches with anything, the bash command associated with it will be executed.

First, we need to check whether the microphone is connected. To do that, run the following command:

```
lsusb
```

This command will show you a list of devices connected on USB. If you see yours on the list, then thumbs up, you are on the right track. Otherwise, try finding it with the connection or maybe try another hardware.

We also need to set the recording volume to high. To do this, go ahead and type the following command on the serial:

```
alsamixer
```

Now once the GUI pops on to the screen, toggle the volume using the arrow keys.

It's best to hear the sound recorded by yourself rather than directly giving it down to the Raspberry. To do that first, we need to record our voice, so we need to run the following command:

```
arecord -l
```

This will check whether the webcam is on the list. Then, write the following command to record:

```
arecord -D plughw:1,0 First.wav
```

The sound will be recorded with the following name, `First.wav`.

Now we would also like to listen to what we just recorded. The simple way to do that is by typing the following command:

```
aplay test.wav
```

Check whether the voice is correct. If not, then you are free to make any adjustments to the system.

Once we are done with checking the sound and the microphone, it's time to install the real software for the job. There are simple ways with which you can do it. The following is a list of commands that you need to run:

```
wget -- no-check-certificate "http://goo.gl/KrwrBa" -O PiAUISuite.tar.gz

tar -xvzf PiAUISuite.tar.gz

cd PiAUISuite/Install/

sudo ./InstallAUISuite.sh
```

Now when you run this, very interesting things will start to happen. It will start to ask you various questions. Some of them will be straightforward. You can use your right mind to give the answers to it in the form of yes or no. Others could be very technical. As these questions might change over time, there seems to be no need to explicitly mention the answers that you need to fill, but as a general rule of thumb—Give it a yes unless it's something you really want to say no to.

Perfect then, we have installed the software. Now before you go any further in that software, let's go ahead and write the following programs:

```
import RPi.GPIO as GPIO
import time
import os
GPIO.setmode(GPIO.BCM)
LIGHT = 2
GPIO.setup(LIGHT,GPIO.OUT)
GPIO.output(LIGHT, GPIO.HIGH)
os.system('echo "LIGHTS TURNED ON "|festival --tts')
```

Whenever this program runs, the light that is connected on PIN number 2 will be turned on. Also, it will read out LIGHTS TURNED ON. Save this file with the name lighton.py:

```
import RPi.GPIO as GPIO
import time
import os
GPIO.setmode(GPIO.BCM)
LIGHT = 23
GPIO.setup(LIGHT,GPIO.OUT)
GPIO.output(LIGHT, GPIO.LOW)
os.system('echo "LIGHTS TURNED OFF "|festival --tts')
```

Similarly, in this program, the light would be turned off and it would read out LIGHTS TURNED OFF. Save it by the name lightoff.py:

```
import RPi.GPIO as GPIO
import time
Import os
GPIO.setmode(GPIO.BCM)
FAN = 22
GPIO.setup(FAN,GPIO.OUT)
GPIO.output(LIGHT, GPIO.HIGH)
os.system('echo "FAN TURNED ON "|festival --tts')
```

Now we are doing the same thing for the fan as well. In this one, the fan will be switched on; save it with the name fanon.py:

```
import RPi.GPIO as GPIO
import time
Import os
GPIO.setmode(GPIO.BCM)
FAN = 22
GPIO.setup(FAN,GPIO.OUT)
GPIO.output(LIGHT, GPIO.LOW)os.system('echo "FAN TURNED OFF "|festival --tts')
```

I don't need to explain the same thing for this do I? As you will have guessed, save it with the name fanoff.py.

All right! When all of this is done, then type the following command to check whether the software is installed properly:

```
voicecommand -c
```

Raspberry Pi responds to the wake word `pi`; let's change it to `jarvis`. All these changes can be made after opening the configuration file using the following command:

```
voicecommand -e.
```

In that file, enter the commands of your own. Here, let's add the following code:

```
LIGHT_ON

LIGHT_OFF

FAN_ON

FAN_OFF
```

Now for each command, define the action. The action would be to run the Python file that contains the code for switching the lights and fan on or off. The code is basic and simple to understand. Add the following to the file:

```
LIGHT ON = sudo python lighton.py

LIGHT OFF = sudo python lightoff.py

FAN ON = sudo python fanon.py

FAN OFF = sudo python fanoff.py
```

Now, let's see what we have done. Whenever you say *Jarvis, light on*, it will convert your speed to text, compare it with the program that it has to run corresponding to it and will do whatever is there in the program. Hence, in this program, whenever we say *Light on*, the lights will be turned on and similarly for the rest of the commands as well. Remember to make it listen to what you are saying. You would have to say the word, *Jarvis*, which will make it attentive to the commands and ready to listen.

Summary

In this chapter, we understood how to interact and make the Jarvis work according to our needs. If this chapter was about verbal communication, then the next chapter is about gesture recognition where, using advanced capacitive techniques, you will be able to control your automation system just by waving at it.

15
Gesture Recognition

Since the beginning of time, humans have communicated with each other using gestures, even before there wasn't any formal language. Hand gestures were the primary way of communication, and it is also evident in the ancient sculptures found all across the world that the signs have been a successful way of transferring a huge amount of data in a very efficient way, sometimes, even more efficient than language itself.

Gestures are natural, and they can occur as a reflex to a certain situation. It also happens subconsciously even without our knowing. So, it becomes an ideal way of communication with various devices. However, the question remains, how?

We have used vision processing in our last few chapters, and we can be sure that if we are talking about gestures, then we would surely have to do a lot of programming to identify the gestures in the videos; furthermore, it would require a huge amount of processing power to make it happen as well. Hence, it is out of the question. We can build some basic gesture-recognition system using an array of proximity sensors. However, the range of gestures recognized would be very limited, and the overall ports being used would be multiple fold.

Hence, we need to find a solution that is easy to work with and does not cost more than what it would deliver.

This chapter will be covering the following topics:

- Electric field sensing
- Using the Flick HAT
- Gesture recognition-based automation

Electric field sensing

Near-field sensing is a very interesting field of sensing. Be prepared for some interesting stuff. If you are feeling a little sleepy, or if you are lacking attention, then get some coffee because the working principle of this system is going to be a little new.

Whenever there is a charge, there is an associated electrical field that comes along with it. These charges propagate through the space and go around an object. When that happens, the electric field associated with it has a specific characteristic. This characteristic will be the same till the time the environment around it is empty.

For the gesture-recognition board that we are using, the field that would be sensed around it is only for about a few centimeters, so anything beyond that point can be disregarded. If there is nothing in that vicinity, then we can safely assume that the pattern of electric field being sensed would be unchanged. However, whenever an object such as our hand comes in the vicinity, then these waves are distorted. The distortion is directly linked to the position of the object and its position. With this distortion, we can sense where the finger is, and with constant sensing, we see what kind of motion is being performed. The board in question looks like this:

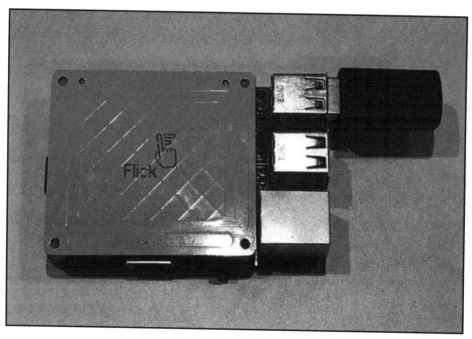

The central criss-crossed area on the board is the transmitter and on the extreme sides are rectangular structures that are four in number. These are the sensing elements. These sense the pattern of waves in the space. Based on it, they can derive what are the x, y, and z coordinates of the object. This is powered by a chip named MGC 3130. This does all the computation and delivers the raw reading to the user, regarding the coordinates.

Using the Flick HAT

Flick HAT comes in the form of a shield, which you can simply plug into your Raspberry Pi and start using. However, once you do that, you will not be left with any GPIO pins. Hence, to save ourselves from that problem, we will be connecting it using male-to-female wires. This will give us access to the other GPIO pins and then we can have fun.

So, go ahead and connect it as follows. The following is a pin diagram of the Flick board:

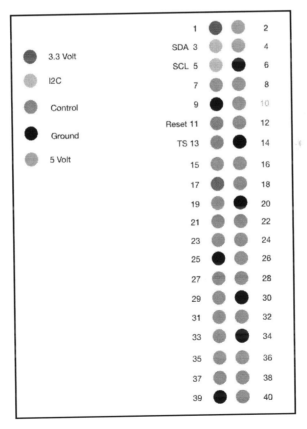

Thereafter, make the connections as follows:

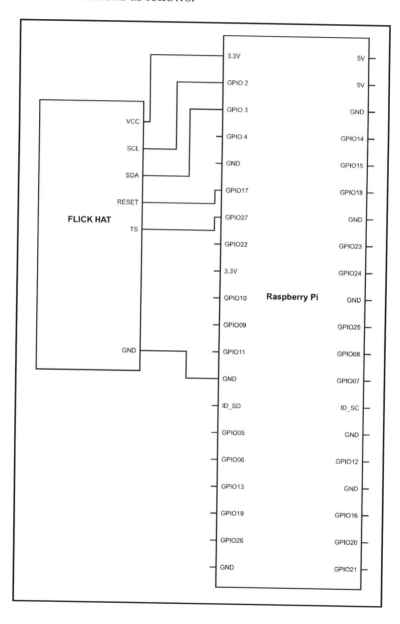

Once the connection is done, simply upload this code and see what happens:

```
import signal
import flicklib
import time
def message(value):
    print value
@flicklib.move()
def move(x, y, z):
    global xyztxt
    xyztxt = '{:5.3f} {:5.3f} {:5.3f}'.format(x,y,z)
@flicklib.flick()
def flick(start,finish):
    global flicktxt
    flicktxt = 'FLICK-' + start[0].upper() + finish[0].upper()
    message(flicktxt)
def main():
    global xyztxt
    global flicktxt
    xyztxt = ''
    flicktxt = ''
    flickcount = 0
    while True:

    xyztxt = ''
    if len(flicktxt) > 0 and flickcount < 5:
        flickcount += 1
    else:
        flicktxt = ''
        flickcount = 0
 main()
```

Now once you have uploaded the code, lets go ahead and understand what this code is actually doing.

We are using a library called `import flicklib` this is provided by the manufacturer of this board. The functions of this library would be used all over in this chapter for communicating with the flick board and getting the data

```
def message(value):
    print value
```

Here, we are defining a function named `message(value)` what this would do is simply print whatever value would be passed on to the function in the argument:

```
@flicklib.move()
```

This has a special concept of decorators. By definition, a decorator is a function that takes another function and extends the behavior of the latter function without explicitly modifying it. In the preceding line of code, we are declaring that it is a decorator `@`.

This has a special job: dynamically defines any function in a program. What this means in plain English is that the function defined using this methodology can work differently depending on how the user defines it.

The function `move()` will further be complimented by the function, which is getting defined after it. These kind of functions are named nested functions. That is functions inside a function:

```
def move(x, y, z):
    global xyztxt
    xyztxt = '{:5.3f} {:5.3f} {:5.3f}'.format(x,y,z)
```

Here, we are defining a function named `move()`, which has arguments as x, y, and z. Inside the function, we have defined a global variable named `xyztxt`; now, the value of `xyztxt` would be in a form of five digit, with a decimal after three places. How did we know that? As you can see, we are using a function named `format()`. What this function does is format the values of a given variable according to the way the user has requested it for. We have declared here the value as `{:5.3f}`. `:5` represents that it would be of five digits, and `3f` represents that the decimal places would be after three digits. Hence, the format would be xxx.xx:

```
def flick(start,finish):
    global flicktxt
    flicktxt = 'FLICK-' + start[0].upper() + finish[0].upper()
    message(flicktxt)
```

Here, we have defined a function named `flick(start, finish)`. It has two arguments: `start` and `finish`. Using the line `flicktxt = 'FLICK-' + start[0].upper() + finish[0].upper()`, this is slicing the characters as recognized by the gesture board. If a south–north swipe is detected, then the start will get south and finish is north. Now we are only using the first characters of the words:

```
global xyztxt
global flicktxt
```

We are again defining the variables named `xyztxt` and `flicktxt` globally. Earlier, what we have done is that we have defined it in the function. Hence, it is important for us to define it in the main program:

```
if len(flicktxt) > 0 and flickcount < 5:
        flickcount += 1
else:
        flicktxt = ''
        flickcount = 0
```

The `flicktxt` variable would get a value corresponding to the gesture when the gesture is detected. In case there is no gesture then `flicktxt` would be left empty. A variable named `flickcount` will count how many times its swiped. If the values are out of the range specified then the `flicktxt` would be cleared to empty string using the line `flicktxt = ''` and `flickcount` would be made 0.

The final output of this would be a text given to user providing in which direction the hand is flicked.

Gesture recognition-based automation

Now we have interfaced the connections as per the following diagram:

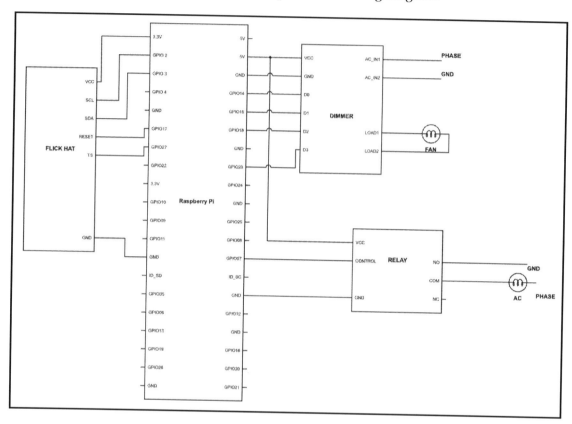

Let's go ahead and upload the following code:

```
import signal
import flicklib
import time
import RPi.GPIO as GPIO
GIPO.setmode(GPIO.BCM)
GPIO.setup(light, GPIO.OUT)
GPIO.setup(fan,GPIO.OUT)
pwm = GPIO.PWM(fan,100)
def message(value):
    print value
@flicklib.move()
def move(x, y, z):
```

```
    global xyztxt
    xyztxt = '{:5.3f} {:5.3f} {:5.3f}'.format(x,y,z)
@flicklib.flick()
def flick(start,finish):
    global flicktxt
    flicktxt = 'FLICK-' + start[0].upper() + finish[0].upper()
    message(flicktxt)
def main():
    global xyztxt
    global flicktxt
    xyztxt = ''
    flicktxt = ''
    flickcount = 0
    dc_inc = 0
    dc_dec = 0
while True:
    pwm.start(0)
    xyztxt = ' '
    if len(flicktxt) > 0 and flickcount < 5:
        flickcount += 1
    else:
        flicktxt = ''

flickcount = 0
if flicktxt =="FLICK-WE":
    GPIO.output(light,GPIO.LOW)
if flicktxt =="FLICK-EW":
    GPIO.output(light,GPIO.HIGH)
if flicktxt =="FLICK-SN":
    if dc_inc < 100:
        dc_inc = dc_inc + 10
        pwm.changeDutyCycle(dc_inc)

else:
    Dc_inc = 10
    if flicktxt =="FLICK-NS":
        if dc_inc >0:
        dc_dec = dc_dec - 10
        pwm.changeDutyCycle(dc_dec)
main()
```

The program is in addition to the program we have done before, as always we have some added functionality of using the data being received by the flick gesture board and using it to switch on or switch off the lights.

Like the previous program, we are taking in the gestures over the board in the form of the directions of swipes, and using a simple condition to switch off the lights, or switch them on. So, let's see what are the additions:

```
if flicktxt =="FLICK-WE":

        GPIO.output(light,GPIO.LOW)
```

The first condition is simple. We are comparing the value of `flicktxt` to a given variable, which in our case is `FLICK-WE`, wherein `WE` stands for **west** to **east**. So when we flick from west to east, or in other words, when we flick from left to right, the lights would be switched off:

```
if flicktxt =="FLICK-EW":
        GPIO.output(light,GPIO.HIGH)
```

As before, we are again taking in a variable named `FLICK-EW`, which stands for flick from east to west. What it does is whenever we flick our hand from east to west, or from right to left, the lights will be switched on:

```
if flicktxt =="FLICK-SN":
    if dc_inc <= 100:
        dc_inc = dc_inc + 20
        pwm.changeDutyCycle(dc_inc)
```

Now we have put a dimmer along with a fan to control the speed of the fan as well; hence, we will have to give it a PWM corresponding to the speed that we want to drive it. Now whenever the user will flick his hand from south to north or from down to up. The condition `if dc_inc <100` will check whether the value of the `dc_inc` is less than or equal to 100 or not. If it is, then it will increment the value of the `dc_inc` by 20 values. Using the function `ChangeDutyCycle()`, we are providing the different duty cycle to the dimmer; hence, changing the overall speed of the fan. Every time you swipe up the value of the fan, it will increase by 20%:

```
else:
    Dc_inc = 10
    if flicktxt =="FLICK-NS":
    if dc_inc >0:
    dc_dec = dc_dec - 10
    pwm.changeDutyCycle(dc_dec)
```

Summary

In this chapter, we are were able to understand the concept of how gesture recognition works via electric field detection. We also understood how easy it is to use a gesture-controlled board and control the home using gestures. We will cover the machine learning part in the next chapter.

16
Machine Learning

Robots and computers from its primitive days to even right now are being programmed to do a set of activities. These activities can be very large. Hence, to develop complex programs, there is a need for a lot of software engineers who work day and night to achieve a certain functionality. This is workable when the problem is well defined. But what about situations when the problem is also way complex?

Learning is something that has made us humans what we are. Our experiences molded us to adapt to situations in a better and a more efficient way. Every time we do something, we know more. This makes us better at doing that task over a period of time. It is said practice makes a man perfect, and it is learning through doing things again and again that makes us better.

However, let us step back and define what learning is? I would like to quote Google here according to it, *It is a knowledge acquired through study, experience or being taught.* So, learning is basically a way of acquiring information from our surroundings to understand a process and its nature.

Now, you must be thinking, wait a minute, haven't we made our system learn a lot of vision data in previous chapters when we were making the guard robot. You would be absolutely correct to think so. However, the learning can be done in different ways. What may work for one kind of problem can be futile for some other kind of problem. Hence, there are various types of learning algorithms and their principles. In this chapter, we will be focusing on an algorithm named **k-nearest neighbor**. It's named the **lazy algorithm**. I love this algorithm personally for classification. Why? Because technically there is no training phase. How?

k-nearest neighbor is actually a smart algorithm. Rather than computing a regression of data provided and do a lot of mathematics calculations, it simply takes a structured data from the dataset provided. Whenever there is new data that has come in for prediction, then it simply searches the closest *k* match of the data provided by the user to the database based on its classification given. So, in this chapter, we will learn how this algorithm will work and how we can use it to make our home smart.

We will cover the following topics in this chapter:

- Making a dataset
- Prediction using dataset
- Making your home learn
- Home learning and automation

Making a dataset

Like in Chapter 10, *Making a Guard Robot*, we have used multiple images for the user to train the model to find out whether the object in the image is a man or something else. In a very similar way, we would have to make a dummy dataset so that the machine learning algorithm can predict based on that data what should be done.

To make a dataset, we need to understand what data is being considered. In this chapter, we will be making a machine learning algorithm based on time and the temperature to predict whether the fan should be on or off. Hence, there are at least two things that should be provided by us to the system one being Temperature, and the other would be Time so that the prediction can take place. But one thing to remember is that we are talking about a supervised learning algorithm, so to train the model, we need to also give the outcome of Temperature and Time onto the state of the fan. Here, the state of the fan would be either on or off. Hence, we can depict it using 0 or 1. Now let's go ahead and make a dataset by ourselves.

Now, to make a dataset, you simply have to open Microsoft Excel and start writing the dataset as follows:

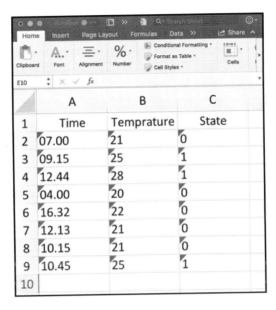

It is always better to have a dataset of more than 20 sets of data. Also, its important that the data has a distinct characteristic and its not random data. For example, in the preceding case, you can see that at 12.44 when the temperature is 28, the fan will be on; however, at the same time, when the time is 12.13 and temperature is 21, then the fan is off.

Once you have created a dataset, then you must save it with the name dataset in the CSV format. There may be some users who would not use a Microsoft Excel, in which case you can write the data with the same format in text editor and finally save it in the CSV format.

Once you have the dataset.csv files, then you must go ahead and copy them into the place where you will be saving the upcoming code. Once you are done, then we can move on to the next step.

Remember that the better the quality of data, the better the learning process. So you may take some time and carefully craft your dataset so that it does make sense.

Predicting using a dataset

Without much talking, let's take a look at the following code:

```
import numpy as np
import pandas as pd
from sklearn.neighbors import KNeighborsClassifier

knn = KNeighborsClassifier(n_neighbors=5)
data = pd.read_csv('dataset.csv')

x = np.array(data[['Time', 'Temp']])
y = np.array(data[['State']]).ravel()

knn.fit(x,y)

time = raw_input("Enter time")
temp = raw_input("Enter temp")

data =. []

data.append(float(time))
data.append(float(temp))

a = knn.predict([data])

print(a[0])}
```

So, let's see what we are doing here:

```
import numpy as np
```

We are importing numpy to our program; this helps us handle lists and matrices:

```
import pandas as pd
```

Here, we are importing a library named pandas; this helps us read files in comma-separated values or in other words, CSV files. We will be using CSV files to store our data and access it for learning process:

```
from sklearn.neighbors import KNeighborsClassifier
```

Here, we are importing `KneighborsClassifier` from the library `sklearn`. `sklearn` itself is a huge library; hence, we are importing only a part of it as we will not be using all of it in this program:

```
knn = KNeighborsClassifier(n_neighbors=5)
```

Here, we are giving value to variable `knn` wherein the value would be `KNeighborsClassifer(n_neighbors =5)`; what this means is that it is using the `KNeighborsClassifer()` function with the argument as `n_neighbors=5`. This argument tells the `KNeighborsClassifer` function that we will be having five neighbors in the algorithm. Further to this using this declaration, the whole function can be called using `knn`:

```
data = pd.read_csv('dataset.csv')
```

Here, we are providing value to a variable called `data` and the value passed is `pd.read_csv('dataset.csv')`; what this means is that whenever `data` is called, then a `pd.read_csv()` function from the `pandas` library will be called. The purpose of this function is to read data from the CSV files. Here, the argument passed is `dataset.csv`; hence, it is indicating which data would be read by the function. In our case, it will read from a file name: `dataset.csv`:

```
x = np.array(data[['Time', 'Temp']])
```

In the following line, we are passing value to the variable x, and the value being passed is `np.array(data[['Time, 'Temp']])`. Now the `np.array` function to make an array through the `numpy` library. This array will store the data by the name of `Time` and `Temp`:

```
y = np.array(data[['State']]).ravel()
```

Just like the previous time, we are storing `State` in an array made through the `numpy` library `.ravel()` function at the end would transpose the array. This is done so that the mathematical functions can be done between two arrays—x and y:

```
knn.fit(x,y)
```

In this small line, we are using the function from the `knn` library called `fit()` what it is doing is fitting the model using the x as the primary data and y as the output resultant data:

```
time = raw_input("Enter time")
temp = raw_input("Enter temp")
```

In this line, we are requesting the data from the user. In the first line, we will be printing `Enter time` and thereafter wait for user to enter the time. After user has entered the time, it will be stored in the variable named `time`. Once that is done, then it would move on to the next line; the code and it would print `Enter temp` once that is prompted to the user it would wait for data to be collected. Once data is fetched by the user, it will store that data in the variable called `temp`:

```
data =. []
```

Here, we are making an empty list by the name of `data`; this list will be used for calculating the resultant state of the output. As all the machine learning algorithm is working in list data type. Hence, the input must be given for decision in the form of a list itself:

```
data.append(float(time))
data.append(float(temp))
```

Here, we are adding data to the list that we just created with the name `data`. First, `time` will be added, followed by `temp`:

```
a = knn.predict([data])
```

Once that is done, a function named `predict` from the `knn` algorithm will be used to predict the output based on the list provided with the name of `data`. The output of the prediction algorithm is fetched to a variable by the name `a`:

```
print(a[0])
```

Finally, once the prediction is done, then we would read the value of `a` and remember that all the data I/O is happening in the form of lists. Hence, the data output given by the prediction algorithm would also be in the list format. Hence, we are printing the first element of the list.

This output will predict which state will be of the fan according to the dataset given by the user. So, go ahead and give a temperature and a time and let the system predict the outcome for you. See if it works fine or not. If it doesn't, then try adding some more datasets to the CSV files or see whether the values in the dataset actually make any sense. I am sure that you end up with a wonderful predictive system.

Making your home learn

Once this constitution is done, go ahead and wire it up, as shown here:

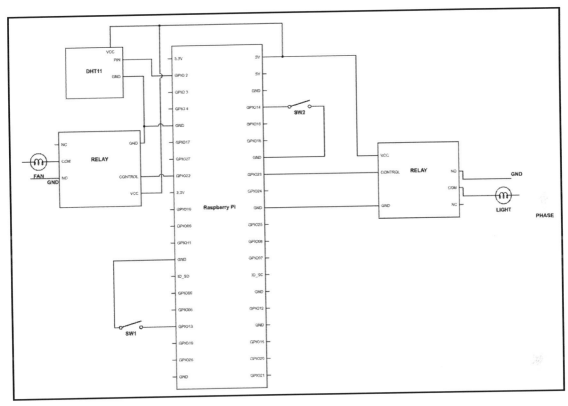

Once that is set, it is time for us to write the following code on to our Raspberry Pi:

```
import Adafruit_DHT
import datetime
import RPi.GPIO as GPIO
import time
import numpy as np
import pandas as pd
import Adafruit_DHT
from sklearn.neighbors import KNeighborsClassifier

GPIO.setmode(GPIO.BCM)
GPIO.setwarnings(False)

fan = 22
```

```
light = 23
sw1 = 13
sw2 = 14

GPIO.setup(led1,GPIO.OUT)
GPIO.setup(led2,GPIO.OUT)
GPIO.setup(sw1,GPIO.IN)
GPIO.setup(sw2,GPIO.IN)

sensor = 11
pin = 2


f = open("dataset.csv","a+")
count = 0
while count < 50:

 data = ""

 H = datetime.datetime.now().strftime('%H')
 M = datetime.datetime.now().strftime('%M')

 data = str(H)+"."+str(M)
 humidity,temperature = Adafruit_DHT.read_retry(sensor,pin)
 data = data + "," + str(temperature)

prev_state = state

 if (GPIO.input(sw1) == 0) and (GPIO.input(sw2) == 0):
     state = 0
     GPIO.output(light,GPIO.LOW)
     GPIO.output(fan,GPIO.LOW)

 elif (GPIO.input(sw1) == 0) and (GPIO.input(sw2) == 1):
     state = 1
     GPIO.output(light,GPIO.HIGH)
     GPIO.output(fan,GPIO.LOW)

 elif (GPIO.input(sw1) == 1) and (GPIO.input(sw2) == 0):
    state = 2
     GPIO.output(light,GPIO.LOW)
     GPIO.output(fan,GPIO.HIGH)

 elif (GPIO.input(sw1) == 1) and (GPIO.input(sw2) == 1):
    state = 3
     GPIO.output(light,GPIO.HIGH)
     GPIO.output(fan,GPIO.HIGH)
```

```
data = ","+str(state)

if prev_state =! state:

        f.write(data)
        count = count+1


    f.close()
```

Now, let's see what we have done here:

```
f = open("dataset.csv","a+")
```

In this line of the code, we have assigned the value `open("dataset.csv", "a+")` to the variable `f`. Thereafter, the `open()` function will open the file that is passed on to its argument, which in our case is `dataset.csv`; the argument `a+` stands for appending the value at the end of the CSV file. Hence, what this line will do is to open the file `dataset.csv` and add a value that we will pass later on:

```
data = ""
```

We are declaring an empty string by the name of `data`:

```
data = str(H)+"."+str(M)
```

We are adding values of hours and minutes to the string, separated by a dot in between for differentiation. Hence, the data will look like `HH.MM`:

```
humidity,temperature = Adafruit_DHT.read_retry(sensor,pin)
```

We are using this line to read the humidity and temperature reading from the DHT 11 sensor and the values that would be passed on to the variables `humidity` and `temperature`:

```
data = data + "," + str(temperature)
```

Once the data is read, we are adding temperature to the variable `data` as well. Hence, now the data would look like this `HH.MM` and `TT.TT`:

```
if (GPIO.input(sw1) == 0) and (GPIO.input(sw2) == 0):
state = 0
elif (GPIO.input(sw1) == 0) and (GPIO.input(sw2) == 1):
state = 1
elif (GPIO.input(sw1) == 1) and (GPIO.input(sw2) == 0):
state = 2
elif (GPIO.input(sw1) == 1) and (GPIO.input(sw2) == 1):
state = 3
```

Here, we have defined different types of states which are corresponding to the switch combinations. The table for it is as follows:

Switch 1	Switch 2	State
0	0	0
0	1	1
1	0	2
1	1	3

Hence, by the value of state, we can understand which switch would be turned on and which would be turned off:

```
data = ","+str(state)
```

Finally, the value of state is also added to the variable named `data`. Now, finally, the data would look like `HH.MM`, `TT.TT`, and `S`:

```
f.write(data)
```

Now, using the `write()` function, we are writing the value of data to the file that we have already defined by the value `f` earlier.

Hence, with every single switch on or off, the data would be collected, and the value would be recorded with the time stamp in that file. This data can then be used to predict the state of the home at any given time without any intervention:

```
if prev_state =! state:

    f.write(data)
    count = count+1
```

Here, we are comparing the state with the `prev_state` as you can see in our program. The previous state is calculated at the start of our program. So, if there is any change in the state of the system, then the value of `prev_state` and `state` would be different. This will lead to the `if` statement to be true. When that happens, the data would be written onto our file using the `write()` function. The argument passed is the value that needs to be written. Finally, the value of count is increased by 1.

Once this is left running for a few hours or may be days, then it would collect some really useful data regarding your switching pattern of the lights and fan. Thereafter, this data can be fetched to the previous program wherein it would be able to to take its own decision based on the time and temperature.

Home learning and automation

Now that in the previous section we have understood how the learning works, it's time to use this concept to make a robot that will automatically understand how we function and make decisions. Based on our decisions, the system will judge what should be done. But this time, rather than giving a set of data by the user, let's make this program create the data for itself. Once the data seems sufficient for itself to function. So, without much explanation, let's get right into it:

```
import Adafruit_DHT
import datetime
import RPi.GPIO as GPIO
import time
import numpy as np
import pandas as pd
from sklearn.neighbors import KNeighborsClassifier

GPIO.setmode(GPIO.BCM)
GPIO.setwarnings(False)

light = 22
fan = 23
sw1 = 13
sw2 = 14

GPIO.setup(light,GPIO.OUT)
GPIO.setup(fan,GPIO.OUT)
GPIO.setup(sw1,GPIO.IN)
GPIO.setup(sw2,GPIO.IN)
```

```
sensor = 11
pin = 2


f = open("dataset.csv","a+")
count = 0

while count < 200:

        data = ""

        H = datetime.datetime.now().strftime('%H')
        M = datetime.datetime.now().strftime('%M')

        data = str(H)+"."+str(M)
        humidity,temperature = Adafruit_DHT.read_retry(sensor,pin)
        data = data + "," + str(temperature)

prev_state = state

  if (GPIO.input(sw1) == 0) and (GPIO.input(sw2) == 0):
      state = 0
      GPIO.output(light,GPIO.LOW)
      GPIO.output(fan,GPIO.LOW)

  elif (GPIO.input(sw1) == 0) and (GPIO.input(sw2) == 1):
      state = 1
      GPIO.output(light,GPIO.HIGH)
      GPIO.output(fan,GPIO.LOW)

  elif (GPIO.input(sw1) == 1) and (GPIO.input(sw2) == 0):
      state = 2
      GPIO.output(light,GPIO.LOW)
      GPIO.output(fan,GPIO.HIGH)

  elif (GPIO.input(sw1) == 1) and (GPIO.input(sw2) == 1):
      state = 3
      GPIO.output(light,GPIO.HIGH)
      GPIO.output(fan,GPIO.HIGH)

data = ","+str(state)

if prev_state =! state:

    f.write(data)
    count = count+1
```

```
Test_set = []
knn = KNeighborsClassifier(n_neighbors=5)
data = pd.read_csv('dataset.csv')

X = np.array(data[['Time', 'Temp']])
y = np.array(data[['State']]).ravel()

knn.fit(X,y)

While Count > 200:

    time = ""

    H = datetime.datetime.now().strftime('%H')
    M = datetime.datetime.now().strftime('%M')

    time = float(str(H)+"."+str(M))

    humidity, temperature = Adafruit_DHT.read_retry(sensor, pin)


  temp = int(temperature)
  test_set.append(time)
  test_set.append(temp)

  a = knn.predict([test_set]])
  Out = a[0]

  If out == 0:
  GPIO.output(light,GPIO.LOW)
  GPIO.output(fan,GPIO.LOW)

  If out == 1:
  GPIO.output(light,GPIO.LOW)
  GPIO.output(fan,GPIO.HIGH)

  If out == 2:
  GPIO.output(light,GPIO.HIGH)
  GPIO.output(fan,GPIO.LOW)

  If out == 3:
  GPIO.output(light,GPIO.HIGH)
  GPIO.output(fan,GPIO.HIGH)
```

Now let's see what we have done here. In this program, the first part of the program inside the condition `while count < 200:` is exactly the same as what we have done in the last code. So, it is just doing the things according to the user, and at the same time, it's taking in the values from the users to understand their working behavior:

```
while count > 200:
```

Thereafter, we have the second part of the code that will start to execute when the count is beyond 200 that is inside the preceding loop:

```
time = ""
```

In this line, we are forming an empty string by the name of time where we would be storing the value of time:

```
H = datetime.datetime.now().strftime('%H')
M = datetime.datetime.now().strftime('%M')
```

We are storing the values of time into the variable named `H` and `M`:

```
time = float(str(H)+"."+str(M))
```

We are now storing the value of time in the string `time`. This would include both hours and minutes:

```
temp = int(temperature)
```

For the sake of ease of calculations and reducing the computing load on the system, we are reducing the size of the temperature variable . We are doing it by removing the decimal places. To do that `TT.TT`; we are simply eliminating the decimal point and converting it into integer. This is done by the function named `int()`. The value of temperature in `int` will be stored in the variable named `temp`:

```
test_set.append(time)
test_set.append(temp)
```

Here, we are adding the value of the time and the temperature to a list named `test_set` if you look in the program, then you will see the declaration of an empty set in the mid of the program. So, now this `test_set` has the value of `time` and `temp`, which can be further used by the prediction algorithm to predict the state:

```
a = knn.predict([test_set]])
```

Using the simple function named `predict()` from the `knn` function, we can predict the value of the state. All we need to do is to pass on the data or `test_set` list over to the predict function. The output of this function will be a list that will be stored in a variable named `a`:

```
Out = a[0]
```

The value of `Out` will be set to the first element of the list `a`:

```
If out == 0:
GPIO.output (light, GPIO.LOW)
GPIO.output (fan, GPIO.LOW)

If out == 1:
GPIO.output (light, GPIO.LOW)
GPIO.output (fan, GPIO.HIGH)

If out == 2:
GPIO.output (light, GPIO.HIGH)
GPIO.output (fan, GPIO.LOW)

If out == 3:
GPIO.output (light, GPIO.HIGH)
GPIO.output (fan, GPIO.HIGH)
```

Using the preceding code block, we are able to switch on the light and fans selectively based on the state predicted by the algorithm. Hence, using this, the program would be able to automatically predict and switch on or off the light and the fans without your intervention.

Summary

In this chapter, we understood how machine learning works even without learning. We understood how datasets can be provided, and we can create a new dataset using the existing system. Finally, we understood how the system can work seamlessly to collect data, learn from that data, and finally, provide the input. Want to build a wheeled self-balancing robot? Well, then see you in the next chapter!

17
Gesture-Controlled Robotic Vehicle

In the previous few chapters, you have learned a lot about sensors—what they do and how they work. The number of sensors on this planet is simply out of bonds. It's ever increasing, and while you are reading this book, there could be some new sensor being launched by some country across the world. This might make you wonder, do you have to learn about all of these sensors coming out on the market every single day?

Thankfully, as you have learned, these sensors are more or less similar and work on a limited set of protocols. This makes working with new sensors easy. You might think that we have covered most of our basic sensors. However, that wouldn't be true—as we are yet to learn one of the most important sensors when it comes to the balancing of robots. These are accelerometers and gyroscope. These two sensors are not only present in all of these robots that have anything to do with balancing, but they have also found their way into our mobile devices. So, now let's learn about the basics of these sensors.

Accelerometers and gyroscope

Let's first start with accelerometers. As the name suggests, these are meant to measure acceleration in any body. Hence, whenever there is any acceleration in any body, then the accelerometers have the work to sense that acceleration and give the corresponding reading.

A gyroscope is a device that uses Earth's gravity to help determine orientation of the robot. An accelerometer is a device designed to measure non-gravitational acceleration. Whenever there is any acceleration, the crystals in the accelerometer excite and provide a voltage corresponding to it.

The main difference between these devices is simple: the gyroscope can sense rotation, whereas the accelerometer cannot. In a way, the accelerometer can gauge the orientation of a stationary item with relation to Earth's surface. When accelerating in a particular direction, the accelerometer is unable to distinguish between that and the acceleration provided through Earth's gravitational pull. The gyroscope measures the rate of rotation around a particular axis. In comparison, the accelerometer measures linear acceleration.

Here in this chapter, we will be using a sensor called MPU 6050, which is one of the most common sensors that has both the accelerometers and gyroscope built into one single package.

Preceding is a photograph of it. As you can see, it has **SCL** and **SDA** lines. Hence, you can be sure that this sensor works on I2C protocol. This is cool because we have already had a good experience working with I2C type sensors.

Interfacing the inertial measurement unit

MPU 6050 is a three-axis accelerometer and three-axis gyroscope. It works on I2C, but the interesting thing about this sensor is that it has a different address for different sensors. What did you just say? Different address for different sensors. Isn't it one single sensor?

Well, yes it is, but if you see the internal construction of the sensor, then you would find that for every different axis, the data is being stored in different registers from where we can acquire the data at our disposal. Hence, if you require just the reading of x axis of accelerometer, then you can do so efficiently rather than getting a whole long string of different values. Now connecting this sensor is super easy. All you have to do is to power it up using Raspberry Pi and simply connect the I2C pins over, as shown in the following diagram:

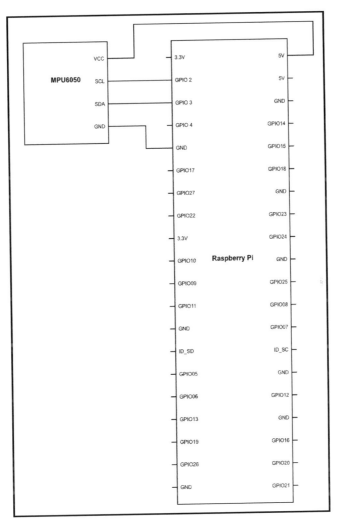

Once the wiring is done, go ahead and upload the following code. Once you do so, run and see what you get:

```
import smbus
from time import sleep
PWR_MGMT_1 = 0x6B
SMPLRT_DIV = 0x19
CONFIG = 0x1A
GYRO_CONFIG = 0x1B
INT_ENABLE = 0x38
ACCEL_XOUT_H = 0x3B
ACCEL_YOUT_H = 0x3D
ACCEL_ZOUT_H = 0x3F
GYRO_XOUT_H = 0x43
GYRO_YOUT_H = 0x45
GYRO_ZOUT_H = 0x47
def MPU_Init():
   bus.write_byte_data(Device_Address, SMPLRT_DIV, 7)
   bus.write_byte_data(Device_Address, PWR_MGMT_1, 1)
   bus.write_byte_data(Device_Address, CONFIG, 0)
   bus.write_byte_data(Device_Address, GYRO_CONFIG, 24)
   bus.write_byte_data(Device_Address, INT_ENABLE, 1)

def read_raw_data(addr):
   high = bus.read_byte_data(Device_Address, addr)
   low = bus.read_byte_data(Device_Address, addr+1)
   value = ((high << 8) | low)
    if(value > 32768):
    value = value - 65536
    return value
   bus = smbus.SMBus(1)
   Device_Address = 0x68

MPU_Init()
print (" Reading Data of Gyroscope and Accelerometer")
while True:
   Ax = read_raw_data(ACCEL_XOUT_H)
   Ay = read_raw_data(ACCEL_YOUT_H)
   Az = read_raw_data(ACCEL_ZOUT_H)
   Gx = read_raw_data(GYRO_XOUT_H)
   Gy = read_raw_data(GYRO_YOUT_H)
   Gz = read_raw_data(GYRO_ZOUT_H)
print ("Ax="+str(Ax)+"Ay="+str(Ay)+"Az="+str(Az)+"Gx="+str(Gx)+"Gy="+str(Gy)+"G
z="+str(Gz))
```

Now it's time to see what we have done:

```
def MPU_Init():

            bus.write_byte_data(Device_Address, SMPLRT_DIV, 7)

            bus.write_byte_data(Device_Address, PWR_MGMT_1, 1)

            bus.write_byte_data(Device_Address, CONFIG, 0)

            bus.write_byte_data(Device_Address, GYRO_CONFIG, 24)

            bus.write_byte_data(Device_Address, INT_ENABLE, 1)
```

In this lines, we are defining a function called `MPU_Init()`. This will be used to initialize the **inertial measurement unit (IMU)** sensor. In this function, we are using a method called `write_byte_data()` from the library `bus`. What it does is that it writes the data to a specific register declared in the argument. The data written using this function would be of a byte in size. Now we are declaring `Device_Address`. That is, the data written would be on the connected device's address. The second argument `SMPLRT_DIV` will tell the address of the register in hexadecimal. Hence, the value of `SMPLRT_DIV` would be used as the address. The last argument is the data that needs to be written, which in our case is 7. Similarly, the following would be the values passed to the device:

- `PWR_MGMT_1`: 1
- `CONFIG`: 0
- `GYRO_CONFIG`: 24
- `INT_ENABLE`: 1

These values would be required to set up the sensor. What these values are doing is not of an importance to us at this point. However, if you wish to know, then you can use the data sheet of the IMU MPU 6050 and get what all these registers are doing in detail:

```
def read_raw_data(addr):
        high = bus.read_byte_data(Device_Address, addr)
        low = bus.read_byte_data(Device_Address, addr+1)
```

Here, we are defining a function called `read_raw_data(addr)` reading the address from the device and then register where we are reading the address from is `addr` for the `high` variable and `addr+1` for the `low` variable.

```
        value = ((high << 8) | low)
```

Once the data has been acquired then it is being processed by the following statement `value = ((high << 8) | low)` what this does is that shifts the value of the high variable hence if the data of the variable high in binary is `10111011`, `(high <<8)` would transform this value to `1011101100000000`. Once that is done the and operator would add the eight digit value to the newly calculated value of high. Making the output a 16 bit integer. Now you must be thinking why did we do this?

The value which is being given by the MPU 6050 for any reading is 16 bit. However the registers of MPU 6050 are 8 bit in size. Now what MPU 6050 does is that it stores the value of any sensor in the registers based on the position of the bits. That is the most significant 8 bits would be stored in the first address and the rest of the least significant 8 bits would be stored in the next address that is `addr+1`:

```
if(value > 32768):
        value = value - 65535
    return value
```

As we understood in the last line, the output data from the sensor would be in a 16 bit format. When the sensor would be in the normal position this reading would be lying somewhere in the middle. If the value is more than the middle reading we would subtract the value by `65535`, hence providing us a negative value for every value which is over the middle reading. This would give us a sense of direction without doing much brain work. If the values are positive the tilt is in one direction and if negative then in other direction.

```
acc_x = read_raw_data(ACCEL_XOUT_H)
acc_y = read_raw_data(ACCEL_YOUT_H)
acc_z = read_raw_data(ACCEL_ZOUT_H)

gyro_x = read_raw_data(GYRO_XOUT_H)
gyro_y = read_raw_data(GYRO_YOUT_H)
gyro_z = read_raw_data(GYRO_ZOUT_H)
```

Now that we have defined the function called `read_raw_data()` we can start reading the data from different sensors. These sensors would be saving the data onto different addresses. These lists of addresses we have mentioned earlier. Hence by passing that data to the function we can get to know the reading of every single sensor. All these readings are being calculated and the data is stored in a variable.

```
print("Ax="+str(Ax)+"Ay="+str(Ay)+"Az="+str(Az)+"Gx="+str(Gx)+"Gy="+str(Gy)+"G
z="+str(Gz))
```

In this line we are simply printing the values of each of the variables corresponding to each of the sensors.

Now once you run this code you will see the values of each of the sensors coming out and this will change as you change the orientation or acceleration. Explore the reading and how they are changing in respect to movement. I'm sure it would give you a plentiful idea about the sensor. So go ahead and enjoy!

Gesture-controlled car

We have seen how we can extract the data from IMU. Now its time to put that data to work. In this chapter we will be controlling our robotic vehicle just with the tilt of our hand. So in essence it will be a gesture-controlled robotic vehicle. Now to do so, lets go ahead and connect the Raspberry Pi as follows:

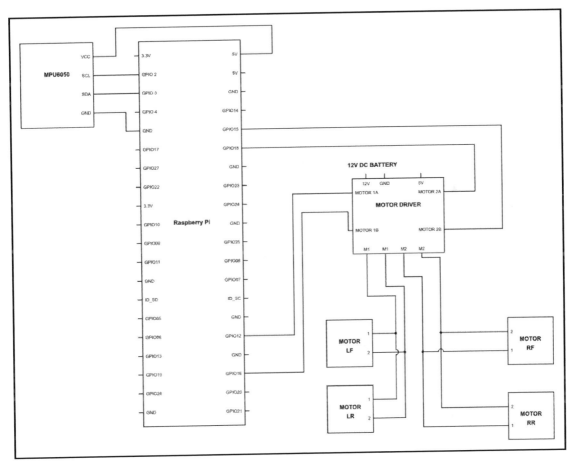

Make sure you attach a sufficiently long wire for the sensor, do not exceed 1 meter at any point and use it as a remote control for your vehicle. Once connected upload the following code:

```
import smbus
from time import sleep
import RPi.GPIO as GPIO
int1 = 12
int2 = 16
int3 = 18
int4 = 15
GPIO.setup(int1, GPIO.OUT)
GPIO.setup(int2, GPIO.OUT)
GPIO.setup(int3, GPIO.OUT)
GPIO.setup(int4, GPIO.OUT)
PWM1 = GPIO.PWM(12, 100)
PWM2 = GPIO.PWM(16, 100)
PWM3 = GPIO.PWM(18, 100)
PWM4 = GPIO.PWM(15, 100)
PWM1.start(0)
PWM2.start(0)
PWM3.start(0)
PWM4.start(0)
PWR_MGMT_1 = 0x6B
SMPLRT_DIV = 0x19
CONFIG = 0x1A
GYRO_CONFIG = 0x1B
INT_ENABLE = 0x38
ACCEL_XOUT_H = 0x3B
ACCEL_YOUT_H = 0x3D
ACCEL_ZOUT_H = 0x3F
GYRO_XOUT_H = 0x43
GYRO_YOUT_H = 0x45
GYRO_ZOUT_H = 0x47

def MPU_Init():
  bus.write_byte_data(Device_Address, SMPLRT_DIV, 7)
  bus.write_byte_data(Device_Address, PWR_MGMT_1, 1)
  bus.write_byte_data(Device_Address, CONFIG, 0)
  bus.write_byte_data(Device_Address, GYRO_CONFIG, 24)
  bus.write_byte_data(Device_Address, INT_ENABLE, 1)

def read_raw_data(addr):
  high = bus.read_byte_data(Device_Address, addr)
  low = bus.read_byte_data(Device_Address, addr+1)
  value = ((high << 8) | low)
  if(value > 32768):
```

```
    value = value - 65536
    return value
  bus = smbus.SMBus(1)
  Device_Address = 0x68

MPU_Init()
while True:
    acc_x = read_raw_data(ACCEL_XOUT_H)
    acc_y = read_raw_data(ACCEL_YOUT_H)
    acc_z = read_raw_data(ACCEL_ZOUT_H)
    gyro_x = read_raw_data(GYRO_XOUT_H)
    gyro_y = read_raw_data(GYRO_YOUT_H)
    gyro_z = read_raw_data(GYRO_ZOUT_H)
    Ax = (gyro_x/327)
    Ay = (gyro_y/327)
    for Ax > 20:
      PWM1.changeDutyCycle(Ax)
      PWM3.changeDutyCycle(Ax)
    for Ax < -20:
      PWM2.changeDutyCycle(Ax)
      PWM4.changeDutyCycle(Ax)

    for Ay > 20:
      PWM1.changeDutyCycle(Ax)
      PWM4.changeDutyCycle(Ax)
    for Ay < -20:
      PWM2.changeDutyCycle(Ax)
      PWM3.changeDutyCycle(Ax)
```

As you would have seen the code is almost the same till the time we reach the `while True` loop. Thereafter we have done a small trick. So let's see what it is.

```
    Ax = (gyro_x/327)
    Ay = (gyro_y/327)
```

When the accelerometer is in the middle or in the flat lying position the value would be close to 32768, which would be the central reading. Hence to find out what percentage we have tilted front or back we are using this line. To do that we are dividing it by 327. What it does is, it gives a reading in between 0 - 100. For example, if raw reading is gryo_x = 21000, gyro_x/327 = 64.22. Now 64.22 would be reading of tilt in the percentage value. This is important step for us as, this reading will help us determine the DutyCycle that we have to provide to the motors drivers.

```
for Ax < -20:
        PWM2.changeDutyCycle(Ax)
        PWM4.changeDutyCycle(Ax)
```

This step is very simple, what we have done is simply taken a threshold for the readings beyond which the PWM would be provided to the motors. The DutyCycle for the PWM being provided to the motors would be directly proportional to the angle of tilt.

```
for Ay < -20:
        PWM2.changeDutyCycle(Ax)
        PWM3.changeDutyCycle(Ax)
```

Just like we did before, in case the tilt is in another direction, then the motor drivers pins corresponding to the rear direction would be made high making it go backwards. The speed as before would be proportional to the tilt.

```
for Ay > 20:
        PWM1.changeDutyCycle(Ax)
        PWM4.changeDutyCycle(Ax)
```

In this line, we are making the robotic vehicle turn in one direction. As before, due to the percentage value of tilt the DutyCycle will change and hence change the rate of turn. As you can see the robot's wheels will turn opposite to each other, hence the turn will be made while being on its axis.

Sometimes while using various libraries, the raw outputs can vary. To make sure your code works fine, firstly see the raw readings which you are getting. Once you get the readings write on a piece of paper what are the flat-line reading and maximum and minimum readings. These readings can change based on the made of the sensors as well. (There are a lot of counterfeits that does not give the same readings.) Once you see the entire span of the reading then you can make the desirable adjustment to the algorithms and make it work.

Go ahead, see how you can control it just by your hand gestures.

Making it more advanced

In the previous chapter we have seen that we are making the car turn in any of the directions just based on our hand movements, however there is a problem with the previous code. Firstly the car is moving in one direction at a time, that is it's going either forward or backward or turning left or right.

It was not able to make a banking turn based on the hand gestures itself. To make it capable of doing so, we need to make the code even smarter. The overall connections to the robot would be exactly the same. But the code would be slightly different, so let's see what it is:

```
import smbus
from time import sleep
import RPi.GPIO as GPIO
int1 = 12
int2 = 16
int3 = 18
int4 = 15
GPIO.setup(int1, GPIO.OUT)
GPIO.setup(int2, GPIO.OUT)
GPIO.setup(int3, GPIO.OUT)
GPIO.setup(int4, GPIO.OUT)
PWM1 = GPIO.PWM(12, 100)
PWM2 = GPIO.PWM(16, 100)
PWM3 = GPIO.PWM(18, 100)
PWM4 = GPIO.PWM(15, 100)
PWM1.start(0)
PWM2.start(0)
PWM3.start(0)
PWM4.start(0)
PWR_MGMT_1 = 0x6B
SMPLRT_DIV = 0x19
CONFIG = 0x1A
GYRO_CONFIG = 0x1B
INT_ENABLE = 0x38
ACCEL_XOUT_H = 0x3B
ACCEL_YOUT_H = 0x3D
ACCEL_ZOUT_H = 0x3F
GYRO_XOUT_H = 0x43
GYRO_YOUT_H = 0x45
GYRO_ZOUT_H = 0x47

def MPU_Init():
    bus.write_byte_data(Device_Address, SMPLRT_DIV, 7)
    bus.write_byte_data(Device_Address, PWR_MGMT_1, 1)
    bus.write_byte_data(Device_Address, CONFIG, 0)
```

```
      bus.write_byte_data(Device_Address, GYRO_CONFIG, 24)
      bus.write_byte_data(Device_Address, INT_ENABLE, 1)
  def read_raw_data(addr):
    high = bus.read_byte_data(Device_Address, addr)
    low = bus.read_byte_data(Device_Address, addr+1)
    value = ((high << 8) | low)
    if(value > 32768):
      value = value - 65536
      return value
  bus = smbus.SMBus(1)
  Device_Address = 0x68
MPU_Init()
while True:
  acc_x = read_raw_data(ACCEL_XOUT_H)
  acc_y = read_raw_data(ACCEL_YOUT_H)
  acc_z = read_raw_data(ACCEL_ZOUT_H)
  gyro_x = read_raw_data(GYRO_XOUT_H)
  gyro_y = read_raw_data(GYRO_YOUT_H)
  gyro_z = read_raw_data(GYRO_ZOUT_H)
  Ax = (gyro_x/160)- 16384
 Ay = (gyro_y/160)-16384
  if Ax > 20:
    if Ay > 20:
      dc1 = Ax - Ay
      PWM1.changeDutyCycle(dc1)
      dc3 = Ax + Ay
      PWM3.changeDutyCycle(dc3)
   elif Ay <- 20:
     dc2 = Ax + Ay
     PWM1.changeDutyCycle(dc)
     dc4 = Ax - Ay
     PWM3.changeDutyCycle(dc4)
   else:
     dc1=Ax
     PWM1.changeDutyCycle(dc)
     dc3=Ax
     PWM3.changeDutyCycle(dc)
   if Ax < -20:
     if Ay > 20:
       dc1 = Ax - Ay
       dc3 = Ax + Ay
       PWM1.changeDutyCycle(dc1)
       PWM3.changeDutyCycle(dc3)
     if Ay <- 20:
       dc2 = Ax + Ay
       dc4 = Ax - Ay
       PWM2.changeDutyCycle(dc2)
       PWM4.changeDutyCycle(dc4)
```

```
    else:
        dc2=Ax
        dc4=Ax
        PWM2.changeDutyCycle(dc2)
        PWM4.changeDutyCycle(dc4)
```

Now let's see all the changes we have done to the code. The entire sensing mechanism is the same, however, data processing has a major overhaul. So let's see what it is:

```
If Ax > 20:
    if Ay > 20:
        dc1 = Ax - Ay
        PWM1.changeDutyCycle(dc1)
        dc3 = Ax + Ay
        PWM3.changeDutyCycle(dc3)
```

Now here we are comparing the value of Ax. If the value of Ax > 20 then the code below it would run. We have done this because, the accelerometer is extremely sensitive and can sense slightest vibration. Due to this there can be erroneous output. So to filter it we have a threshold value of 20. That is till the time the accelerometer is 20% tilted, this code will not come into effect. Similarly we are doing this for the y axis as well. Once that is done that percentage value is given to the line dc1 = Ax - Ay. What this is doing is taking the tilt in x axis which is the forward axis and subtracting it with movement of Y. In the second line we are doing the same thing with the other side of the motors however rather than subtracting the value of Y we are adding it. Hence what it would do is to create a difference of speed in between the speed of motors on the opposite ends. This speed difference would be directly proposal to the angular tilt of the Y axis. Hence more the tilt, the more would be the change in the speed and more would be the angle of the turn.

```
    elif Ay <- 20:

        dc2 = Ax + Ay
        PWM1.changeDutyCycle(dc)
        dc4 = Ax - Ay
        PWM3.changeDutyCycle(dc4)
```

In the next line what we have done is that we have made a condition for the tilt on the other side of the accelerometer by sensing Ay < -20. If the value is smaller than -20 then the following algorithm would come into play.

Here the lines are exactly the same. However the mathematical operators have been inverted. Hence for the first motor, instead of subtracting the value of Y now we are adding it. On the other hand for the second motor rather than adding the value we are subtracting it.

```
Else:

    dc1=Ax
    PWM1.changeDutyCycle(dc)
    dc3=Ax
    PWM3.changeDutyCycle(dc)
```

Finally, if the value of Ax is greater than 20 but the value of Ay is between −20 and +20 then we will assume that the car has to go straight. Hence the value of the Ax is directly getting passed on to both the motors, making it go entirely straight.

Summary

In this chapter, we have understood on how accelerometer and gyros functions. We have taken the raw data of the gyro and accelerometer and utilized it to make a gesture-controlled robot. Finally, onto the next and final chapter of the book, where we will continue our journey with the most exciting chapter you were looking forward to.

18
Making a Robotic Arm

Finally, we are where most of us have wanted to be since the start of this book. Making a robotic arm! In this chapter, we will learn the concepts behind the working of a robotic arm. Undoubtedly, we will also be making a robotic arm for our personal use as well that can do limitless things for us.

Basics of a robotic arm

If you see a human body, then one of the most distinctive parts that makes us able to be different than most other species is the arm. It is the part of the body that we use to do most of the work.

The human arm is a very complex mechanism of joints and muscles that work in tandem to give it the dexterity that we know it for. Take an example of our shoulder joint. If you pay attention, then you will notice that it has the ability to move up and down, right and left, and even rotate on its own axis, and all this while it just has one single joint, which we know as a ball joint.

When we talk about a robotic arm on a robot, we are undoubtedly talking about a complex arrangement of actuators with the body, otherwise known as a chassis, to get the desired motion in a three-dimensional space.

Now, let's understand some of the basic parts of any robotic arm. The first parts are the actuators. We can use motors to control the robotic arm; however, as we have studied earlier, using the motors we have used before will not be the ideal solution for it as it cannot hold its position neither does it have a feedback mechanism. So we are left with only one option, that is, to use servo motors. As we know, they have a handful of torque and have the ability to know where it is and to hold its position for as long as we want.

The second part of the robot is the chassis, that is, the part that holds all the motors together and provides structural support to the robot. This has to be made in such a way that it provides motion in all the desirable axis to any given joint. This is important as a single servo can only provide motion in one single axis. However, there are multiple places in which complex arrangement can be used to make the robot traverse in multiple axes. Also, the chassis should be rigid, which is extremely important. As we all know, all the material on this planet have certain level of flexibility. Also, the construction of the material depends on how noncompliant the material would be. This serves a very important purpose of repeatability.

Now, what is repeatability? As you might have seen in industries or any manufacturing units, the robots are installed and they do the same task over and over again. This is possible as the robots are programmed to perform a specific set of functions under specific circumstances. Now, let's say that the chassis of the robot is not rigid. In such a case, even if the servos are 100% precise and get to the exact same position over and over again, still the robot may actually differ from its actual goal position. This happens as there may be some flexibility in the chassis, which is why the final position may differ. Hence, a right chassis is a must. It becomes even more important when we are talking about large robots, as even the slightest of deformation can lead to a very large change in the final position of the arm.

One very common terminology which we use while talking about the robot arm is the end effector. This is basically the end of the robot arm, which will be doing all the final work for us. End effector in the case of a real human arm can be considered the hand. This is at the top of the arm and all the movement of the arm is basically to articulate the position of the hand in a three-dimensional space. Also, it is the hand that picks up the objects or does the necessary physical action. Hence, the term end effector.

Now, as the robotic arm is moving in a three dimensional space, it becomes a real big problem to define the axis in which the motion is happening. Hence, instead of using the axis to define the motion, we generally use the type of motion being performed, which gives us a realistic idea of what the motion is and in which axis it may be on. To analyze the motion, we use the concept of **Yaw Pitch and Roll (YPR)**.

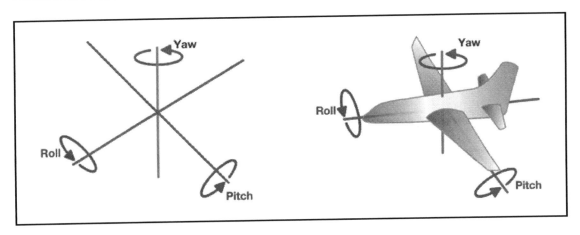

The preceding diagram will clear most of the doubts about YPR. This concept is generally used in aircrafts; however, it is an essential part of a robotic hand as well. So, as you can see from the preceding figure, when the nose of the plane goes up or down, it will be considered as pitch movement. Similarly, if the aircraft changes the heading, then the **Yaw** can be considered to change accordingly—the **Yaw** is nothing but the movement of aircraft in the *y* axis. Finally, we have something called **Roll**. It is used to understand the angel of rotation. As you can see, all these three entities are independent to each other and chasing any of it will not have any effect on the other. This concept is also useful as no matter what the orientation of the aircraft is, the YPR would still be unchanged and very much understandable. Hence, we take this concept straight from the aircraft directly to our robots.

Finally, how can we forget about the processing unit? It is the unit that commands all the actuators and does the coordination and the decision making. This processing unit in our case is Raspberry Pi, which will command all the actuators. All of these preceding components make up a robotic arm.

Degrees of freedom

Not every robotic arm is the same. They have different load ratings, that is, the maximum load that the end effector can take, the speed and reach, that is, how far the end effector can reach. However, one very important part of a robotic arm is the number of motors it has. So, for every axis, you need at least one motor to make the robot traverse in that axis. For example, a human arm has three-dimensional freedom in the shoulder joint. Hence, to mimic that joint, you will need a motor for every axis, that is, a minimum of three motors are required for the arm to move in all the three axis, independently. Similarly, when we talk about the elbow joint of our hand, it can only traverse in two dimensions. That is the closing and opening of the arm and the finally the rotation of the arm—the elbow does not move in the third dimension. Hence, to replicate its motion, we need at least two motors, so that we an move the robot in the w axis.

From what we have understood so far, we can safely assume that the more the number of motors, the more dexterous the robot would also be. This is mostly the case; however, you may use multiple motors to make the robot turn in a single axis itself. In such a scenario, the basic concept of counting the number of actuators to determine the dexterity of the robot will not work. So how do we determine how dexterous the robot is?

We have a concept called **degrees of freedom** (DOF). If I go by the standard definition, then I can be very sure that you will be left confused as to what it actually means. If you are not convinced, then try finding out on Google yourself. A DOF, in very simple and plain English, is a joint that can independently move on any given axis. So, for example, if we are talking about a shoulder joint, then we have movement in all the three axis. Hence, the degrees of freedom would be three. Now, let's take into consideration the elbow joint of our arm. As it can only move in pitch and roll, hence there are two DOFs that we end up with. If we connect the shoulder joint with the elbow joint, then the DOF will be added up and the whole system would be called to have six DOFs. Keep in mind that this definition is a very simplified one. There are multiple complexities that you will encounter should you choose to dig deeper.

Now, most of the robotic arms that you will encounter would be having close to six DOFs. Though you may say that it is less than what human arms have, in practicality, it does most of the work and obviously having less DOFs means less number of motors leading to lower cost and obviously lower complexity in programming. Hence, we try to use as few DOFs as possible.

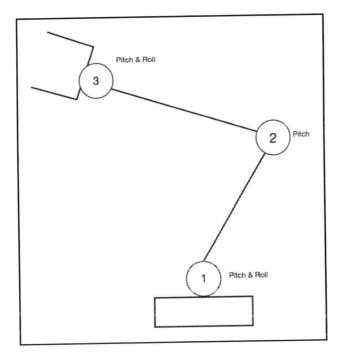

Now, in the preceding diagram, you can see a typical robotic arm which has six DOFs. The base actuator marked by number **1** gives the freedom of rolling and altering the pitch. The elbow actuators marked by number **2** add only one DOF of the pitch to the robot. Furthermore, joint number **3** is has the ability to travel in **Pitch & Roll**. Finally, we have the end actuator as the gripper here; the gripper in itself has one DOF. So, cumulatively, we can say that the robot is a six-DOF robot.

Power house

There is one unit that we have been using in all our projects, but I want to emphasize on it in this chapter. This unit is the power unit. The reason we are talking about it is because in this chapter we will be controlling multiple servos. When we are talking about multiple servos, naturally we will be talking about a lot of power consumption. In the robot arm, we have six servo motors. Now, depending upon the make and model of the motor, the power consumption will vary. But keeping yourself on a safer side and assuming every servo's power consumption to be around 1 amp would be a good idea. Most of the power supply you would be using might not be able to give you this much of burst current. So what should we do?

We can take the easy approach of taking a higher power output. But, instead, we can take the unconventional route. We can have a battery that can deliver this much of power when needed. But, the question is, will any battery solve our purpose? Obviously, the answer would be no.

There are multiple types of batteries that exist. These batteries can be distinguished based on the following parameters:

- Voltage
- Capacity
- Power to weight ratio
- Maximum charge and discharge rate
- Chemical composition

These are covered in detail in the upcoming subsections.

Voltage

Voltage is the overall potential difference that the battery can create. Every battery has a specific voltage that it delivers. One thing to remember is that this voltage will vary slightly based on the charge condition of the battery. That is, when a 12V battery is fully charged, it may be giving an output of 12.6V. However, when it gets fully discharged, it may reach up to 11.4V. So, what battery voltage means is the nominal voltage that the battery would be providing.

Capacity

Now, the second parameter is the capacity. Generally, when you buy a battery, you will see its capacity in **milliampere hour (mAh)** or in **ampere hours (Ah)**. This is a very simple term. Let me explain this term to you using an example. Let's say you have a battery with a capacity of 5 Ah. Now, if I draw 5 amperes continuously for 1 hour, then the battery will be completely discharged. On the contrary, if I draw 10 amperes continuously, then the battery will be discharged in half an hour. With this, we can also derive the overall power that the battery has using the following simple formula: *Overall Power in Watts = Nominal Voltage of Battery x Overall battery capacity of battery in amperes*

Hence, if you have a battery of 12V, which has a capacity of 10 Ah, then the overall capacity in watts will be 120 watts.

Power-to-weight ratio

In the previous chapter, we have understood that weight plays a very crucial role in robotics and if we increase the weight of the robot, then the force required to move it can exponentially go up. Hence, the concept of power to weight ratio comes into play. We always prefer a battery, which is extremely lightweight and delivers a large sum of power in respect to the weight. The equation for the power-to-weight ratio can be defined as follows: *Power to weight ratio in watt hour/kg = Maximum Power in watts / Overall weight of battery in kg.*

Now, let's say a battery is providing a power of 500 watts and the weight is 5 kg, then the power to weight ratio will be 100 Wh/kg. The higher the power to weight ratio, the better the battery is.

Maximum charge and discharge rate

This is perhaps one of the most crucial parts of the battery. Often the batteries are capable of running the robot for a span of 1 hour. However, the power consumption of robots is not constant. Let's say for 90% of the time, our robotic arm is consuming 2 amperes of power, so the battery capacity is of 2 Ah. However, at some points of time during the operation, the robot needs all the motors to work on peak power. The peak power consumption of the robot is around 6 amperes. Now, the question is, will the battery of 2 Ah be able to provide 6 amperes power to the robot?

This is a very practical challenge. You may say, it is better to go with a battery that is much bigger than a 2 Ah battery. But, as you know, it will increase the weight phenomenally. So what's the solution?

There is something called peak discharge current. This is denoted by C rating. So, if our battery is of 1 C rating then a 2 Ah battery will only be able to give us a maximum of 2 Ah of power supply at any given time. However, if the battery is of 10 C rating, then it should be able to provide a burst power supply of up to 20 amperes. These days, you can find batteries that can give a burst power supply of up to 100 C or even more. The reason we have this is because the peak power consumption of robots can be exponentially higher than their constant power consumption. If, at any point, the battery is not able to pull ample amount of power, then the robot would behave erroneously and can even shut down.

The second part of this story is the charge rating. This is the maximum charge current that you can provide to the battery. It is also denoted by the same C rating. So, if the C rating is 0.5, then you can provide a max of 1 ampere of charge to a 2 Ah battery.

In other words, the fastest you can charge a battery would be in 2 hours.

Chemical composition

There are different types of batteries that you can find on the market these are broadly segregated by their chemical composition. All of these batteries have their own pros and cons. Hence, we cannot say that one is better than the other. It is always a trade-off between various factors. The following is a list of batteries you can find on the market along with their pros and cons:

Battery	Peak power output	Power-to-weight ratio	Price
Wet cell	Low	Extremely low	Cheapest
Nickel metal hydride	Medium	Low	Cheap
Lithium ion	High	Good	High
Lithium polymer	Extremely high	Extremely good	Extremely high

As you can see from this table, the peak power output is something which we highly want and so is the good power-to-weight ratio; hence, spending a good amount of money on a lithium polymer battery makes sense.

These batteries, at a minimum, have a 20 C rating with a power-to-weight ratio around five times higher than the normal wet cell batteries. However, they can be up to 10 times more expensive than the normal wet cell batteries.

Now we know which batteries to choose for those higher current requirements. A lithium polymer battery of 11.1V and 2200 mAh will not cost you more than $20 and will provide you with immense power that you may never need. So, we have the power supply issue sorted. Now it's time to go ahead and make the robotic hand operational.

Finding the limits

The robotic arm kit is a fairly easy one to procure from eBay or Amazon. This is not very difficult to assemble and will require a few hours to prepare. Some of the robotic arm kits might not ship with servo motors, in which case, you may have to order it separately. I would say go for the kit that comes bundled with the servos, as there can be compatibility issues if you choose to order servos separately.

As you know, these servos will work using PWM and it's not hard to control them either. So, let's go straight onto it and see what we can do. Once you have assembled the robotic arm kit, connect the wires of the servos as follows:

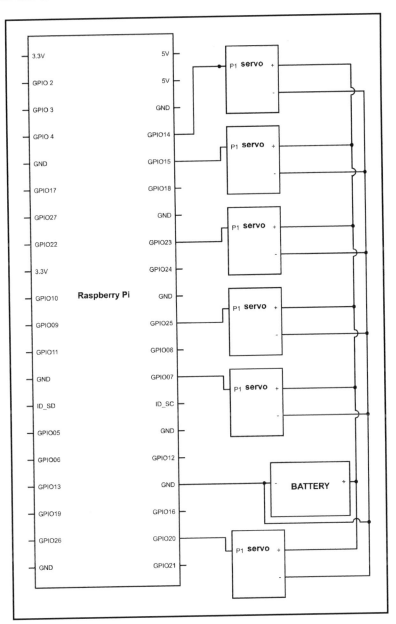

Now, firstly, we need to know what are the maximum physical limits of every single servo connected on our robot. There are various techniques to do that. The very basic one is to measure it physically. This method can be good but you won't be able to ever utilize the full potential of the servo motor as you would be having some degree of error in measuring. Hence, the value you put in the servo will be slightly less than what you think it can go to. The second method is by manually feeding the data and finding out the exact angle. So, let's go ahead with the second way of doing things and upload the following code:

```
import RPi.GPIO as GPIO
import time

GPIO.setmode(GPIO.BCM)
GPIO.setup(14,GPIO.OUT)
GPIO.setup(16,GPIO.OUT)
GPIO.setup(18,GPIO.OUT)
GPIO.setup(20,GPIO.OUT)
GPIO.setup(21,GPIO.OUT)
GPIO.setup(22,GPIO.OUT)


GPIO.setwarnings(False)

pwm1 = GPIO.PWM(14, 50)
pwm2 = GPIO.PWM(16, 50)
pwm3 = GPIO.PWM(18, 50)
pwm4 = GPIO.PWM(20, 50)
pwm5 = GPIO.PWM(21, 50)
pwm6 = GPIO.PWM(22, 50)

pwm1.start(0)
pwm2.start(0)
pwm3.start(0)
pwm4.start(0)
pwm5.start(0)
pwm6.start(0)

def cvt_angle(angle):
    dc = float(angle/90) + 0.5
    return dc

while 1:

 j = input('select servo')

 if j == 1:

  i = input('select value to rotate')
```

```
pwm1.ChangeDutyCycle(cvt_angle(i))
time.sleep(2)
pwm1.ChangeDutyCycle(cvt_angle(90))

elif j ==2:

i = input('select value to rotate')
pwm2.ChangeDutyCycle(cvt_angle(i))
time.sleep(2)
pwm2.ChangeDutyCycle(cvt_angle(90))


elif j ==3:

i = input('select value to rotate')
pwm3.ChangeDutyCycle(cvt_angle(i))
time.sleep(2)
pwm3.ChangeDutyCycle(cvt_angle(90))

elif j ==4:

i = input('select value to rotate')
pwm4.ChangeDutyCycle(cvt_angle(i))
time.sleep(2)
pwm4.ChangeDutyCycle(cvt_angle(90))

elif j ==5:

i = input('select value to rotate')
pwm5.ChangeDutyCycle(cvt_angle(i))
time.sleep(2)
pwm5.ChangeDutyCycle(cvt_angle(90))

elif j ==6:

i = input('select value to rotate')
pwm6.ChangeDutyCycle(cvt_angle(i))
time.sleep(2)
pwm6.ChangeDutyCycle(cvt_angle(90))  }
```

Now, let's see what this code is doing. This code may look pretty elaborate, but what it is doing is extremely simple.

```
j = input('select servo from 1-6')
```

Using the preceding line of code, we are printing the statement for the user `select servo from 1-6`. When the user enters a value of the servo, this value gets stored in a variable `j`:

```
if j == 1:

    i = input('select value to rotate')
    pwm1.ChangeDutyCycle(cvt_angle(i))
    time.sleep(2)
    pwm1.ChangeDutyCycle(cvt_angle(90))
```

This `if` condition here checks for the value of `j`. If in this line, `j=1`, then it will run the code corresponding to the servo number 1. Inside this code, the first line will print `select value to rotate`. Once this is done, the program will then wait for user input. Once the user inputs any value, then it will be stored in a variable called `I`. Thereafter, using the `cvt_angle(i)` function, the value which the user has input into the system will be converted to its corresponding duty cycle value. This duty cycle value will be fetched to the `pwm1.ChangeDutyCycle()` argument thereby giving the robot that very certain angle in the particular joint that you want. Due to the `time.sleep(2)` function, the servo will wait to go over to the next line. Thereafter, we are using the line `pwm1.ChangeDutyCycle(cvt_angle(90))`, which will bring it back to 90 degrees.

You may ask, why are we doing this? This is for a very important reason. Let's say you have given it a command to go beyond its physical limit. If that's the case, then the servo will keep on trying to move in that direction no matter what. However, due to the physical constrain, it will not be able to go ahead. Once this happens, then, within a few seconds, you will see blue smoke coming out of your servo indicating its death. The problem is that making such type of errors is very easy and the loss is quite noticeable. Hence, to prevent this, we quickly bring it back to the central position where it does not have any possibility of burning up.

Now, as per the preceding code, the same is done for servos 1-6 through the robot. Now that you know what is happening, it's time to take a pen and a paper and start giving servos the angular values. Do remember that the final goal of this code is to find out the maximum limits. So, let's start doing it starting from 90 degrees onwards. Give it a value on either side and not down until which value you can take it. Make a list on a paper as we will require it for our next code.

Making the robot safe

In the previous part of the chapter, with our multiple attempts, we have been able to find the maximum positions for each of the servos. Now it's time to use these values. In this chapter, we will be programming the servos for what its absolute maximums are. In this program, we will make sure that servos will never need to travel even a degree beyond the defined parameters on both the sides. If the user gives a value beyond it, then it will simply choose to ignore the user inputs instead of causing self damage.

So, let's see how to get it done. There are some parts of this program, where the numeric values have been bold. These are the values that you need to replace with the values which we have noted in the previous section of this chapter. For example, for servo 1, the values noted down are 23 and 170 as the maximum values for either side. Hence, the change in the code will be from if a[0] < 160 and a[0] > 30 to ifa[0] < 170 and a[0] > 23. Similarly, for every servo, the same procedure has to be followed:

```
import RPi.GPIO as GPIO
import time

GPIO.setmode(GPIO.BCM)
GPIO.setup(14,GPIO.OUT)
GPIO.setup(16,GPIO.OUT)
GPIO.setup(18,GPIO.OUT)
GPIO.setup(20,GPIO.OUT)
GPIO.setup(21,GPIO.OUT)
GPIO.setup(22,GPIO.OUT)


GPIO.setwarnings(False)

pwm1 = GPIO.PWM(14, 50)
pwm2 = GPIO.PWM(16, 50)
pwm3 = GPIO.PWM(18, 50)
pwm4 = GPIO.PWM(20, 50)
pwm5 = GPIO.PWM(21, 50)
pwm6 = GPIO.PWM(22, 50)

pwm1.start(cvt_angle(90))
pwm2.start(cvt_angle(90))
pwm3.start(cvt_angle(90))
pwm4.start(cvt_angle(90))
pwm5.start(cvt_angle(90))
pwm6.start(cvt_angle(90))

def cvt_angle(angle):
```

```
    dc = float(angle/90) + 0.5
    return dc

while True:

    a = raw_input("enter a list of 6 values")
    if a[0] < 160 and  a[0] > 30:
        pwm1.ChangeDutyCycle(cvt_angle(a[0]))

    if a[1] < 160 and  a[1] > 30:
        pwm2.ChangeDutyCycle(cvt)angle(a[1]))

    if a[0] < 160 and  a[0] > 30:
        pwm3.ChangeDutyCycle(cvt_angle(a[2]))

    if a[0] < 160 and  a[0] > 30:
        pwm4.ChangeDutyCycle(cvt_angle(a[3]))

    if a[0] < 160 and  a[0] > 30:
        pwm5.ChangeDutyCycle(cvt_angle(a[4]))

    if a[0] < 160 and  a[0] > 30:
        pwm6.ChangeDutyCycle(cvt_angle(a[5]))}
```

Now, in this code, we have done something very rudimentary. You can safely say that all we have done is put the `ChangeDutyCycle()` function inside an `if` statement. This `if` statement will govern whether the servo will move or stay still in its own position. To some, it may seem very naive to have this program in a special section. But, trust me, it is not. This statement will now be used as a part of every program from here on. All the code written for the movement of the servos will have to check the final values going to the servos through this `if` statement; hence, a basic visualization of code is extremely necessary.

Now that the explanation is done, it's time for you to give different commands and see whether they are working within the safe working limits.

Programming multiple frames

In the previous chapter, we have learned the basics of how to make sure that the robot is working under safe limits. In this chapter, we will be looking at how a robot can be made to do different activities at a click of a button, instead of typing the values one by one.

To do this, we will need to understand some advanced concepts of motion. Whenever you watch any video or play any video games, then you must have come across the term **frames per second** (**FPS**). If you haven't heard this term, then let me explain it for you. Every video made right now is actually made by still images. These still images are captured by cameras that click 25-30 times in a second. When these images are played back on the screen at the same rate at which they are captured, it forms a smooth video.

Similarly, in robots, we do have the concept of frames. These frames, however, are not images but instead multiple steps that the robot has to follow to achieve a specific motion. In a simple robotic program, there could be simply two frames, that is, the initial frame and the final frame. These two frames will correspond to the initial position or the final position.

However, in the real world, this is not always possible, as whenever the robot goes directly from the initial position to the final position, it tends a specific path with a specific curvature. However, there can be obstacles in that path or this path would not be desired as the path that needs to be followed could be a different one. Hence, we need frames. These frames not only define the robot's motion from the initial position to the final position, but also break down the transition from these two positions into multiple steps making the robot follow the desired path.

This can be referred as frame programming, which we will cover in this chapter. One thing to keep in mind is that more the number of frames, smoother will be the functioning of the robot. Do you remember the CCTV footage we saw? We could say it's not smooth and has a lot of jerkiness. This is due to the low frame rate of the CCTV camera. Instead of working on 30 FPS, they work on 15 FPS. This is done to reduce the storage space of the video. However, if you see the latest videos, there are some games and videos with much higher frame rate than normal. Some of our latest camera works on 60 FPS, making the video even smoother and enjoyable to watch. The same will be the case with the robot. The more the number of frames, the smoother and controlled the motion would be. However, make sure you don't go into overkill.

Now, to move from one position to another, we will have to put the values of the angles of every single servos in the very beginning. Once fetched, it will automatically start to execute these values one by one. To do this, go ahead and write the following code:

```
import RPi.GPIO as GPIO
import time

GPIO.setmode(GPIO.BCM)
GPIO.setup(14,GPIO.OUT)
GPIO.setup(16,GPIO.OUT)
GPIO.setup(18,GPIO.OUT)
GPIO.setup(20,GPIO.OUT)
```

```
GPIO.setup(21,GPIO.OUT)
GPIO.setup(22,GPIO.OUT)


GPIO.setwarnings(False)

pwm1 = GPIO.PWM(14, 50)
pwm2 = GPIO.PWM(16, 50)
pwm3 = GPIO.PWM(18, 50)
pwm4 = GPIO.PWM(20, 50)
pwm5 = GPIO.PWM(21, 50)
pwm6 = GPIO.PWM(22, 50)

pwm1.start(0)
pwm2.start(0)
pwm3.start(0)
pwm4.start(0)
pwm5.start(0)
pwm6.start(0)

def cvt_angle(angle):
    dc = float(angle/90) + 0.5
    return dc

prev0 = 90
prev1 = 90
prev2 = 90
prev3 = 90
prev4 = 90
prev5 = 90

while True:

    a = raw_input("enter a list of 6 values for motor 1")
    b = raw_input("enter a list of 6 values for motor 2")
    c = raw_input("enter a list of 6 values for motor 3")
    d = raw_input("enter a list of 6 values for motor 4")
    e = raw_input("enter a list of 6 values for motor 5")
    f = raw_input("enter a list of 6 values for motor 6")


    for i in range(6):

        if a[i] > 10 and a[i]< 180 :
            pwm1.ChangeDutyCycle(cvt_angle(a[i]))

        if b[i] > 10 and b[i] < 180:
            pwm2.ChangeDutyCycle(cvt_angle(b[i]))
```

```
if c[i] > 10 and c[i] < 180:
    pwm3.ChangeDutyCycle(cvt_angle(c[i]))

if d[i] > 10 and d[i] < 180:
    pwm4.ChangeDutyCycle(cvt_angle(d[i]))

if e[i] > 10 and e[i] < 180:
    pwm5.ChangeDutyCycle(cvt_angle(e[i]))

if f[i] > 10 and f[i] < 180:
    pwm6.ChangeDutyCycle(cvt_angle(f[i]))
```

In this program, you can see that we have replicated the previous program with some very minor changes. So, let's see what these changes are:

```
a = raw_input("enter a list of 6 values for motor 1")
b = raw_input("enter a list of 6 values for motor 2")
c = raw_input("enter a list of 6 values for motor 3")
d = raw_input("enter a list of 6 values for motor 4")
e = raw_input("enter a list of 6 values for motor 5")
f = raw_input("enter a list of 6 values for motor 6")
```

Here, we are taking the input values for each servo and storing it in a different list. For servo 1, the list a will be used; similarly, b will be used for servo 2, and so on until f. In the preceding lines of code, the robot will prompt the user to fill in the six frame values for motor 1. Then, it will ask six values for motor 2 and similarly until motor 6:

```
for i in range(6):
```

The entire program for giving PWM to the servo is concentrated in this for loop. This loop will check the value of i and increment it every time. The value of i will start from 1 and the loop will run and increment the value of i until it reaches 6.

```
if a[i] > 10 and a[i]< 180 :
    pwm1.ChangeDutyCycle(cvt_angle(a[i]))
```

In this line of the program, the value contained in the list is headed based on the value of 1. So, for the first time it will read the value of `a[1]`, which will correspond to the first value of the list `a[]`. This value should be between the safe working limits, hence the `if` loop. If it is within safe working limits, then the program in the `if` condition will work, else it won't. Inside the `if` loop, we have a simple statement:

`pwm1.ChangeDutyCycle(cvt_angle(a[I]))`. This will simply take the value of `a[1]` and convert it into the corresponding PWM value and fetch it to the `ChangeDutyCycle()` function, which will change the PWM for servo 1.

A similar program is made for the rest of the servos as well going on from servo 1 to servo 6. Hence, all of these will read the values of their corresponding list one by one and change the angle of the servo the way the user has programmed it. Furthermore, as the loop gets executed, the value of `i` will increase, hence making the program read the different values fetched in the list. Every value of the servo in the list will correspond to a different frame, hence parsing the robot through it.

So go ahead and have some fun making your robot do some awesome moves. Just take care that you be gentle to it!

Speed control

It's amazing to have made a robotic arm so easily, and with just a bit of code, we are now able to control it the way we want. However, there is one problem you might have noticed, that is, the robot is moving the way we want but not at the speed at which we want it to move. This is a very common problem while using the digital PWM-based servos.

These servos do not have a built-in speed control. Their control system is programmed to move the servo as fast as they can to reach the goal position. Hence, to control the speed, we will have to play with the program itself and give it a smooth linear progression.

The speed control can be done through a few different techniques. So, without much talking, let's go and see the code. Before you write it, read it and go through the code once and then see the following explanation to it. Thereafter, you will have a better idea of what we are doing. This will make writing the code faster and easier. So, let's take a look at it:

```
import RPi.GPIO as GPIO
import time

GPIO.setmode(GPIO.BCM)
GPIO.setup(14,GPIO.OUT)
GPIO.setup(16,GPIO.OUT)
GPIO.setup(18,GPIO.OUT)
GPIO.setup(20,GPIO.OUT)
GPIO.setup(21,GPIO.OUT)
GPIO.setup(22,GPIO.OUT)


GPIO.setwarnings(False)

pwm1 = GPIO.PWM(14, 50)
pwm2 = GPIO.PWM(16, 50)
pwm3 = GPIO.PWM(18, 50)
pwm4 = GPIO.PWM(20, 50)
pwm5 = GPIO.PWM(21, 50)
pwm6 = GPIO.PWM(22, 50)

pwm1.start(0)
pwm2.start(0)
pwm3.start(0)
pwm4.start(0)
pwm5.start(0)
pwm6.start(0)

def cvt_angle(angle):
    dc = float(angle/90) + 0.5
    return dc

prev0 = 90
prev1 = 90
prev2 = 90
prev3 = 90
prev4 = 90
prev5 = 90

pwm1.ChangeDutyCycle(cvt_angle(prev0))
pwm2.ChangeDutyCycle(cvt_angle(prev1))
pwm3.ChangeDutyCycle(cvt_angle(prev2))
```

```
pwm4.ChangeDutyCycle(cvt_angle(prev3))
pwm5.ChangeDutyCycle(cvt_angle(prev4))
pwm6.ChangeDutyCycle(cvt_angle(prev5))


while True:

  a = raw_input("enter a list of 6 values for motor 1")
  b = raw_input("enter a list of 6 values for motor 2")
  c = raw_input("enter a list of 6 values for motor 3")
  d = raw_input("enter a list of 6 values for motor 4")
  e = raw_input("enter a list of 6 values for motor 5")
  f = raw_input("enter a list of 6 values for motor 6")

    speed = raw_input("enter one of the following speed 0.1, 0.2, 0.5, 1")


  for i in range(6):

    while prev0 =! a[i] and prev1 =! b[i] and prev2 =! c[i] and prev3 =!
d[i] and prev4 =! e[i] and prev 5 =! f[i]

      if a[i] > 10 and a[i]< 180 :

        if prev0 > a[i]
            prev0 = prev0 - speed

        if prev0 < a[i]
            prev0 = prev0 + speed

        if prev0 = a[i]
            prev0 = prev0

        pwm1.ChangeDutyCycle(cvt_angle(prev0))



    if b[i] > 10 and b[i] < 180:

        if prev2 > b[i]
            prev2 = prev2 - speed

        if prev2 < b[i]
            prev2 = prev2 + speed

        if prev2 = b[i]
            prev2 = prev2
```

```
    pwm2.ChangeDutyCycle(cvt_angle(b[i]))


if c[i] > 10 and c[i] < 180:

    if prev3 > c[i]
        prev3 = prev3 - speed

    if prev3 < c[i]
        prev3 = prev3 + speed

    if prev3 = c[i]
        prev3 = prev3

    pwm3.ChangeDutyCycle(cvt_angle(c[i]))



if d[i] > 10 and d[i] < 180:

    if prev4 > d[i]
        prev4 = prev4 - speed

    if prev4 < d[i]
        prev4 = prev4 + speed

    if prev4 = d[i]
        prev4 = prev4

pwm4.ChangeDutyCycle(cvt_angle(d[i]))



if e[i] > 10 and e[i] < 180:
    if prev5 > e[i]
        prev5 = prev5 - speed

    if prev0 < e[i]
        prev5 = prev5 + speed

    if prev5 = e[i]
        prev5 = prev5

pwm5.ChangeDutyCycle(cvt_angle(e[i]))



if f[i] > 10 and f[i] < 180:
```

```
        if prev6 > f[i]
            prev6 = prev6 - speed

        if prev6 < f[i]
            prev6 = prev6 + speed

      if prev6 = f[i]
          prev6 = prev6

    pwm6.ChangeDutyCycle(cvt_angle(f[i]))


  flag = 0
```

In this program, there are quite a few things. We should go through them one by one to have an understanding of it. So, let's see what we are doing:

```
prev0 = 90
prev1 = 90
prev2 = 90
prev3 = 90
prev4 = 90
prev5 = 90
```

Here, we have defined six new variables with the name `prev0` to `prev5` and all of them have been allowed a value of 90. The term `prev` here stands for previous, so this will be there to indicate the previous value.

```
        while prev0 =! a[i] and prev1 =! b[i] and prev2 =! c[i] and prev3
  =! d[i]   and prev4 =! e[i] and prev 5 =! f[i]
```

After the code line `for i in range 6`, we have the preceding line of code, which is basically checking the value of `a[i]` with `prev0`. Similarly, it is checking the values of `b[i]` with `prev1` and so on. Until the time all of these are not true the `while` loop will be true and will loop the program inside it until the condition is not false. That is, all the `prev` values are exactly equal to the values of the corresponding values of the list.

Again, this may seem a little odd to you, but, trust me, it will be quite useful, which we will see in a while:

```
    if a[i] > 10 and a[i]< 180 :

      if prev0 > a[i]
          prev0 = prev0 - speed

      if prev0 < a[i]
```

```
        prev0 = prev0 + speed

    if prev0 = a[i]
        prev0 = prev0

    pwm1.ChangeDutyCycle(cvt_angle(prev0))
```

Now, here comes the real deal. This is the main program that will control the speed of the servo. In this, the first line is simple; it will check whether the value given to it is valid, that is, between the safe limits. Once that is done, it will then check whether the value of `a[Ii]` is less than or greater than the previous value. If it is greater than `a[i]`, then it will take in the previous value and decrement it with the speed specified by the user. If it is less than the value of `a[i]`, then it will increment the previous value with the speed specified.

So, if you look at it, the code is simply incrementing or decrementing the previous value every time the `while` loop is running. Now, the `while` loop will run until the value of `prev` is equal to the corresponding list value. That is, the loop will keep incrementing the value until it reaches the specified position.

Hence, lower the value of the speed, lower will be the increments every single time, thereby slowing down the speed all together.

This is the same process which will happen for all other servos as well. It may sound very complicated, but it is not! Programming is easy and will continue to remain easy each time you break it down into small pieces and understand them one by one!

Summary

In this chapter, we have understood the basics of robotic arm, its power source, and its programming. With a very simple program, we were able to find out the limits of the servos and then apply these limits to make sure the servo did not damage itself. We got a basic idea of what frames are and did some programming based on frames. Finally, we also went ahead and controlled the speed of the servo using our very own program on a basic level.

Other Books You May Enjoy

If you enjoyed this book, you may be interested in these other books by Packt:

ROS Robotics Projects
Lentin Joseph

ISBN: 978-1-78355-471-3

- Create your own self-driving car using ROS
- Build an intelligent robotic application using deep learning and ROS
- Master 3D object recognition
- Control a robot using virtual reality and ROS
- Build your own AI chatter-bot using ROS
- Get to know all about the autonomous navigation of robots using ROS
- Understand face detection and tracking using ROS
- Get to grips with teleoperating robots using hand gestures
- Build ROS-based applications using Matlab and Android
- Build interactive applications using TurtleBot

Mastering ROS for Robotics Programming - Second Edition
Lentin Joseph, Jonathan Cacace

ISBN: 978-1-78847-895-3

- Create a robot model with a seven-DOF robotic arm and a differential wheeled mobile robot
- Work with Gazebo and V-REP robotic simulator
- Implement autonomous navigation in differential drive robots using SLAM and AMCL packages
- Explore the ROS Pluginlib, ROS nodelets, and Gazebo plugins
- Interface I/O boards such as Arduino, robot sensors, and high-end actuators
- Simulate and motion plan an ABB and universal arm using ROS Industrial
- Explore the latest version of the ROS framework
- Work with the motion planning of a seven-DOF arm using MoveIt!

Leave a review - let other readers know what you think

Please share your thoughts on this book with others by leaving a review on the site that you bought it from. If you purchased the book from Amazon, please leave us an honest review on this book's Amazon page. This is vital so that other potential readers can see and use your unbiased opinion to make purchasing decisions, we can understand what our customers think about our products, and our authors can see your feedback on the title that they have worked with Packt to create. It will only take a few minutes of your time, but is valuable to other potential customers, our authors, and Packt. Thank you!

Index

Printed in Great Britain
by Amazon